Desserts

Mediterranean Flavors, California Style

Cindy Mushet

Photographs by Paul Franz-Moore

Illustrations by Wendy Wray

SCRIBNER

NEW YORK LONDON TORONTO SYDNEY SINGAPORE

SCRIBNER
1230 Avenue of the Americas
New York, NY 10020

SCRIBNER and design are trademarks of Macmillan Library Reference USA, Inc.,
used under license by Simon & Schuster, the publisher of this work.

Designed by Richard Oriolo
Set in Dante

Manufactured in the United States of America

10   9   8   7   6   5   4   3   2   1

Library of Congress Cataloging-in-Publication Data
Mushet, Cindy, 1960–
Desserts : Mediterranean flavors, California style / Cindy Mushet ; photographs by Paul
Franz-Moore ; illustrations by Wendy Wray.
p.   cm.
Includes index.
1. Desserts. 2. Cookery, Mediterranean. 3. Cookery, American—California style. I. Title.
TX773.M933 2000
641.8'6—dc21   00-030810

ISBN 0-684-80054-3

To Miguel,
for believing in magic,
the power of love,
and me

And to Isabella,
who makes the sun rise
each day

Acknowledgments

To Marah Stets, my editor, who allowed my voice to shine through and whose insightful suggestions and dry sense of humor made each conversation a bright spot in the day. I am so lucky to have had the editor of my dreams for my first book.

To Paul Franz-Moore, for his sensuously captivating photography and for understanding both what I wanted and what the book needed. And to stylist George Dolese, for sharing my vision of the natural beauty of food.

To Richard Oriolo, for his beautiful book and cover design—the mark of a gifted designer is the ability to make the complex job of designing a book look simple and elegant and he has done that masterfully here.

To Wendy Wray, for her lovely photographic illustrations (my hands never looked so good) and for her professionalism under fire.

To the entire team at Scribner, who supported my vision and managed to make me feel as if I was its only writer, especially Erich Hobbing, for his insight into design and his patient willingness to help me see the light on the beautiful eggplant color that graces these pages. To John Fontana, for his advice and some wonderful conversations about Italian food; to Ginny Croft and Jay Schweitzer, for their thorough and gentle copyediting; and to Jeff Wilson, for his kind legal counsel.

To friends who offered recipes and lent their shoulders, especially Brigit Binns, Laurie Connor, Michelle Fagerroos, Joanne Fusco, Heidi Insalata Krahling, Evan Kleiman, Theresa Maranzano, Ellen Rose, and Joanne Weir.

To the members of the Bakers Dozen, for comradery, inspiration, and advice, but mostly for their enormously generous spirit.

To the organic farmers and food artisans of California, who make it such a pleasure to shop, cook, and eat here.

To my grandmother, whose love of baking started it all.

To my mother and father who deserve the Pulitzer Prize for parenthood. For their endless love and encouragement that included, but was not limited to, enthusiastically tasting yet another dessert (sometimes as many as five or ten), lending me at various times their kitchen, car, fax machine, and computer, and on occasion acting as my personal patrons of the arts. There are no words to express my love and gratitude.

To my brothers and sisters and their spouses and children, who provide me with enough birthdays, anniversaries, and special occasions to run my own "minibakery," and who offer honest critiques of my latest creation (whether I like it or not).

To Miguel for his patience, understanding, and unending support these past seventeen years—especially the last few, when he would have much preferred I test recipes for a book about steak and shrimp.

To Isabella, who was as patient as a baby could be during this process, and who now gleefully stands on a stool beside me kneading dough (or eating handfuls of chocolate if I get distracted), certain that her presence in the kitchen is a necessary component of any recipe—which it is.

Contents

Introduction

I grew up in a suburb of Los Angeles, part of a large, boisterous family presided over by my Italian maternal grandparents. Mealtime was never dull, and the ritual of food, family, and friends around the dining table was as natural a part of my life as going to school or riding my bike to the park. My mother's and grandmother's baking skills were legendary throughout our extended family, so it is no surprise that I was drawn to the craft from a very early age.

I took my first step beyond the family hearth and into my life as a professional cook when I was fifteen and started to work at a local bakery. There I learned the rhythm of a kitchen, the delight and daily grind of a small business, and even some rudimentary cake decorating. From then on, I continued to work with food while pursuing my education, and when I graduated from college with a degree in anthropology, I was certain of two things: food is as much a barometer of culture as tools or dwellings or language, and I intended to pursue my love of food as a vocation—my own personal anthropological study—rather than taking a more traditional scholarly road. There was no better place to begin than my own backyard; the food and culture of California has been influenced by myriad ethnic groups from many different parts of the world. But to me, none speaks to my sense of home or my culinary soul more than the Mediterranean, for the food and surroundings of my childhood were a mosaic of Mediterranean flavors, sights, and sounds.

Los Angeles has been greatly influenced by both the native Mexicans and the Spanish colonizers of Mexico, and the effect of these cultures was ubiquitous during my childhood. Spanish missionaries introduced citrus to California, and my neighborhood was once the site of orange groves as far as the eye could see. Although the citrus ranches are long gone, virtually every house has at least one orange, lemon, or kumquat tree, and their colorful fruits can be seen hanging over fences, their branches shading porches all year long. Other echoes of the Mediterranean that resonate in my old neighborhood include the summertime aroma of jasmine (a popular flavor in Sicilian desserts), which is planted in almost every garden. Olive trees abound, their ridged and gnarled trunks and tiny silvery gray leaves setting the tone in the front yard of many a white-washed Mediterranean-style home. Rosemary is a favorite hedge plant, and its robin's egg blue flowers can be seen everywhere.

Though I didn't realize it when I was young, the climate and culinary tradition I grew up with in sunny California paralleled those of my ancestors who lived in the Mediterranean. When I traveled in the area as an adult, I found the surroundings surprisingly comfortable, with olive and citrus trees, chaparral and rolling hills, and an abundance of delicious food and goodwill. Despite the difference in language, I discovered familiarity in the tanned, happy faces and rough hands of the working-class people I met. In both places people can often be found outdoors walking, bicycling, shopping, and enjoying family and friends. There is a spirit that Californians share with people of the Mediterranean, which comes not only from the similarity in climate, terrain, and agricultural products but also from the outdoor-oriented lifestyle that lends itself to an intimate relationship with nature and a more casual, open, and friendly attitude toward entertaining.

California Style

Through the years, I've been fortunate to live all over California, from Los Angeles to San Francisco, Santa Barbara to the Napa Valley, Davis to Berkeley. In each of these places I've been delighted to find cuisine that blends food and agriculture in a menu that is, like the population, eclectic yet close to the earth, much like that of the Mediterranean. Desserts are no exception. In California and the Mediterranean alike, they tend to be fruit or nut oriented, rustic in appearance, and gutsy in flavor. The connection between California and the Mediterranean is a natural one, for both boast a market basket of intensely flavored foods for the dessert maker—fruits, nuts, herbs, honeys, chocolates, cheeses, preserves, wines, and spirits—enough to inspire sweet and happy endings for a lifetime of feasts.

In writing this book, I've tried to capture the flavors and spirit of the Mediterranean while satisfying the dessert desires of American taste buds. The recipes included here are not, for the most part, "authentic" Mediterranean desserts. I've worked as a pastry chef for more than fourteen years in California, creating desserts in restaurants featuring Mediterranean-inspired food made with the bounty of California products. And it has been my experience that while Americans may be adventurous eaters when traveling the Mediterranean, they want something closer to their own tastes when they return home. This means that the syrup-laden baklava that was magical on that sultry, moonlit night in Morocco is just too sweet when eaten back home. And the bowl of figs that was so perfect on the terrace in Sicily is too plain when entertaining friends in America. Much of the enjoyment of eating while on vacation comes from the unique combination of time, place, and the romance of travel converging at mealtime. This is why the experience can never be truly replicated at home.

The Mediterranean dishes we prepare in this country cannot be completely authentic, for we are American cooks with biases and ingredients unique to this country. This doesn't mean that the dishes are not good here—they can be utterly delicious and entirely satisfying, but they are not the same. This is why I say my desserts convey the "spirit" of the Mediterranean rather than authenticity (though people are often surprised to hear the dessert they just finished is not a regional specialty—such is the power of flavor and context).

Desserts are often deliciously predictable abroad, steeped as the Mediterranean culture is in tradition. Tradition provides a solid base from which to move forward in food as in life, and my style as a pastry chef is grounded in my formal training in classic French pastry techniques. I love the classic desserts of the Mediterranean, so nearly everything I do is based on these traditions, whether it is flavor combinations or methods of preparation. But I'm also American, which means I'm open to new ideas and new ways of looking at things. Here in California we've practically elevated this philosophy to a lifestyle. When it comes to food, we like to explore a new cuisine, then look for those flavors or preparations that speak to us, our lifestyle, and our Californian-American tastes, then meld them into our kitchens. Possibilities tantalize us—How does this taste with that? What if I combine this cooking method with that new ingredient? Frankly, the experiment doesn't always work. But when tradition is spiked with imagination and transformed into something both new and familiar, the results can be exciting and very satisfying.

The best examples of this blending of cultures and cuisine occur when new flavors are incorporated into traditional forms (or when classic flavors and classic forms not usually combined are gently blended). This is how I create desserts. I call my method "tradition with a twist." Pomegranate Dacquoise (68) is a good example. Dacquoise is a classic French cake made of two crispy almond meringue discs sandwiching a filling of silky buttercream. My version takes this classic French form and imbues it with vibrant Middle Eastern flavor by replacing the almonds with pistachios and flavoring the buttercream with the complex tartness of pomegranate molasses. It works because I've taken a classic form and simply changed the flavors to reflect the traditions of a different culture. In Siena Tart with Almonds, Cherries, Honey, and Spices (107), I begin with the traditional flavors and ingredients of panforte—a classic nut, honey, and spice confection made in Siena—and translate them to a tart (with some American dried sour cherries thrown in for fun). The flavors are familiar, as is the tart shell—it's pairing the two that makes it all seem new. Similarly, Orange Flower and Pine Nut Armadillos with Apricot Sauce (51) is a favorite American pound cake with traditional Mediterranean flavorings added, along with a visual twist, for the cakes are baked in individual custard cups lined with the pine nuts so the exterior of each cake is a textured, pebbly delight. Pistachio and Apricot Baklava with Orange Cardamom Syrup (209) is another example of my California style. Baklava is a classic in Turkey and the Middle East, as are the flavors in this recipe, for pistachios, apricots, orange, and cardamom are much loved in this region of the world. Nothing is new in this dessert except the way the components are combined. Would you find a baklava like this in the Mediterranean? No. But somehow it seems very natural, because everything is already familiar within the context of the traditional cuisine. Truly wonderful and satisfying desserts can be made when we step outside the bounds of convention and adapt the foods and flavors of the Mediterranean to our tastes, so long as we respect the style and flavor combinations particular to the region.

Likewise, my finishing touches and presentations are simple and natural, reflecting the food and people of both the Mediterranean and California. You'll find no caramel cages, chocolate sculpture, or architectural constructions here, for I find such presentations difficult to eat. Dessert is about pleasure, not figuring out how to take the first bite without everything scattering or collapsing under the weight of a fork. Such architectural feats have no place next to the earthy, Mediterranean fare I enjoy, which requires vibrant finishes, with flavors and construction that complement the assertively flavored food that precedes it— food that takes its cue from the rugged beauty of the landscape and the sun that illuminates all within it.

Mediterranean Flavors

Creating desserts in the Mediterranean spirit necessitates an understanding of the flavors common to the Mediterranean and more specifically to each country within that region. Once you learn to think creatively, and carefully weave together traditional flavors and forms, you can easily create your own Mediterranean endings, just as you improvise combinations of flavors common to that region in your main courses. For instance, you may make pasta with summer chanterelles, pancetta, and Parmesan, then create an Italian dessert to follow by choosing complementary flavors from the list below and adding them to your favorite pound cake or ice cream to round out the meal with a dessert whose flavors enhance and continue the spirit of the main course—perhaps a cornmeal pound cake with peaches and honey cream, or a hazelnut and shaved-chocolate ice cream with a shot of Frangelico-spiked espresso poured over the top. Are these traditional desserts? No, but unless you are a culinary historian or are specifically creating a traditional meal, there is little reason to obsess about the most "authentic" version of this or that; realize, instead, that while food at its most basic is about survival and nourishment, it is also about pleasure. This means that if it pleases you to put a little American in with your Middle Eastern food, a touch of French in with your Greek dishes, or a bit of North African in with your Spanish cooking, it's okay. After all, the countries of the Mediterranean—including for the discussion at hand France, Greece, Italy, North Africa, Spain, Turkey, and the Middle East—which we think of as having such distinct cuisines, share much food history, for they have all been heavily influenced by common occupying forces, which accounts for the overriding sense of place that permeates the Mediterranean.

Before the first millennium there was the great Greek empire that set up trade settlements and influenced culture throughout the Mediterranean, then the mighty Roman empire for the next five hundred years, followed by the expansion of the Arab Moors, who dominated until the late 1400s and were succeeded by the Turkish Ottoman empire, which remained until the early 1800s. These two thousand years of trading and conquering led to the widespread distribution of not only the agricultural crops and spices we associate with the Mediterranean today but also the cooking techniques and specific flavor combinations. Even those areas not occupied were influenced by those that were, so it is not surprising that many common ingredients can be found throughout the area.

Although ingredients may be shared, each country seems to have its own style of combining those ingredients. For example, oranges and almonds can be found in every country in the Mediterranean, but they may be used in a dense cake in Italy, an egg yolk–rich custard in Spain, a classic cookie in Morocco, a tart in France, a baklava in Greece, or a marzipan confection in Turkey or the Middle East. Of course, each country also has its own distinct ingredients or preparations, which speak clearly of locale and cultural traditions. An understanding of the flavors specific to a country can aid you in creating your own Mediterranean-style desserts at home, so I have included here a list of ingredients for each country compiled during my travels and studies. These are the tastes that—to me— most represent this region. The first list consists of dessert-friendly flavors common throughout the Mediterranean, and the lists that follow contain ingredients that I feel give a real sense of the essence of each country.

The Mediterranean: Almonds, anise, apples, apricots, cherries, cinnamon, cloves, coffee or espresso, crystallized fruit, dates, deep-fried pastries (showered with sugar or honey), dried fruit, figs, grapes, hazelnuts, honey, jams and preserves, lemons, melons, mint, nutmeg, olive oil, oranges, orange flower water, peaches, pears, pine nuts, pistachios, plums, pomegranates, pumpkins, quinces, raisins, red wine, rice (rice pudding), rose water, semolina, sesame seeds, walnuts, and white wine.

France (including Corsica): Anisette (anise-flavored liqueur), bay leaves, blackberries, caramel, champagne, chestnuts, chocolate, comfit (whole fruits whose water has been replaced by sugar in a long, multilayered cooking process), cornmeal (in Corsica), crème fraîche, currants, fennel seed, goat cheese, grapefruit, lavender, lemon balm, lemon verbena, limes, muscat de Beaumes de Venise (a fortified dessert wine), nougat, pastis (anise-flavored liqueur), praline, prunes, raspberries, ricotta, rose geranium, rosemary, rum, Sauternes (dessert wine), strawberries, tarragon, thyme, and vanilla.

Greece: Chestnuts, coconuts, fennel seed, filo, *kataifi* (shredded filo), *manouri* (a soft unsalted white cheese similar to ricotta), *mastic* (gum arabic—small anise-flavored crystals from a resinous bush or tree), *mizithra* (a soft unsalted white cheese similar to ricotta), ouzo (anise-flavored liqueur), retsina (wine flavored with pine resin), strawberries, sugar syrups, thyme, and yogurt.

Italy (including Sicily and Sardinia): *Amarene* (wild cherries preserved in syrup), amaretti cookies, amaretto (almond liqueur), basil, bay leaves, blackberries, candied citrus peel, caramel, cardamom, chestnuts (and chestnut flour), chocolate, coriander, cornmeal, fennel seed, jasmine, limoncello (lemon-flavored liqueur), mace, Madeira, maraschino (cherry liqueur), Marsala, marzipan, Moscato de Pantelleria (dessert wine), mulberries, praline, ricotta, rosemary, rum, saffron, sambuca (an elderflower-flavored liqueur that tastes of anise), strawberries, *torrone* (nougat), vin santo (dessert wine), and watermelons.

North Africa: Allspice, almond milk, bananas, buttermilk, caraway, cardamom, coriander, filo, ginger, loquats, marzipan, poppyseeds, prickly pears, saffron, *smen* (clarified butter), strawberries, tangerines, *warka* (or *ouarka,* a paper-thin pastry sheet).

Spain: Anise del mono (anise-flavored liqueur), bananas (from the Canary Islands), blackberries, brandy, candied squash, caramel, chocolate, coconuts, empanadas (similar to turnovers), flans, fried custard squares, Gran Torres (orange liqueur), hard cider, marzipan, Mistela (dessert wine), port, prunes, saffron, sangria, sherry, strawberries, thyme, *torrijas* (similar to French toast), and *turron* (nougat).

Turkey and the Middle East (including Egypt, Israel, Lebanon, and Syria): Allspice, bananas, bay leaves, cardamom, coconuts, coriander, dried fruit pastes and confections, filo, ginger, guavas, *kaymak* (a clotted cream thick enough to cut with a knife, made from buffalo milk), *konafa* (shredded filo), mangoes, marzipan, *mastic* (gum arabic—small anise-flavored crystals from a resinous bush or tree), *ouarka* (or *warka,* a paper-thin pastry sheet), pomegranate molasses, prunes, raki (anise-flavored liqueur), *smen* (clarified butter), sugar syrups, tahini (sesame paste), tangerines, and yogurt.

Brandies, Eaux-de-Vie, and Liqueurs

Brandies, eaux-de-vie (fruit brandies), and liqueurs are used freely in the Mediterranean, except in those areas dominated by conservative Islamic culture. They are an integral part of daily life, and this extends naturally to desserts as well. Many of the recipes in this book call for a small amount of liqueur or eau-de-vie, and for good reason. Their intense flavorings add a nuance to a dish that is at once both subtle and indispensable. Their presence can heighten flavors or add a contrasting note, while their alcoholic content is often just the right amount to slightly cut the perceived richness of a dish.

You may have large, elegant (and expensive) bottles of these elixirs on your pantry shelves, but if you do not, everything called for in this book is available in small airline-size bottles at fine liquor stores.

If you are unfamiliar with liqueurs and eaux-de-vie, here is a short list of the types I use most often, listed by their names and flavors. Quality is of the utmost importance, and since these spirits are usually called for in small amounts, the smallest available bottle will be all you need. Inexpensive supermarket brands or other knock-offs of the intensely flavored originals are generally very sweet and lack depth or character of flavor. I urge you to avoid them.

Brandies: These are liquors distilled from fruit and aged in oak casks, which gives them a lightly caramel color.

Calvados—an apple brandy distilled from cider rather than fresh apples and aged in oak casks.

Armagnac—a very fine French brandy distilled from grapes and aged in oak casks. Cognac is another. While their flavors are excellent, good American brandies may be substituted.

Eaux-de-vie: These are usually clear brandies distilled from fresh fruit.
Kirsch—cherries
Framboise—raspberries
Poire William—pears

Liqueurs: These consist of a flavorless base alcohol that is sweetened and flavored with either herbs, seeds or plants, or fruit. Occasionally the base is whiskey or brandy (such as Drambuie or Southern Comfort), but these varieties are not called for in this book.

Amaretto di Saronno—a highly aromatic almond liqueur that derives its flavor from the tiny bitter almond kernel nestled inside apricot pits. Another good brand is Amaretto Lazzaroni, made by the same company that produces the famous red tins of amaretti cookies.

Anisette—a clear liqueur flavored with aniseed (not licorice, as is commonly thought). Marie Brizard is the favorite brand in France.

Crème de Menthe—a liqueur, either clear or colored green, that derives its flavor from mint leaves.

Frangelico—an intense hazelnut liqueur.

Grand Marnier—the best orange liqueur, blended with cognac for a richer, more complex flavor. Other good choices are Cointreau or Curaçao.

Kahlua—a Mexican coffee-flavored liqueur with a touch of cocoa. Tia Maria is another good brand.

Sambuca—a clear liqueur with a strong anise flavor but actually made with elderflower, not aniseed. Molinari is a good brand.

Using Herbs in Desserts

Herbs are an indispensable ingredient in the culinary dictionary of the Mediterranean and of California as well. We tend to think of herbs as an integral part of savory dishes, but they can be wonderful paired with fruit in desserts and are often found in such guise throughout the Mediterranean. Though their perfume can lend just the right note to a dish, herbs must be used with a restrained and judicious hand, always in harmony with the other flavors, and never for the sake of shock, for too much can quickly taste medicinal. Like any other product of nature, herbs vary greatly in their intensity, so taste, taste, and taste. My favorite herbs for use in desserts belong mainly to the Labiatae family, which includes basil, lavender, lemon balm, the mints, rosemary, and thyme. Lemon verbena is a wonderfully enticing perennial that makes a delicious tea and is an enhancement to sorbets, ice creams, puddings, and the like. And scented geraniums should be noted not only for their beauty in the garden (they grow easily and prolifically) but for the wide range of subtle and exotic nuances they can lend to desserts. Rose geranium is especially lovely, much easier to come by than bushels of organic fragrant rose petals and more subtle than rose water.

A Few Notes About Using This Book

The recipes here are written to ensure your success in baking. This means that sometimes they may seem a bit long, but don't be intimidated, especially if you are new to baking. It means that I am walking you gently through the entire process, encouraging your skills, and giving you tips on how to repair the mistakes that inevitably happen to all of us. If you are an experienced baker, you will know when the egg whites are whipped to the correct consistency or how to combine the ingredients for tart dough and can skip past my comments, but if you are a novice, you will find the instructions helpful in building your confidence.

It is difficult to bake good pastries if your oven is not at the correct temperature. You might be shocked to know how often home ovens are out of calibration—sometimes by as much as 50° to 100°F! Buy a mercury-based oven thermometer and keep it in your oven, for it is a small investment in peace of mind. Admittedly, these thermometers can be difficult to find; if your local cookware store does not carry them, order one from Sur La Table (327). Do not be tempted to substitute one of the round dial-style stainless-steel thermometers—some are not accurate to begin with, and they all eventually break down and register the wrong temperature (the problem is, you don't know whether your oven or the thermometer is out of whack). To use the mercury thermometer for the first time, place it in the center of the oven on a rack, set your oven to the desired temperature, then wait 20 minutes. Check the thermometer and adjust your oven up or down if needed to reach the desired temperature.

Be sure to read a recipe all the way through before beginning to bake. It's crucial to know what lies ahead so you can plan your time in the kitchen efficiently. Each recipe in this book has the following parts, which will help you organize your baking time in the kitchen.

Equipment and Advance Preparation: Here you will find the type and size of pan needed for the pastry, in addition to any special equipment you may need, such as a soft-bristle brush or a pastry bag for piping. I do not list saucepans, whisks, rubber spatulas, or other common kitchen equipment. This section also includes any preparation that needs to occur before proceeding with the recipe. This may include notes about thawing filo, prebaking a tart shell, or shelling pistachios if you have to buy them in shells. Much of the equipment called for is not fancy—the custards here were baked in Pyrex custard cups, available in many supermarkets and large drugstores; the baklavas were baked in an inexpensive 8 x 8-inch pan (not foil) I bought in the baking aisle of the supermarket; the propane torch I use is the same one that sits on my husband's workbench; my ice cream machine is an inexpensive electric salt-and-ice model that I bought years ago; and my double boiler is improvised from a bowl that sits on top of a saucepan. I like to put my money where it counts—the ingredients—though I do splurge on equipment that makes my life easier, like a KitchenAid mixer, a food scale, a food processor, the best zester (145), an oven thermometer . . . and the occasional, irresistible set of beautiful dessert plates or compote bowls.

The Ingredient List: Here is a list of all the ingredients you will need. Some entries have a page number following them. This page number refers you to one of three things: a method (for example, how to toast the nuts); a recipe (such as Honey Cream); or an explanation or exploration of the listed ingredient (such as pomegranate molasses).

Mediterraneans and Californians love fruit desserts, and many of the recipes in this book call for fresh, ripe produce, so it's best to choose a recipe whose ingredients are in season. I like to shop every week at the farmers' market, which provides me with constant inspiration, as well as a bounty of locally grown ripe, organic fruit at very reasonable prices. If you can't make it to the farmers' market (or it's winter in your part of the country and there is no market), ask the produce manager in the supermarket for a taste of the fruit you are considering before you buy it. If it doesn't taste good, choose another recipe.

If you aren't sure which supermarket fruits are in season, keep the following general guidelines in mind. In spring, look for strawberries, rhubarb, tropical fruit (like mangoes and pineapples), and citrus; summer brings apricots, some early apples, all types of berries, cherries, figs, peaches and nectarines, early pears, plums, melons, and strawberries; fall offers apples, cranberries, dates, figs, melons, pears, persimmons, pomegranates, pumpkins, quinces, and the end of summer's stone fruits and melons; winter's offerings are sparse but potent, such as dried fruit and citrus (including blood oranges, lavender gems, lemons, limes, grapefruit, and tangerines), as well as fall storage fruit, like apples, pears, and quinces.

Serving and Storage Notes: Here are my suggestions on the best methods for cutting, serving, and presenting your dessert. Of course, you may have your own ideas on presentation, and I encourage your creativity. Most pastries are at their best the same day they are baked. With this in mind, I have also included notes on the best way to store the dessert and the length of time that I would recommend keeping it.

Getting Ahead: There's a lot in these recipes that can be done in advance. To help you plan your time when entertaining, I have included notes on which parts of the recipe can be done in advance, how long in advance, and how they should be stored until needed.

Variations: Sometimes another enticing dessert can be made by substituting almonds for walnuts; orange flower water for rose water; or nectarines for strawberries. When I feel the substitution creates an equally good dessert, I have included amounts and directions for the variation. Notes under this heading may trigger some ideas of your own. Feel free to experiment, keeping in mind that the quantities of ingredients should stay consistent.

In addition to the recipes, you will find scattered throughout the book a series of in-depth explorations and explanations of the ingredients used in Mediterranean desserts, from fruits to herbs to spices, as well as discussions that range from what makes good ice cream to how to use a propane torch in dessert making to what type of cocoa powder to purchase.

I hope this book will lure you into the kitchen to create luscious endings for your Mediterranean-inspired meals. The greatest compliment you could pay me would be a well-worn and dirty book, its pages spattered with cream, stained from buttery fingers, and darkened with bits of melted chocolate. It would mean that you took it, and me, into the kitchen and that we became friends. So while you, like I, enjoy reading cookbooks curled up on the sofa, I hope that we will wind up in the kitchen together, baking for people you love. In the true spirit of the Mediterranean, relish the food, enjoy the conversation, and raise your glass to another celebration of family and friendship. Salud!

Cakes

More than any other dessert, cakes are the stuff of which celebrations are made. Birthdays, weddings, welcome home celebrations, good-bye commemorations—the grand events of our lives have many beginnings, but they almost always end with a cake. Because of this, cakes have a resonance that can turn the everyday into something special simply by virtue of their presence.

Cakes are used for celebrations in the Mediterranean as well, though to a lesser degree. Sometimes the celebration there calls for a baklava or other filo dessert, or tradition may dictate that a particular cookie or candy be served for the upcoming holiday or feast. Even so, cakes still find their way into every kitchen in the Mediterranean. Simple cakes are baked at home and eaten as a snack in the morning or afternoon, while more elaborate affairs are usually purchased from the neighborhood bakery. The cakes in this chapter harken to the Mediterranean with their flavor combinations and French-derived techniques, but their exuberance is purely American. There are some simple cakes here, as well as some showstoppers that require an extra level of effort but whose results will help to make an occasion unforgettable. Whether a traditional dessert takes on a delightful new flavor, as in Pomegranate Dacquoise, or familiar flavors turn up in a new shape, as in Grilled Coconut Cake with Double-Lime Ice Cream or Chocolate Soufflé Roll with Rum Mascarpone Cream, you will find a cake here for your special celebration. You may want something soft and sweet, like Strawberry Mascarpone Layer Cake, or perhaps you prefer a study in textural contrasts, as in Almond Brown Butter Cakelettes with Raspberries or the Orange Flower and Pine Nut Armadillos with Apricot Sauce. Or maybe even a knock-'em-out fruitcake for people who never thought they'd eat fruitcake again—California Fruitcake with Dates, Apricots, and Walnuts. In this chapter you will find cakes to delight and cakes to surprise for those important—and everyday—events of our lives.

Chocolate, Hazelnut, and Orange Torte

serves 10 to 12

In Italy the combination of chocolate and hazelnuts is so popular that it has its own name, gianduia. *This duo can be found in all manner of sweets, from gelato to candies to cakes, and with good reason—it is a flavor match made in heaven. This dense, moist torte, fragrant with hazelnuts and speckled with bittersweet chocolate chips, was created by my friend Joanne Fusco while working at a bakery in Italy. The addition of orange zest to the cake offers a bright counterpoint and intensifies the earthy richness of hazelnuts and chocolate.*

Over the years I have served this cake hundreds of times, in dozens of guises, and it's a real crowd pleaser. But my favorite way to eat it is the simplest and just as I present it here—topped with a silken cloud of bittersweet chocolate frosting. The frosting is so easy—a combination of melted butter and chocolate—and so good, you'll want to use it again and again in your baking.

EQUIPMENT AND ADVANCE PREPARATION: One 9-inch springform pan • Line the bottom of the pan with a round of parchment paper or wax paper. Alternatively, brush the sides and bottom of the pan with a thin, even coat of melted butter, then dust the pan with flour, tapping out any excess.

FOR THE CAKE

1¼ cups (6 ounces) hazelnuts, toasted and skinned (227)

¾ cup (5¼ ounces) plus 2 tablespoons (1 ounce) sugar

2 sticks (8 ounces) unsalted butter, softened

2 tablespoons finely chopped orange zest (145), about 2 large oranges

2 large eggs

4 large eggs, separated

½ cup (2½ ounces) unbleached all-purpose flour

1¼ teaspoons baking powder

4 ounces (about ¾ cup) miniature bittersweet chocolate chips (274)

6 ounces bittersweet chocolate, finely chopped

12 tablespoons (6 ounces) unsalted butter

Softly whipped cream (54) flavored with Frangelico

Miniature chocolate curls (106), optional

Preheat the oven to 350°F. Position an oven rack in the center of the oven.

To make the cake, place the hazelnuts and ¾ cup sugar in a food processor and process until the nuts are finely ground, about 20 to 30 seconds. In the bowl of an electric mixer fitted with the paddle attachment (a handheld mixer is fine; just allow a little extra time to reach each stage in the recipe), cream the butter until light in color, about 2 minutes on medium speed. Add the ground hazelnut-sugar mixture and beat on medium speed for an additional 2 minutes, or until the mixture looks very light and fluffy. Beat in the orange zest.

In a small bowl, combine the whole eggs and egg yolks and whisk just until blended. With the mixer running, dribble the eggs into the butter mixture a couple of tablespoons at a time, allowing each addition to blend in fully (about 15 to 20 seconds) before adding the next. Stop the mixer and use a rubber spatula to scrape down the sides of the bowl a couple of times during this process. In a separate small bowl, whisk the flour and baking powder to blend. Add the flour mixture to the batter and mix thoroughly on medium speed, about 20 to 30 seconds. Stop the mixer and scrape down the sides, then add the chocolate chips and blend well. The batter will be very stiff.

In a clean mixing bowl, using a clean whisk attachment, whip the egg whites on medium-high speed until soft peaks form, about 1½ to 2 minutes. With the mixer running, slowly add the remaining 2 tablespoons of sugar, tablespoon by tablespoon, and continue beating just until the whites hold firm peaks and are glossy, another 1 to 2 minutes. To check the whites, dip a spoon into the bowl and scoop out some beaten whites—the whites should sit firmly on the spoon, and the peaks that formed in the bowl when the spoon was lifted should hold their shape (the very tips of the peaks may bend slightly—this is okay). Be careful not to overbeat the whites, or they will begin to clump and separate.

Use a rubber spatula to stir one-third of the beaten whites into the cake batter to loosen and lighten the mixture, then gently fold in the remaining whites.

Scrape the batter into the cake pan, level the top, and bake for 45 to 55 minutes, or until the center of the cake springs back when gently touched with a fingertip or until a toothpick inserted into the center comes out with a few moist crumbs clinging to it. Remove from the oven and place on a rack to cool completely.

To make the frosting, place the chopped chocolate in a medium bowl. In a small saucepan over low heat, heat the butter until it is completely melted and has just come to a boil. Immediately pour the butter over the chocolate, then let the mixture sit for 2 minutes. Gently whisk the frosting until it is blended and smooth (if the chocolate still has lumps, place the bowl over a pot of barely simmering water and stir constantly until the lumps have melted).

Place the bowl of frosting in the refrigerator. Every 5 minutes or so, remove the bowl and whisk the frosting to blend in any patches that have cooled and are beginning to harden on the sides and bottom of the bowl. Continue until it reaches a spreadable consistency, about 30 minutes. If the frosting gets too hard, simply place the bowl over a pot of simmering water and whisk until the desired consistency is reached (this will happen quickly, so don't walk away).

To unmold the cake, run a thin, sharp knife around the edges of the cake to loosen any areas that may have stuck to the pan. As you do this, gently press the knife into the side of the pan to avoid gouging the cake. Then pop the sides off the springform pan and set aside. Gently set a plate or cake cardboard on top of the cake, then flip it over and remove the bottom of the pan and the parchment paper. Place your serving dish or a cake cardboard on the bottom of the cake, then turn the cake right side up. To frost the cake, scrape the frosting from the bowl onto the center of the cake and use an icing spatula or the back of a spoon to spread it evenly over the top, just to the edges—do not spread any frosting down the sides. Use the tip of the spatula or spoon to make swirls in the frosting.

SERVING AND STORAGE NOTES: Serve at room temperature accompanied by a spoonful of softly whipped cream. I like to flavor the cream with a bit of Frangelico (hazelnut liqueur). If you like, garnish each plate by sprinkling it with some miniature chocolate curls. Store the cake at room temperature. There is no need to wrap the entire cake with plastic; instead, simply press a piece of plastic wrap against the cut surfaces. Though the cake is at its best the same day it is baked, it keeps well for 3 to 5 days.

Chocolate, Walnut, and Orange Torte: Substitute 1¾ cups (6 ounces) walnuts for the hazelnuts above. Toast the walnuts according to the instructions for toasting almonds (254).

Chocolate, Almond, and Orange Torte: Substitute 1 cup plus 2 tablespoons (6 ounces) whole, natural, toasted (254) almonds for the hazelnuts above.

Gianduia

Gianduia is a sensuous blend of chocolate and hazelnuts that originated in the Piedmont area in northern Italy. Like many inventions, its creation was a serendipitous meeting of necessity and ingenuity. In the early 1800s, the chocolate makers of Piedmont were faced with a shortage of cacao beans. As part of the war effort against Napoleon, the English navy was preventing trade ships bringing the beans from South America from arriving at their final destinations in Europe. In an effort to augment what little chocolate they could obtain, Piedmont chocolate makers added ground hazelnuts to their chocolate, and a taste sensation was born. It received an official name when it was introduced at the carnival of Turin and given the same name as one of the popular festival masks—*gianduia.* Though gianduia is technically a paste, or butter, of chocolate and hazelnuts, the term is applied to all manner of sweets that contain this uniquely satisfying combination of nuts and chocolate.

Pistachio Layer Cake
with Nougat Cream

serves 10 to 12

Nougat (33), a sometimes chewy, sometimes crunchy candy made of egg whites, sugar, honey, almonds, and pistachios is a much-loved treat in the south of France, Italy, Spain, and Syria. This beautiful special occasion cake echoes those flavors in layers of pistachio sponge cake filled with orange, honey, and almond-flavored whipped cream. I love to serve this in the springtime, especially at Easter, when the lovely pastel green cake and honey-toned cream seem especially evocative of nature's rebirth.

EQUIPMENT AND ADVANCE PREPARATION: One 16½ x 11½-inch baking sheet with sides (if your pan is slightly smaller, the cake will take a bit longer to bake; if the pan is larger, the cake will be finished more quickly) • Line the bottom of the pan with parchment paper. Do not grease the sides of the pan. • If you find only pistachios in shells, buy double the weight given below and shell them by hand.

FOR THE CAKE

8 large eggs, separated

6 tablespoons (2¾ ounces) sugar plus 6 tablespoons (2¾ ounces) sugar

1¾ cups (8 ounces) raw unsalted shelled pistachios

¼ cup (1¼ ounces) unbleached all-purpose flour

1 teaspoon baking powder

FOR THE SOAKING LIQUID

½ cup (5 ounces) low-sugar apricot jam (Smucker's brand if available)

2 tablespoons (1 ounce) water

2 tablespoons (1 ounce) Amaretto di Saronno

FOR THE NOUGAT CREAM

3 cups (24 ounces) heavy cream

5 tablespoons (3¾ ounces) honey

2 teaspoons orange oil (see Note) or 1½ to 2 tablespoons orange liqueur

¼ teaspoon pure almond extract

²/₃ cup (2 ¾ ounces) raw unsalted shelled pistachios, toasted (213)

FOR SERVING

Powdered sugar, optional

Candied orange zest (236), optional

NOTE: Orange oil is a very concentrated, natural flavoring extracted from the rind of oranges, with a much purer and cleaner flavor than orange extract. Orange oil is available in fine cookware stores, or is available by mail order from general baking and equipment suppliers (327).

Preheat the oven to 350°F. Position an oven rack in the center of the oven.

To make the cake, place the egg yolks and 6 tablespoons of sugar in the bowl of an electric mixer fitted with the whisk attachment (a handheld mixer is fine; just allow a little extra time to reach each stage in the recipe). Whip on high speed until the mixture is very thick, light in color, and ribbons when it falls from the whisk to the surface of the batter, about 3 to 4 minutes.

Place the pistachios, flour, and baking powder in the bowl of a food processor and process until the nuts are finely ground, about 30 seconds.

In a clean mixing bowl, using a clean whisk attachment, whip the egg whites on medium-high speed until soft peaks form, about 1½ to 2 minutes. With the mixer running, slowly add the remaining 6 tablespoons of sugar, tablespoon by tablespoon, and continue beating just until the whites hold firm peaks and are glossy, another 1 to 2 minutes. To check the whites, dip a spoon into the bowl and scoop out some beaten whites—the whites should sit firmly on the spoon, and the peaks that formed in the bowl when the spoon was lifted should hold their shape (the very tips of the peaks may bend slightly—this is okay). Be careful not to overbeat the whites, or they will begin to clump and separate.

Use a rubber spatula to stir one-third of the egg whites into the yolks to loosen and lighten the mixture, then gently fold in half of the ground pistachios. When the nuts are almost incorporated, fold in half of the remaining egg whites. Then fold in the last of the pistachios, followed by the remaining egg whites. Scrape the batter into the sheet pan and use an offset spatula or the back of a spoon to gently spread it evenly in the pan. Bake for 18 to 20 minutes, or until the center of the cake springs back when gently touched with a fingertip or until a toothpick inserted into the center comes out free of crumbs. Remove from the oven and place on a rack to cool completely.

To make the soaking liquid, combine the apricot jam, water, and amaretto in a small saucepan. Cook over low heat, stirring frequently, until the mixture is hot and very liquid (do not let it boil).

To make the nougat cream, place the cream, honey, orange oil or orange liqueur, and almond extract in the bowl of an electric mixer fitted with the whisk attachment and whip on medium speed to firm peaks. Be careful not to overwhip the cream, or it will begin to separate and look curdled. If this happens, remove the bowl from the mixer and use a rubber spatula to gently stir in several tablespoons of cream, just until the whipped cream has smoothed out again.

To assemble the cake, run a thin, sharp knife around the edges of the cake to loosen it from the pan. As you do this, gently press the knife into the side of the pan to avoid gouging the cake. Then grab hold of the parchment paper on one of the short sides and slide the cake, still attached to the parchment paper, out of the pan and onto your work surface. Trim ¼ inch off each side of the cake and discard these dry edges. Using a sharp serrated knife, cut the cake crosswise into 4 equal pieces (each about 4 inches wide), making sure to cut all the way through the parchment paper. Leaving the cake on the paper makes it much easier to maneuver the layers into position without breaking them.

Place the first layer of cake on the serving platter or cake cardboard, parchment paper upward. Once the cake is in position, gently peel back the paper and discard. Brush the cake with one quarter of the soaking liquid. Spread a ½-inch-thick layer of the nougat cream on top of the cake. Place the second cake layer on top, parchment paper upward, and gently peel off the parchment. Apply another layer of soaking liquid and nougat cream. Repeat with the next cake layer and another layer of soaking liquid and cream. Before you add the final layer of cake, brush the top of it with the remaining soaking liquid, then turn it over and place it on top of the last layer of cream and peel off the parchment. (This layer is different from the rest because the moistened side is downward, which leaves a clean, dry surface on which to finish icing the cake).

Set aside ½ to ⅔ cup of nougat cream to pipe around the edges of the cake, and use the remaining cream to frost the top and sides of the cake as smoothly as possible. Use a bit more cream on the top and a bit less on the sides, as the sides will be covered with nuts (and they will adhere to the barest coating of cream).

To finish the cake, place the ⅔ cup pistachios in the bowl of a food processor and pulse until finely ground. To press the nuts into the sides of the cake, put a small mound of nuts in the palm of your hand. With your other hand, tilt the cake toward the nuts as you tilt your hand toward the cake, gently pressing them into the cream and letting the excess nuts fall onto your work surface or platter. Proceed around the cake until the sides are coated evenly with the ground pistachios. Gently brush away any excess nuts around the bottom of the cake. Spoon the reserved nougat cream into a pastry bag fitted with a small star tip and pipe a border around the top and bottom edges of the cake. Refrigerate until serving time.

SERVING AND STORAGE NOTES: Slice the cake with a serrated knife into ¾-inch-thick pieces. I like this cake served simply, but if you want to dress up the plate, sprinkle it with powdered sugar and garnish the cake with a few strands of candied orange zest. Store the cake in the refrigerator with a piece of plastic wrap pressed firmly against the cut edge. The cake is at its best 8 hours after assembly, but will keep for 3 to 4 days.

GETTING AHEAD: The pistachio sponge cake may be made 2 days in advance, wrapped tightly in plastic (still in the pan), and stored at room temperature. It may also be made up to 3 weeks in advance and frozen—remove the cake from the pan but leave the parchment paper on the cake. Wrap tightly twice with plastic and freeze on a flat surface. Thaw at room temperature, still wrapped in plastic, for 2 hours before using.

Nougat

Nougat, also known as *torrone* in Italy, *turron* in Spain, and *noga* in Syria, is a light almond- and pistachio-filled confection made with whipped egg whites and sweetened with honey, though in Damascus the preferred flavors are either a firm peppermint variation or a soft rose water nougat with pistachios and walnuts. Believed to be a descendant from a praline-like confection made of caramelized honey and pine nuts, nougat may be soft and chewy or hard and crunchy, depending upon the traditions of the region. Until recently nougat was available only during the Christmas season, when its nuts are a symbol of abundance, and its honey is considered an omen for sweetness in the coming year.

In Provence *nougat blanc* (the light nougat described above) and *nougat noir* (caramelized honey with nuts and sometimes herbs, closely related to the praline-like original nougat) are two of the traditional thirteen desserts, *les treize desserts de Noël,* enjoyed at the end of a long ritualistic dinner that is eaten before attending midnight mass on Christmas Eve. While visiting Nice, I became fascinated with nougat and sampled dozens of varieties at charming old-fashioned candy shops down narrow streets in the old section of the city. Cake pedestals in the windows were piled high with "bars" of nougat, each wrapped with edible rice paper, the cut ends exposed to show a minikaleidoscope of the candy's ingredients. Flavors ranged from the versions described above to others containing walnuts, hazelnuts, candied fruits or spices, even chocolate—every mouthful a sweet, chewy taste of tradition.

California Fruitcake with Dates, Apricots, and Walnuts

serves 8 to 10

A dense confection with just three basic ingredients—walnuts, dates, and dried apricots—this cake explodes with flavor as the sweetness of the dates blends with the puckery tartness of the apricots and the earthy crunch of walnuts. There is only enough batter to hold the fruits and nuts in place—so little, in fact, that the first time I made the cake, I was sure I had done something wrong. But one taste will tell you that everything is very right—this is one fabulous fruitcake. The recipe comes from friend and creative chef Evan Kleiman of Angeli Caffè in Los Angeles.

EQUIPMENT AND ADVANCE PREPARATION: One 9 x 5 x 3-inch loaf pan • Butter the pan, then line the bottom and sides with foil or parchment paper. Butter the foil or parchment with a thin, even coat of melted butter, then dust the pan with flour, tapping out any excess. • A roasting pan large enough to hold the bread pan with at least 2 inches between the sides of the pans

FOR THE CAKE

1½ cups (9 ounces) tightly packed moist, pitted dates, preferably the Medjool variety

2 cups (8 ounces) walnut halves, toasted (follow the instructions for toasting whole almonds on page 254)

¾ cup (3¾ ounces) unbleached all-purpose flour

¾ cup (6 ounces) tightly packed light brown sugar

¼ teaspoon baking soda

3 large eggs

1 teaspoon pure vanilla extract

1½ cups (9 ounces) tightly packed dried apricot halves, preferably California, each half cut in quarters

FOR SERVING

Honey cream (53) flavored with a few drops of orange flower water (260), optional

Preheat the oven to 300°F. Position an oven rack in the center of the oven.

To make the cake, stuff each date with a walnut half (or a couple pieces of walnut if the halves are broken).

In a separate large bowl, whisk the flour, brown sugar, and baking soda to blend. Don't worry about any lumps of sugar—they will dissolve when the eggs are added. Whisk in the eggs and vanilla, and continue stirring until a thin batter has formed. Add the dates, walnuts, and apricots to the bowl and use a large spoon or your hands to mix the ingredients until the fruits and nuts are evenly coated with the batter. Scrape the mixture into the prepared loaf pan. Place the loaf pan in the center of the roasting pan. Place in the oven, then and add enough hot water to come halfway up the sides of the loaf pan. Bake for 1½ hours, or until a toothpick inserted into the center comes out free of crumbs. The cake will be a deep brown color and feel firm to the touch in the center. Lift the cake out of the water bath, and place it on a rack to cool completely, about 2 hours. Don't try to remove the cake from the pan while it is the least bit warm, or you'll have a big mess on your hands.

To unmold the cake, turn the loaf pan upside down and allow the cake to slide out onto your work surface or a plate. Gently peel the foil or parchment from the surface of the cake. Turn the cake right side up and place on a serving platter or cake cardboard.

SERVING AND STORAGE NOTES: Cut the cake into very thin slices (about ¼ inch thick) with a thin, sharp knife—I find that a good serrated knife is best. This cake is lovely served plain with a cup of coffee or tea. To dress it up a bit, serve with a spoonful of honey cream flavored with a few drops of orange flower water. If you will not be serving the cake within a few hours, wrap it tightly in plastic wrap and store it at room temperature until needed.

GETTING AHEAD: This recipe can be doubled, tripled, or more for holiday gift giving. Wrap the cake tightly in plastic wrap and store at room temperature for 2 to 3 weeks. For longer storage, wrap twice with plastic wrap, then seal with foil or place in a freezer bag, and freeze for up to 3 months.

Though I enjoy snacking on dried fruits throughout the year, I rely on them in my baking most heavily during the winter, when fresh fruit is sparse. By winter, apples and pears, while good keepers, have been in cold storage for months, and though citrus is wonderful, its uses in baking are limited. It can be tempting to buy raspberries from New Zealand and apricots from Chile when you've just fought blizzard conditions to get to the grocery store, but those foreign fruits are picked hard and unripe to survive the long trip from fields to packing houses to airports. And while that first bite may seem delightful, you'll soon realize that you've spent a small fortune on some pretty tasteless stuff.

Dried fruit, on the other hand, is relatively inexpensive, readily available, and intensely flavorful. Why isn't it used more often? Did it simply go out of fashion when fresh fruit flown in from around the world became available? The fact is, dried fruit is now better than ever, and there is an amazing variety to choose from. If your supermarket selection seems limited, check out the local natural food store, which usually carries an inspiring array. And if there are farmers' markets in your area that continue through the winter, there are sure to be at least a few farmers specializing in dried wares.

When choosing dried fruit, make sure it is moist and pliable. Extremely dry or brittle fruit may never rehydrate properly, and hard bits of fruit can ruin an otherwise lovely dessert. Store dried fruit in plastic zip-top bags or airtight storage containers in a cool, dry location to prevent mold or fermentation. You can also store dried fruit in the refrigerator or freezer, where it will keep for at least a year.

Strawberry Mascarpone Layer Cake

Spiked with a bit of liqueur and made extraluscious with the addition of mascarpone, this towering melt-in-your-mouth dessert is somewhere between a child's nursery trifle and an adult's tiramisu. Four layers of sponge cake moistened with amaretto and layered with cream and strawberries are all dressed up and ready for a party. This cake is great for entertaining because it needs to be prepared a day ahead so the flavors have a chance to meld. In fact, some of the components can be made weeks in advance, then simply assembled the day before your party. The ultimate success of this cake relies on sweet, ripe, peak-of-the-season strawberries, so enjoy it during the spring and early summer months, and be sure to choose berries that are shiny and a deep red from top to bottom.

EQUIPMENT AND ADVANCE PREPARATION: Two 9 x 2-inch round cake pans • Brush the bottom of the pans with a thin, even coat of butter—do not butter the sides. Line the bottoms of the pans with a piece of parchment paper cut to fit. • If you wish to make your own mascarpone (42), you will need to begin at least 3 days before assembling the cake.

FOR THE SPONGE CAKES

6 large eggs, separated

¾ cup plus 2 tablespoons (6 ounces) sugar

1 ¾ cups (4 ounces) cake flour, sifted, then spooned gently into the cups for measuring

FOR THE MOISTENING SYRUP

½ cup (3½ ounces) sugar

½ cup (4 ounces) water

¼ cup (2 ounces) Amaretto di Saronno

FOR THE STRAWBERRIES

1 pint basket strawberries

2 teaspoons sugar

2½ cups (20 ounces) heavy cream

1 pound mascarpone

3 tablespoons (1¼ ounces) sugar

FOR FINISHING

1 cup (3 ounces) sliced almonds, either natural or blanched, toasted (254)

FOR SERVING

Powdered sugar, optional

Whole strawberries, optional

Preheat the oven to 350°F. Position an oven rack in the center of the oven.

To make the sponge cakes, place the egg yolks and half the sugar (7 tablespoons) in the bowl of an electric mixer fitted with the whisk attachment (a handheld mixer is fine; just allow a little extra time to reach each stage in the recipe). Whip on high speed until the mixture is very thick, light in color, and ribbons when it falls from the whisk to the surface of the batter, about 3 to 4 minutes. Set aside while you whip the egg whites.

In a clean mixing bowl, using a clean whisk attachment, whip the egg whites on medium-high speed until soft peaks form, about 1½ to 2 minutes. With the mixer running, slowly add the remaining 7 tablespoons of sugar, tablespoon by tablespoon, and continue beating just until the whites hold firm peaks and are glossy, another 1 to 2 minutes. To check the whites, dip a spoon into the bowl and scoop out some beaten whites—the whites should sit firmly on the spoon, and the peaks that formed in the bowl when the spoon was lifted should hold their shape (the very tips of the peaks may bend slightly—this is okay). Be careful not to overbeat the whites, or they will begin to clump and separate.

Use a rubber spatula to fold half of the beaten whites into the egg yolks (there should still be a few streaks), then sift half of the cake flour over the mixture and fold this in as well. Repeat with the remaining whites and cake flour. Divide the batter between the cake pans and use an offset spatula or the back of a spoon to gently spread it evenly in the pans. Bake for 20 to 23 minutes, or until the center of the cake springs back when gently touched with a fingertip or until a toothpick inserted into the center comes out free of crumbs. Remove from the oven and place on a rack to cool completely.

To unmold the cakes, run a thin, sharp knife around the edges of the cake to loosen any areas that may have stuck to the pan. As you do this, gently press the knife into the side of the pan to avoid gouging the cake. Turn each pan upside down and let the cake slide out (give the pan a sharp rap on the counter if necessary). Set the cakes right side up on your work surface. Leave the parchment paper attached at this point, as it will make it easier to slice the cakes in half.

Use a serrated knife to trim the top crust from each cake and then carefully slice each cake in half horizontally. To do so, set the cake layer close to the edge of your work surface, then bend over so that you are at eye level with the center of the cake. Place one hand on top of the cake to hold it steady, then make a shallow slice at the center point with the serrated knife as shown. Using the original slice as a guide, slowly turn the cake by twisting the hand on top and continue to make a shallow slice all the way around the cake.

Once you have the center marked all the way around, repeat the procedure, slicing a little deeper into the cake. Always keep both the tip of your knife and the handle edge in view—if the tip of your knife disappears into the center of the cake, that's usually when things go awry. Just continue in this manner, slicing deeper and deeper each time you turn the cake, and in just a few minutes you will have 2 equal layers. Repeat with the second cake to make 4 layers.

To make the moistening syrup, place the sugar and water in a small saucepan over medium heat and cook, stirring occasionally, until the sugar is completely dissolved and the liquid is clear. Remove from the heat and cool completely. Add the amaretto and stir to blend.

To prepare the strawberries, rinse them with water and pat dry. Remove their green tops and discard. Slice the berries thinly and place in a medium bowl. Add the 2 teaspoons sugar and stir well. Set aside while you prepare the filling.

To make the filling, place the heavy cream in the bowl of an electric mixer fitted with the whisk attachment and whip on medium speed to soft peaks. Be careful not to overwhip the cream, or it will begin to separate and look curdled. If this happens, remove the bowl from the mixer and use a rubber spatula to gently stir in several tablespoons of cream, just until the whipped cream has smoothed out again. Set aside. Place the mascarpone and sugar in a medium bowl and use a rubber spatula or a wooden spoon to blend until smooth (this can also be done in an electric mixer fitted with the paddle attachment on medium speed). Stir in about 1 cup of the whipped cream to lighten the mascarpone and make it easier to combine with the remaining cream. Then fold in the rest of the whipped cream until the mixture is homogeneous. It should be the consistency of thick pudding. If it seems thin, beat vigorously with the wooden spoon until it thickens. If it seems too thick or grainy, stir in a few tablespoons of cream to smooth it out. Divide the filling in half, reserving one-half for use in frosting the cake. Fold the strawberries into the remaining half, which will be divided into thirds for filling the cake layers.

To assemble the cake, set aside one of the cake layers with a bottom crust to use last. Place a cake layer on a 9-inch cake cardboard or your serving plate. Lightly brush the cake with one quarter of the moistening syrup. Spread one-third of the strawberry mascarpone filling on top. Place the second cake layer on top, moisten the cake, and spread it with half the remaining mascarpone filling. Place the third cake layer on top and repeat the process for the final time, using half of the remaining syrup and all of the remaining filling. Top with the reserved cake layer, placing it bottom crust up. Moisten it with the remaining syrup.

Use an icing spatula to frost the cake with the reserved mascarpone mixture, holding aside 1 cup for decorating. To press the sliced almonds into the sides of the cake, put a small mound of nuts in the palm of your hand. With your other hand, tilt the cake toward the nuts as you bring your hand toward the cake, gently pressing them into the cream and letting the excess nuts fall onto your work surface or platter. Proceed around the cake until the sides are coated evenly with the sliced almonds. Gently brush away any excess nuts around the bottom of the cake. Spoon the reserved mascarpone cream into a pastry bag fitted with a small star tip and pipe a border around the top edge of the cake. Refrigerate for at least 8 hours, preferably overnight, before serving.

SERVING AND STORAGE NOTES: Slice the cake with a serrated knife. I like this cake served simply, but if you want to dress up the plate, sprinkle it with powdered sugar and garnish each plate with a whole strawberry. Store the cake in the refrigerator with a piece of plastic wrap pressed firmly against the cut edge. The cake is at its best the first 2 days, but will keep for 3 to 4 days.

GETTING AHEAD: The sponge cakes may be made 2 days in advance, wrapped tightly in plastic (still attached to the parchment), and stored at room temperature. They may also be made up to 3 weeks in advance and frozen—remove the cakes from the pan but leave the parchment paper on the cakes. Wrap tightly twice with plastic and freeze on a flat surface. Thaw at room temperature, still wrapped in plastic, for 2 hours before using.

The moistening syrup may be prepared up to 2 weeks in advance. Keep refrigerated.

VARIATION

Nectarine Mascarpone Layer Cake: Substitute 4 large ripe nectarines (about 26 ounces) for the strawberries. Halve and pit the nectarines and cut into very thin slices (no larger than ¼ inch thick). Place the slices in a bowl and toss with 2 tablespoons freshly squeezed orange juice (to prevent the fruit from browning). Make the cake exactly as directed above, except for the following change. When you divide the mascarpone filling in half, reserve one-half for frosting and decorating and the second half for filling the layers, but do not stir the nectarines into the second half. As you assemble the cake, spread one-third of the filling on each cake layer, then top the filling with one-third of the sliced nectarines, laying them in a spiral pattern, each slice slightly overlapping the one before it. Finish the cake by topping with the fourth cake layer and decorating as directed above.

Making Mascarpone

makes about 1 pound

Mascarpone is a thick, unctuous fresh cheese made from the sweet cream of cows. It has a light, fresh flavor and is thick enough to stand on its own, though very soft in texture. It can be found in recipes all over Italy, but is used most frequently in desserts. Often referred to as the cream cheese of Italy, mascarpone bears little resemblance in flavor or texture to the cream cheese in this country, and the two should not be used interchangeably. If resemblances are to be drawn, mascarpone is more like the clotted cream of the English countryside, often served as the rich accompaniment to scones at teatime.

Mascarpone can be found in Italian markets and, thanks to its current popularity, even in many supermarkets. It is very easy to make at home, though you will need a thermometer and a couple of special ingredients. Most people will find it simpler to run to the local market, but those intrepid culinary adventurers who want to make their own (or those who need a large quantity and don't wish to pay a king's ransom) will make good use of the following recipe.

The best cream to use for mascarpone is manufacturing cream, which has a higher butterfat content (up to 40 percent or more) than heavy whipping cream (36 percent), which means a richer, denser cheese. Also, manufacturing cream is not ultrapasteurized, which means it doesn't have the cooked milk flavor that typical supermarket creams have. Manufacturing cream is the cream that bakeries and restaurants use and is available in most of the stores that cater to those businesses (restaurant supply stores, large membership stores, and "open to the public" supply stores). If manufacturing cream is unavailable, heavy whipping cream may be substituted. You will also need tartaric acid, which is used to "clot" the cream. It is also used in making wine. It is available from cheese-making and wine-making sources (see Mail-Order Sources, 327) and may be found in some pharmacies.

EQUIPMENT AND ADVANCE PREPARATION: A double boiler (or a medium saucepan coupled with a medium stainless-steel mixing bowl that will fit about halfway into the saucepan when sitting on top of it) • An instant-read thermometer • Enough cheesecloth to line a medium strainer with 2 thicknesses • You will need to begin the mascarpone at least 3 days before you want to use it.

4 cups (32 ounces) heavy cream
¼ teaspoon tartaric acid

Place the cream in the top of the double boiler. Bring 2 inches of water to a boil in the bottom of the double boiler and place the cream on top (the top of the double boiler should not touch the water). Heat the cream to 180°F. Remove the cream from the heat, add the tartaric acid, and stir gently for 1 minute. Let the cream cool for 30 minutes, then cover with plastic wrap and refrigerate for 2 days (the cream may be transferred to a storage container if you don't want to put a bowl in your refrigerator). Line a medium strainer with 2 layers of cheesecloth. Set the strainer over a medium bowl or storage container (it should be at least 1 inch from the bottom of the bowl or container) and pour the cream into the strainer. Cover with plastic wrap and allow the cheese to drain, refrigerated, for 24 hours.

STORAGE NOTES: Transfer the finished cheese to an airtight container. The mascarpone will hold for 5 to 7 days in the refrigerator. The recipe may be doubled, tripled, or more to your liking. In one restaurant where I worked, we used to make mascarpone with 3 gallons of cream at a time!

Fregolotta with Almonds and Jam

serves 8 to 10

This cake could not be easier or more beautiful in its rustic simplicity and straight-forward flavor. Really more like a big cookie, this type of "cake" is popular in northern Italy in the areas around Venice and is the perfect nibbling partner for an amiable visit— before you know it, all that's left is an empty plate. A crumbly shortbread-like dough is pressed in a thin layer in a tart pan and topped with the sheerest glaze of jam (I prefer a tart jam like apricot or grapefruit marmalade), then additional cookie dough is dotted over the surface and sprinkled with sliced almonds. Golden brown and homey, fregolotta is quick, easy, and the kind of dessert that everyone loves. What more could you want?

EQUIPMENT AND ADVANCE PREPARATION: One 9- or 9½-inch fluted tart pan with removable bottom

> 12 tablespoons (6 ounces) unsalted butter, softened
>
> ½ cup (3½ ounces) sugar
>
> ¼ teaspoon pure almond extract
>
> 1½ cups (7½ ounces) unbleached all-purpose flour
>
> ⅛ teaspoon salt
>
> ¼ cup (2 ounces) low-sugar apricot jam (Smucker's brand if available)
>
> ⅓ cup (1 ounce) sliced natural almonds
>
> **FOR SERVING**
> Powdered sugar, optional

Preheat the oven to 350°F. Position an oven rack in the center of the oven.

To make the cake, place the butter and sugar in the bowl of an electric mixer fitted with the paddle attachment (a handheld mixer is fine; just allow a little extra time to reach each stage in the recipe). Beat on medium speed until the mixture is very light in color, about 3 to 4 minutes. Use a rubber spatula to scrape down the sides of the bowl. Add the almond extract and blend well, another 30 seconds.

In a separate bowl, whisk together the flour and salt. Add the dry ingredients to the butter mixture and combine on low speed just until the dough is thoroughly blended, about 30 to 40 seconds. Measure out ½ cup of the dough and set it on a small plate, pressing it into a thin layer, then place the plate in the freezer (this will chill the dough just enough to make it easier to crumble).

Press the remaining dough into the tart pan in an even layer (the edges can be a little higher than the rest, just be careful that the center is not the thickest point). Use a small offset spatula or the back of a spoon to spread the jam in a thin, even layer over the surface of the dough, leaving a border of about 1 inch around the edges. Remove the reserved dough from the freezer and crumble it into small pieces over the layer of jam, allowing some of the jam to peek through. Sprinkle the sliced almonds evenly over the top of the cake. Bake for 40 to 50 minutes, or until the topping is a beautiful golden brown. Remove from the oven and place on a rack to cool completely.

To unmold, center the tart pan on top of a large can (I use a large can of tomatoes) so that it balances midair as the rim of the tart pan falls to the counter (see illustration, 77). Leave the bottom of the pan under the cake for support, or run a large spatula between the crust and the pan, using the spatula to guide the cake onto a plate.

SERVING AND STORAGE NOTES: Dust with a bit of powdered sugar, if you like, and use a large sharp knife to cut the cake into pie-like wedges. Alternatively, just let everyone break off pieces and nibble to their heart's content. Store the cake, covered with plastic wrap, at room temperature for 3 to 4 days.

GETTING AHEAD: The cake can be assembled ahead and frozen for up to 1 month. Assemble the cake in the tart pan, then wrap tightly twice in plastic wrap and freeze on a flat surface. To bake, unwrap the cake and place it in the preheated oven—allow a few extra minutes for baking.

Chocolate Soufflé Roll with Rum Mascarpone Cream

serves 10 to 12

When I was young, Hostess Ho-Hos were my favorite snack—neat little spirals of "cream" (what was that stuff?) inside chocolate cake, covered with a thin chocolate coating. I'd be afraid to read the ingredient label today, and besides, my tastes have changed for the better. Now I want the real chocolate, heavy cream, and whole egg version. In this recipe, a thin and heavenly flourless chocolate espresso cake is rolled around a filling of mascarpone and whipped cream flavored with vanilla and dark rum. I call it the "Italian Ho-Ho."

The amount of mascarpone in the filling may be small, but don't leave it out (well, okay, you could leave it out, but the filling is so much better for its presence). Besides adding a sensual richness and lovely flavor to the filling, the mascarpone acts as a stabilizer for the cream, keeping it firm yet silky for up to 5 days. Needless to say, this cake is great for a party. It can be made several days in advance, feeds a crowd, and any leftovers are just as delicious in the days following the fête.

EQUIPMENT AND ADVANCE PREPARATION: One 16½ x 11½-inch baking sheet with sides (if your pan is slightly smaller, the cake will take a bit longer to bake; if the pan is larger, the cake will be finished more quickly). Do not use a sheet pan that is too much larger because the layer of batter is already thin. • Line the bottom of the pan with a piece of parchment paper cut to fit. • A double boiler (or a medium saucepan coupled with a medium stainless-steel mixing bowl that will fit about halfway into the saucepan when sitting on top of it)

FOR THE CAKE

4 ounces bittersweet or semisweet chocolate, chopped into small pieces

3 tablespoons (1½ ounces) warm water

1½ teaspoons instant espresso granules, preferably Medaglia d'Oro brand

4 large eggs, separated

⅓ cup (2¼ ounces) plus 2 tablespoons (1 ounce) sugar

¾ cup (6 ounces) heavy cream

2 tablespoons (1 ounce) sugar

1 teaspoon pure vanilla extract

1 teaspoon dark rum

¼ cup (2 ounces) mascarpone

2 to 3 tablespoons unsweetened Dutch-process cocoa powder (262)

FOR SERVING

Unsweetened Dutch-process cocoa powder (262), optional

Raspberry sauce (149), optional

Fresh raspberries, optional

Preheat the oven to 350°F. Position an oven rack in the center of the oven.

To melt the chocolate, place the chopped chocolate in the top of the double boiler or a medium bowl. In a separate small bowl, blend the warm water and instant espresso until the granules have completely dissolved, then pour this mixture over the chocolate. Bring 2 inches of water to a boil in the bottom of the double boiler, then turn off the heat and place the chocolate over the hot water (the top of the double boiler should not touch the water). Stir occasionally until the chocolate is melted and smooth. Remove from the heat.

To make the cake, place the egg yolks and ⅓ cup sugar in the bowl of an electric mixer fitted with the whisk attachment (a handheld mixer is fine; just allow a little extra time to reach each stage in the recipe). Whip on high speed until the mixture is very thick, light in color, and ribbons when it falls from the whisk to the surface of the batter, about 3 to 4 minutes. Use a rubber spatula to gently fold the warm melted chocolate into the beaten yolks. Set this mixture aside while you whip the egg whites.

In a clean mixing bowl, using a clean whisk attachment, whip the egg whites on medium-high speed until soft peaks form, about 1½ to 2 minutes. With the mixer running, slowly add the remaining 2 tablespoons of sugar, tablespoon by tablespoon, and continue beating just until the whites hold firm peaks and are glossy, another 1 to 2 minutes. To check the whites, dip a spoon into the bowl and scoop out some beaten whites—the whites should sit firmly on the spoon, and the peaks that formed in the bowl when the spoon was lifted should hold their shape (the very tips of the peaks may bend slightly—this is okay). Be careful not to overbeat the whites, or they will begin to clump and separate.

Using a rubber spatula, gently stir one quarter of the egg whites into the chocolate mixture to lighten the batter, then carefully fold in the remaining whites. Pour the batter into the prepared pan and use an offset spatula or the back of a spoon to gently spread it in an even layer—it will be thin. Bake for 13 to 17 minutes, or until the cake feels firm in the center when lightly pressed with a fingertip. Remove from the oven and place on a rack to cool slightly (about 5 to 8 minutes). Do not let it cool completely, as you will need to roll the cake while it is lukewarm.

To make the filling, place the cream, sugar, vanilla, and rum in the bowl of an electric mixer fitted with the whisk attachment and whip on medium speed until the cream holds soft peaks. Turn the mixer to low and gently blend in the mascarpone, then turn the mixer to medium and continue beating until the cream holds firm peaks. Do not overwhip the cream, or it will begin to separate and look curdled. If this happens, remove the bowl from the mixer and use a rubber spatula to gently stir in several tablespoons of cream, just until the whipped cream has smoothed out again.

While the cake is still lukewarm, run a thin, sharp knife around the edges to loosen it from the pan. Sift the cocoa powder over the cake in a thin, even layer. Place a large piece of parchment paper or waxed paper on the cake—it should be big enough to completely cover the surface of the cake and hang over the short edges of the pan. Grip the paper and the short sides of the pan together, then flip the pan over and set it down with one of the long sides parallel to the edge of your work surface. Allow the cake to fall out of the pan and onto the clean paper. Remove the pan, then carefully and slowly peel back the baking parchment from the cake (this is easiest, and least damaging to the cake, when done on an angle, from corner to corner). Don't worry if you have a few cracks in the surface of the cake— once the cake is rolled and sliced, no one will know.

To assemble the cake, use an offset spatula or a kitchen knife to spread the filling evenly over the surface except for a 1-inch border along the long side opposite you as shown on the previous page. Starting at the long side closest to you, fold the edge of the cake over the filling and then begin to carefully roll the cake into a log, pulling upward and slightly forward on the paper as shown on the previous page. Use the paper as a tool to help roll the cake over on itself—do not press down as you do this, or the cake will break and filling will ooze out. Keep rolling until the long side farthest from you is squarely at the bottom of the roll. Use a long metal spatula (or 2 short ones) to carefully slide the roll onto a cake cardboard or serving platter (if this is too tricky, just cut the cake roll in half to make it easier). Refrigerate, covered with plastic, until ready to serve.

SERVING AND STORAGE NOTES: Before serving, trim the ends of the cake, which may be dry. Cut into ½-inch-thick slices with a thin, sharp knife, occasionally wiping the knife clean with a warm towel as you work. Serve 2 slices per person. For a dressier presentation, lightly dust each plate with cocoa powder, serve with raspberry sauce, and garnish with a few fresh raspberries. Store the cake in the refrigerator, covered with plastic wrap.

GETTING AHEAD: The cake may be completed up to 2 days in advance—store in the refrigerator, covered with plastic wrap. The cake will hold well for up to 5 days but is at its best within the first few days.

Orange Flower and Pine Nut Armadillos with Apricot Sauce

serves 6

I call these little cakes "armadillos" because their pine nut–studded exteriors resemble a cobblestone mosaic of armor covering a soft, moist interior. Similar to pound cake, with semolina substituted for part of the flour, these cakes have a slightly nubby texture and a golden hue. The addition of orange flower water adds an enchanting floral note that perfectly complements the nuts and grain, setting this dessert's roots firmly in the center of the Mediterranean. Semolina, a slightly granular wheat flour used chiefly for making pasta, can be found in the bulk section of natural food stores (see Mail-Order Sources, 327).

EQUIPMENT AND ADVANCE PREPARATION: Six 6-ounce custard cups (I use Pyrex) or ramekins

FOR THE CUSTARD CUPS

4 tablespoons (2 ounces) unsalted butter, room temperature

¾ cup (3¾ ounces) pine nuts, toasted (252)

FOR THE CAKE

12 tablespoons (6 ounces) unsalted butter, room temperature

⅔ cup plus 1 tablespoon (5 ounces) sugar

1 tablespoon finely chopped orange zest (145), about 1 large orange

3 large eggs, room temperature

⅔ cup plus 1 tablespoon (3½ ounces) unbleached all-purpose flour

⅓ cup plus 2 tablespoons (2½ ounces) fine semolina

½ teaspoon baking powder

¼ teaspoon salt

⅓ cup (2¾ ounces) whole milk, room temperature

1 tablespoon orange flower water (260)

1 teaspoon pure vanilla extract

1 cup (10 ¾ ounces) low-sugar apricot jam (Smucker's brand if available)

¼ cup (2 ounces) freshly squeezed orange juice or water

⅛ teaspoon ground cardamom

FOR SERVING

Powdered sugar

Honey cream (53)

To prepare the custard cups for baking, use a pastry brush to heavily coat the inside of each custard cup with 2 teaspoons of the softened butter (you will think it's too much, but you need it for the nuts to adhere). Add 2 tablespoons pine nuts to each cup and rotate the cup so the nuts cover the bottom and sides of the cup evenly.

Preheat the oven to 350°F. Position an oven rack in the center of the oven.

To make the cake batter, place the butter and sugar in the bowl of an electric mixer fitted with the paddle attachment (a handheld mixer is fine; just allow a little extra time to reach each stage in the recipe). Beat on medium speed until the butter is light in color, about 2 to 3 minutes. Beat in the orange zest. In a small bowl, whisk the eggs just until blended. With the mixer running, dribble the eggs into the butter a couple tablespoons at a time, allowing each addition to blend in fully (about 15 to 20 seconds) before adding the next. Stop the mixer and use a rubber spatula to scrape down the sides of the bowl a couple of times during this process. The mixture may look slightly curdled or broken, but it will smooth out as you add the flour.

In a small bowl, whisk together the flour, semolina, baking powder, and salt. In a liquid measuring cup, whisk together the milk, orange flower water, and vanilla. Add one-third of the flour to the batter and mix on low for 6 to 8 seconds, then add half the milk and mix again for 6 to 8 seconds. Scrape down the bowl and continue adding the flour and milk alternately, first half of the remaining flour, then the rest of the milk, and finally the rest of the flour, beating for 6 to 8 seconds after each addition. Turn the mixer to medium and beat for 15 seconds, then scrape down the bowl and beat again for 10 to 15 seconds, or until the batter is very smooth and well blended.

Place the prepared custard cups on a sheet pan—this makes it easy to transfer the cakes in and out of the oven and to rotate the cakes, if necessary, for even baking. Divide the cake batter among the custard cups. Bake for 30 to 35 minutes, or until the center of the cakes spring back when gently touched with a fingertip or until a toothpick inserted into their centers comes out free of crumbs. Remove from the oven and place on a rack to cool for 5 minutes. Then turn the cakes out of the custard cups onto the rack to finish cooling completely (the pine nut–covered areas should be facing upward).

To make the apricot sauce, combine the apricot jam, orange juice (or water), and cardamom in a small saucepan. Place over low heat and cook, stirring occasionally and breaking up any large lumps of fruit with the spoon, just until the mixture begins to simmer. Remove from the heat and use immediately, or place in a container and refrigerate until needed. Warm gently before use.

SERVING AND STORAGE NOTES: Place a cake in the center of each plate and surround with 2 to 3 tablespoons of the warm apricot sauce. Should you be lucky enough to have an orange tree (or access to one), orange blossoms are the perfect garnish. Otherwise, a light dusting of powdered sugar enhances the pebbly texture of the cake's surface. Place a spoonful of honey cream on top or just to the side of each cakelette. Store the cakelettes, wrapped individually in plastic wrap, at room temperature. Though the cakes are at their best the same day they are baked, they will keep for 2 to 3 days.

Honey Cream

makes about 1½ cups

This silky, softly draping cream is perfumed with the flavor of honey, making it a fine accompaniment to Mediterranean-style desserts. Used throughout the region, honey is an ancient sweetener whose flavor depends upon the flowers visited by the honeybee. Standard supermarket honey (clover or orange blossom) is fine here, but for an extra nuance of flavor, experiment with "varietal" honeys, which can be found in upscale markets and at farmers' markets. Good choices include lavender honey, wildflower honey, rosemary or thyme honey, or even the strongly flavored chestnut honey, which has a bitter edge and a deep, earthy, almost herbal flavor. If your honey has crystallized, warm it in a saucepan of hot water until it melts into a liquid state again.

1 cup heavy cream, very cold

2 to 4 teaspoons honey, to taste

Place the cream and honey in a mixing bowl and whip to soft peaks—the cream should look smooth, satiny, and sensuous and barely hold its shape. If you remove a spoonful, the peaks that formed in the bowl when the spoon was lifted should bend over gently and gracefully, like a swan's neck when it drinks from the water. If you are using an electric mixer, set the speed to medium for a more stable whipped cream, as cream whipped on high begins to break down and becomes watery much more quickly. Do not overwhip the cream, or it will begin to separate and look curdled. If this happens, remove the bowl from the mixer and use a rubber spatula to gently stir in 1 to 2 tablespoons of cream, just until the whipped cream has smoothed out again. Store until needed in a covered container in the refrigerator. Whipped cream is best when used the same day, preferably within a few hours. If the cream seems too soft when you use it, beat it lightly with a hand whisk to firm it up.

VARIATIONS

Softly Whipped Cream: This is the type of whipped cream that we know and love. Follow the recipe above, substituting white sugar for the honey. You may add the variations described below as well, if you like.

Flavored Creams: Flavor the honey cream with ⅛ teaspoon of spice, such as cardamom, cinnamon, ginger, or cloves. For another layer of flavor, either with spices or alone, try a teaspoon or two of liqueur, such as Amaretto di Saronno (almond), Frangelico (hazelnut), or Grand Marnier (orange). A few drops of orange flower water or rose water can add a wonderful floral dimension to the cream.

Grilled Coconut Cake with Double-Lime Ice Cream

serves 8

Coconut is popular in the Mediterranean and is especially well loved in the Middle East. This cake is perfect as the ending to a meal featuring the spicy, sometimes fiery foods of North Africa or the Middle East, but it would be just as welcome at an all-American feast like a Fourth of July barbecue. A tender coconut cake, reminiscent of a giant macaroon, is cut into thick slices and grilled over barbecue coals, then served warm with a scoop of brac-ingly tart lime ice cream. The grilling forms a crisp crust on the outside of the cake, con-trasting with its meltingly moist center. The warm sweetness of the coconut set off by the refreshing acidity of the ice cream makes a dynamite ending for an outdoor summer menu.

If there is no barbecue available, simply sauté the cake slices in a skillet to warm and crisp them before serving (see the variation at the end of the recipe). I like to serve this with plump boysenberries or blackberries or with slices of mango, depending on what is in season.

EQUIPMENT AND ADVANCE PREPARATION: One 9 x 5 x 3-inch loaf pan • Brush the bottom and sides of the pan with a thin, even coat of melted butter, then dust the pan with flour, tapping out any excess.

FOR THE CAKE

¾ cup (2¼ ounces) finely shredded unsweetened coconut (available in the bulk section of natural food stores; see Note)

1 stick (4 ounces) unsalted butter, room temperature

1 cup (7 ounces) sugar

3 large eggs, room temperature

1¾ cups (6 ounces) cake flour, sifted, then spooned gently into the cups for measuring

1 teaspoon baking powder

¼ teaspoon salt

2 teaspoons pure vanilla extract

½ cup (4 ounces) whole milk, room temperature

FOR GRILLING

4 tablespoons (2 ounces) unsalted butter, very soft

FOR SERVING

Double-Lime Ice Cream (309)

Blackberries or mango slices, optional

NOTE: If the only coconut you can find is the large-shred variety, pulse it in the food processor until it is finely chopped.

Preheat the oven to 350°F. Position an oven rack in the center of the oven.

To toast the coconut, place a dry 10-inch skillet over medium heat. When the pan is hot, add the coconut and cook, stirring every 5 to 10 seconds, until it begins to turn a very light golden brown—it will not color evenly but will be a mixture of beige and golden brown. Remove the pan from the heat and immediately pour the coconut onto a plate or baking sheet to cool. If left in the skillet, it will continue to cook from the residual heat and could get too dark. Set aside until needed.

To make the cake, place the butter and sugar in the bowl of an electric mixer fitted with the paddle attachment (a handheld mixer is fine; just allow a little extra time to reach each stage in the recipe). Beat on medium speed until the butter is light in color, about 2 to 3 minutes. Add the eggs one by one, allowing each addition to blend in fully (about 15 to 20 seconds) before adding the next. Stop the mixer and use a rubber spatula to scrape down the sides of the bowl once during this process.

In a medium bowl, whisk together the flour, cooled coconut, baking powder, and salt. Add the vanilla to the milk in your measuring cup. Add one-third of the flour to the batter and mix on low speed for 10 seconds, then add one-half of the milk and mix again for 10 seconds. Scrape down the bowl and continue adding the flour and milk alternately, first half of the remaining flour, then the rest of the milk, and finally the rest of the flour, beating for 10 seconds after each addition. Turn the mixer to medium and beat for 15 seconds, then scrape down the bowl and beat again for 10 to 15 seconds, or until the batter is thoroughly blended.

Scrape the batter into the prepared pan and use the edge of your spatula to gently spread it in an even layer. Bake for 50 to 55 minutes, or until the center of the cake springs back when gently touched with a fingertip or until a toothpick inserted into the center comes out free of crumbs. Remove from the oven and place on a rack to cool for 5 minutes. Then turn the cake out of the pan onto the rack to finish cooling completely.

To grill the cake, if you have a gas grill, heat it to medium-low. If you have a charcoal grill, wait until the coals are completely covered with gray ash and are beginning to cool down rather than at the height of their heat, when the fire would burn the cake. You want a medium-low to low heat, which means you can hold your hand about 5 inches above the grilling surface for 3 to 5 seconds (about 40 to 50 minutes after the coals were lit). Before you grill the cake, make sure your grill is clean by scrubbing it briskly with a wire grill brush, allowing any debris to fall into the fire. Brush or wipe the grill with a little melted butter or flavorless vegetable oil.

Cut the cake into 1-inch-thick slices and spread each side with just enough of the softened butter to cover the surface in a thin layer. Place the slices on the prepared grill. The cooking time will vary depending on the heat of your coals— you want the cake to be hot and lightly toasted before turning over to cook the other side (if the grill is hot enough to create grill marks on the cake without burning it, so much the better, but the marks are not necessary), about 2 to 4 minutes per side over medium-low coals.

SERVING AND STORAGE NOTES: Have your ice cream and fruit (if using) nearby as you grill the cake. Serve the cake slices hot off the grill, topped with a scoop of Double-Lime Ice Cream. Scatter the fruit around the plate. Store the unsliced cake, wrapped in plastic wrap, at room temperature. Though the cake is at its best the same day it is baked, it will keep well for 3 days.

GETTING AHEAD: You can make the Double-Lime Ice Cream several days ahead. Homemade ice cream may get very hard after several days in the freezer. If this happens, let it soften in the refrigerator for 15 to 30 minutes before serving.

VARIATION

Skillet-Grilled Coconut Cake: Melt 1 tablespoon butter in a 10-inch skillet over medium heat. When the pan is hot and the butter is bubbling, cut the cake into 1-inch-thick slices and place 4 in the pan. Cook for 2 to 3 minutes, or until golden brown. Remove the slices from the pan, melt another tablespoon of butter in the pan, then turn the slices over and return them to the pan. Cook another 2 to 3 minutes, or until golden brown on the second side. Serve immediately with the ice cream. Repeat with the remaining 4 slices of cake.

Caramelized Apple Cake with Rosemary

serves 8 to 10

Crowned with a crunchy crumble topping, this cake contains a true harmony of enchanting and earthy flavors. Though it can be made year-round, I like this cake best warm from the oven on a cool fall or winter evening, served with a bit of Crème Fraîche Ice Cream or good store-bought vanilla ice cream.

EQUIPMENT AND ADVANCE PREPARATION: One 9-inch springform cake pan • Brush the sides and bottom of the pan with a thin, even coat of melted butter. Line the bottom of the pan with a round of parchment paper cut to fit. Alternatively, dust the greased pan with flour, tapping out any excess.

FOR THE CRUMBLE TOPPING

⅓ cup (1 ¾ ounces) unbleached all-purpose flour

½ cup (3½ ounces) sugar

½ teaspoon ground cinnamon

4 tablespoons (2 ounces) cold butter, cut into ½-inch pieces

3 tablespoons (generous ½ ounce) coarsely chopped walnuts, toasted (follow the instructions for toasting whole almonds on page 254)

FOR THE CARAMELIZED APPLE

1 tablespoon (½ ounce) unsalted butter

1 tablespoon (½ ounce) sugar

1 large firm, tart-sweet apple (8 to 10 ounces), peeled, cored, and chopped into ¼-inch pieces (a Granny Smith is good, but if you can find an antique apple like Gravenstein, Northern Spy, or Ashmead's Kernel, so much the better)

FOR THE CAKE

1 stick (4 ounces) unsalted butter, softened

1 cup (7 ounces) sugar

2 large eggs, room temperature

1 teaspoon pure vanilla extract

1½ cups (7½ ounces) unbleached all-purpose flour

1 teaspoon baking powder

¾ teaspoon very finely chopped fresh rosemary

¼ teaspoon salt

½ cup (4 ounces) milk

FOR SERVING

Powdered sugar

Crème Fraîche Ice Cream (302) or softly whipped cream (54)

Fresh rosemary sprigs

To make the crumble topping, place the flour, sugar, and cinnamon in the bowl of an electric mixer fitted with the paddle attachment (or use a mixing bowl and a pastry blender, 2 knives, or your fingertips to cut the butter into the flour mixture). Beat on medium-low speed until blended, about 1 minute. Add the cold butter pieces and continue on medium-low until the mixture looks like wet sand and starts to form small to medium clumps, about 1 to 2 minutes. Transfer to a small bowl, stir in the chopped walnuts, and refrigerate until needed.

To caramelize the apple, place the butter in an 8-inch sauté pan over medium heat and cook until it is melted. Swirl the pan to completely coat the bottom with the butter. Add the sugar and cook for 1 minute without stirring (the sugar may look clumpy—that's okay). Add the apple pieces (they should form a single layer), turn the heat to high, and cook without stirring until the bottom of the apples are nicely browned, about 4 minutes. Toss or stir the apples and continue to cook for another 3 to 4 minutes, stirring occasionally, until they are an even golden brown color. Remove from the heat and transfer the apples to a plate or baking sheet to cool completely before continuing with the recipe.

Preheat the oven to 350°F. Position an oven rack in the center of the oven.

To make the cake, place the butter and sugar in the bowl of an electric mixer fitted with the paddle attachment (a handheld mixer is fine; just allow a little extra time to reach each stage in the recipe). Beat on medium speed until the butter is light in color, about 2 to 3 minutes. Use a rubber spatula to scrape down the bowl. Add the eggs, one at a time, allowing the first to blend in fully (about 15 to 20 seconds) before adding the second. Add the vanilla and blend well.

In a medium bowl, whisk together the flour, baking powder, rosemary, and salt. Add one-third of this mixture to the batter and mix on low for 10 seconds, then add half the milk and mix again for 10 seconds. Scrape down the bowl and continue adding the flour and milk alternately, first half of the remaining flour, then the rest of the milk, and finally the rest of the flour, beating for 10 seconds after each addition. Turn the mixer to medium and beat for 15 seconds. Gently fold in the cooled apple pieces.

Scrape the batter into the prepared pan and use the edge of your spatula to smooth and level the top. Sprinkle the crumble topping evenly over the surface of the cake. Bake for 55 to 65 minutes, or until the topping is a light golden brown and a toothpick inserted into the center of the cake comes out clean of crumbs. Remove from the oven and place on a rack to cool completely.

To unmold the cake, run a small, sharp knife around the edges of the cake to loosen any areas that may have stuck to the pan. As you do this, gently press the knife into the side of the pan to avoid gouging the cake. Then pop the sides off the springform pan and set aside. Gently set a plate or cake cardboard on top of the cake, then flip it over and remove the bottom of the pan and the parchment paper. Place your serving dish or a cake cardboard on the bottom of the cake, then turn the cake right side up.

SERVING AND STORAGE NOTES: Dust the cake lightly with powdered sugar. Serve each slice accompanied by a scoop of Crème Fraîche Ice Cream or a spoonful of softly whipped cream. If you like, garnish each plate with a small sprig of fresh rosemary. Though the cake is at its best the same day it is baked, it may be stored, wrapped in plastic, at room temperature for 3 to 4 days.

GETTING AHEAD: The crumble topping may be made in advance and refrigerated in an airtight container for up to 5 days or in the freezer for up to 1 month.

Apples

Apples may be one of our nation's most popular fruits, as well as a national icon ("as American as apple pie"), but their origins are halfway around the world. The first "modern" apples grew in the Caucasus in western Asia and were cultivated by Neolithic farmers at least 8,000 years ago. Certainly they were in the Mediterranean by the time of Homer, but it was the Romans who left us descriptions of cultivation and grafting that are still relevant today. The fall of the Roman empire was a disaster for agriculture on many levels, and fruit culture entered a dark and uneventful period. It was only when Islamic conquerors invaded Spain and France in the early 700s that Roman horticultural methods were put to use once again and apples became an integral part of the medieval diet.

The cultivation of sweet eating apples became an art in Europe, with the French pioneering important innovations in growing techniques. They perfected the training of trees onto trellises, or *espaliers*. They also developed the dwarf tree by grafting cultivated branches onto the trunk of a native wild apple. When large numbers of Huguenots immigrated to Great Britain in the late 1600s, they brought with them their apple-growing experience, along with the varieties they had enjoyed in France, leading to an apple explosion in England. Early American colonists brought apple seeds with them, though the fruit was used mainly to produce their favorite beverage—hard cider. Still, it was from those first seedling orchards that some of the best American apples were born, such as the Roxbury Russet, the Rhode Island Greening, and the Newton Pippin. After the Revolutionary War, grafting techniques became common knowledge, and acres of the most popular local varieties sprang up across the country.

In the early 1900s more than a thousand types of apples were available in America. Today, less than a century later, there are only about one hundred. Wonderful local apples fell out of favor with the advent of cold storage, which meant there was no longer any need for apples that ripen successively from summer through winter. Supermarkets demanded the perfect, blemish-free apple for their shelves (many of the best varieties are mottled, striped, or otherwise unlike the primer picture of a red, shiny specimen), and juice and canning companies required vast tonnage of only limited varieties. Luckily, there are home gardeners and farmers across the country who appreciate many of the "antique" or "heirloom" varieties.

Yes, Virginia, there is a whole world of apples beyond Red Delicious, Granny Smith, and Gala, and it is a world full of exciting flavors, textures, and colors. Among the varieties, you may find are apples with names like Arkansas Black, Ashmead's Kernel, Gravenstein, Northern Spy, Pink Pearl, Spitzenburg, and Stayman Winesap. Search out heirloom apples at your farmers' market or roadside stand. You'll enjoy some of the best apples of your life, and you'll help local farmers keep both the genetic diversity and the tradition of flavor alive. To track down farmers in your area growing heirloom apples, contact your local extension service or agricultural experiment station. If you would like to grow your own antique apples, contact the nurseries listed in Mail-Order Sources (327) for a catalog and suggestions on the varieties most appropriate for your locale.

Almond Brown Butter Cakes with Raspberries

serves 6

These individual cakes are similar to the classic French financiers—little almond cakes that are crisp on the outside and meltingly tender on the inside, baked in rectangular pans to resemble mini bars of gold. What I like best about these cakes is the contrast between the crisp crust that forms during the first few minutes of baking and the soft, nutty interior, so I bake the batter in individual tartlet pans for a greater crust-to-crumb ratio. Raspberries sprinkled on top perfume the batter during baking and are the perfect complement to the almonds and brown butter. Though blanched almonds are traditional, I like to use almonds with their skins intact for both the extra layer of almond flavor and the lovely speckled appearance they give the batter. The batter takes only about 5 minutes to prepare, and the cakes bake very quickly, so it's easy to serve them at their best—fresh from the oven. I've even served them for breakfast, with a few extra raspberries on the plate and a bit of crème fraîche; they are heavenly alongside a cup of good coffee.

EQUIPMENT AND ADVANCE PREPARATION: Six 4½-inch fluted tartlet pans with removable bottoms • Brush the sides and bottom of each pan with a thin, even coat of melted butter.

FOR THE CAKES

1⅔ cups (4¾ ounces) powdered sugar, sifted and spooned gently into the cups for measuring

1 cup (5½ ounces) whole natural almonds, toasted (254)

⅓ cup (1¾ ounces) unbleached all-purpose flour

5 large egg whites

12 tablespoons (6 ounces) unsalted butter

1 half-pint basket (about 6 ounces) raspberries

FOR SERVING

Powdered sugar

Crème fraîche (303), optional

Whole raspberries, optional

Preheat the oven to 450°F. Position an oven rack in the center of the oven.

To make the cake batter, place the powdered sugar, almonds, and flour in the bowl of a food processor fitted with the steel blade and process until the nuts are finely ground, about 20 to 30 seconds. Transfer the mixture to a medium mixing bowl. Add the egg whites and whisk them into the flour and almonds until well blended. Set aside.

To brown the butter, melt it in a small saucepan over low heat, swirling the pan occasionally. When the butter is completely melted, turn the heat to medium and cook for about 6 minutes. First it will bubble vigorously, then the solids at the bottom will turn a dark brown—do not let them blacken, or they will be bitter. Immediately pour the butter into the batter and gently whisk the mixture to blend thoroughly.

Place the prepared tartlet pans on a sheet pan—this makes it easy to transfer the cakes in and out of the oven and to rotate the cakes, if necessary, for even baking. Divide the batter among the tartlet pans. Sort through the raspberries and discard any debris or moldy berries (do not wash fresh raspberries, as they will absorb the water and disintegrate and are virtually impossible to dry, which leads to mushy berries with watered-down flavor). Divide the berries evenly among the pans, sprinkling them over the surface of each tartlet.

Bake for 7 minutes, then reduce the oven temperature to 400°F and continue baking for 7 minutes more. Turn the oven off and leave the cakes in the oven for an additional 7 minutes. Remove from the oven and place on a rack to cool briefly. Serve warm.

SERVING AND STORAGE NOTES: Dust lightly with powdered sugar. Place a warm cake on each serving plate. If you like, serve with a spoonful of crème fraîche and scatter a few raspberries around the plate. These little cakes are best served warm from the oven or within a few hours of baking. Store, uncovered, at room temperature overnight—do not wrap in plastic, as it softens the crust.

VARIATION

Hazelnut Brown Butter Cakes with Raspberries: The earthiness of toasted hazelnuts is a lovely counterpoint to the sweet perfume of raspberries. Substitute 1¼ cups (5 ounces) whole hazelnuts, toasted and peeled (227), for the almonds in the recipe above.

Mocha Chiffon Cake with Cinnamon and Orange

Though the chiffon cake is a purely American invention, the flavors here transport you to a sidewalk cafe in the Mediterranean, where a cup of coffee and a "little chocolate something" serve to revive your spirits. I like to serve this towering cake with a puddle of toasted almond caramel sauce, which complements the deep, mellow flavors of espresso and bittersweet chocolate blended lusciously with an underpinning of orange and a familiar note of cinnamon. Moist, rich, yet light as air, this cake is perfect for a crowd.

EQUIPMENT AND ADVANCE PREPARATION: One 10-inch tube pan with removable bottom (do not grease) • This cake is similar to angel food cake in that it needs to cool upside down for several hours. You will need a long-necked bottle over which to invert the cake while it cools. You could also use 3 coffee cups of the same size: set them upside down on the counter, then invert the cake pan, setting the metal "feet" of the pan on the bottoms of the evenly spaced cups.

FOR THE CAKE

¾ cup (6 ounces) water

⅓ cup plus 2 tablespoons unsweetened Dutch-process cocoa powder (262), spooned lightly into the cup for measuring (don't worry about lumps)

2 teaspoons instant espresso granules, preferably Medaglia d'Oro brand

1¾ cups plus 2 tablespoons (6½ ounces) cake flour, sifted, then spooned gently into the cups for measuring

1¼ cups (8¾ ounces) plus ¼ cup (1¾ ounces) sugar

2 teaspoons baking powder

1½ teaspoons ground cinnamon

½ teaspoon salt

½ cup (4 ounces) flavorless vegetable oil, preferably safflower oil

6 large egg yolks

2 tablespoons very finely chopped orange zest (145), about 2 large oranges

1 tablespoon pure vanilla extract

9 large egg whites

1 teaspoon cream of tartar

½ cup (3 ounces) miniature bittersweet chocolate chips (274)

FOR SERVING

Powdered sugar, optional

Toasted almond caramel sauce (67), optional

Preheat the oven to 325°F. Position an oven rack in the lower third of the oven.

To make the cake, place the water in a small saucepan over medium heat and bring just to a boil. Place the cocoa and espresso granules in a small bowl and pour the boiling water over them, stirring with a metal spoon until blended and smooth. Set aside.

Sift the cake flour, 1¼ cups sugar, baking powder, cinnamon, and salt into a large mixing bowl. Pour the vegetable oil, egg yolks, cocoa mixture, orange zest, and vanilla into the center of the dry ingredients and use a whisk to blend the mixture until it is very smooth.

Place the egg whites and cream of tartar in the very clean bowl of an electric mixer fitted with the whisk attachment (a handheld mixer is fine, but allow a little extra time to reach each stage in the recipe). Whip the whites on medium-high speed until soft peaks form, about 2 to 3 minutes. With the mixer running, add the remaining ¼ cup of sugar in a slow, steady stream and continue beating just until the whites hold firm peaks and are glossy, another 2 to 4 minutes. To check the whites, dip a spoon into the bowl and scoop out some beaten whites—the whites should sit firmly on the spoon, and the peaks that formed in the bowl when the spoon was lifted should hold their shape (the very tips of the peaks may bend slightly—this is okay). Be careful not to overbeat the whites, or they will begin to clump and separate.

Use a rubber spatula to stir one-third of the beaten whites into the chocolate batter to loosen and lighten the mixture, then gently fold in the remaining whites until no streaks of white remain. Gently but thoroughly fold in the miniature bittersweet chocolate chips. Scrape the batter into the tube pan and level the top with the spatula or the back of a spoon. Bake for 50 to 60 minutes, until the center of the cake springs back when gently touched with a fingertip or until a toothpick inserted into the center comes out free of crumbs. Remove the cake from the oven and immediately invert it over the long-necked bottle (or set it on the coffee cups) to cool for 2 to 3 hours.

To unmold the cake, run a thin, sharp knife around the edges of the cake to loosen it from the pan. As you do this, gently press the knife into the side of the pan to avoid gouging the cake. Push the removable bottom upward to free the cake from the pan. Then run the same knife around the inside tube and along the bottom of the cake, if necessary, to finish loosening it. Place a plate on top of the cake and invert it, removing it from the pan. Set the cake right side up on a serving plate or cake cardboard.

SERVING AND STORAGE NOTES: Dust with powdered sugar, if desired, slice with a serrated knife, and serve at room temperature. Serve plain or with a pool of toasted almond caramel sauce. Store the cake at room temperature, wrapped in plastic wrap. It will keep well for 3 to 5 days or up to a week in the refrigerator.

Caramel Sauce

makes about 2 cups

I use caramel sauce much more often than chocolate sauce because I feel that its silken, sweet, and yet almost bitter presence enhances nearly every dessert. Here's a recipe for a cold caramel sauce that is smooth and pourable even when refrigerated. It's great to keep on hand for last-minute desserts and will hold in the refrigerator for at least 2 weeks. If the sauce seems a bit thick when you use it, stir in a tiny bit of warm water or cream until you get the consistency you want. And you can always warm it in the microwave or over low heat in a saucepan. Crazy for nuts? Try the variations at the end.

¼ cup (2 ounces) water

1 cup (7 ounces) sugar

1 ¾ cups (14 ounces) heavy cream

Place the water in a medium saucepan, then add the sugar and set the pan over medium-low heat. Stir constantly with a wooden spoon or swirl the pan frequently until the sugar is dissolved and the liquid is clear. Turn the heat to high and boil rapidly, swirling the pan occasionally (do not stir at this point) so that the sugar cooks evenly, until the syrup turns a deep golden brown. Remove the pan from the heat and immediately add the cream—be careful, the mixture will rise dramatically in the pan and sputter, so you may want to wear an oven mitt on the hand holding the pan. Stir with the wooden spoon to blend. If the caramel has solidified, set the pan back over low heat and stir until it melts again. Cool to room temperature. Place in an airtight container and refrigerate until needed.

GETTING AHEAD: The caramel sauce may be made up to 2 weeks in advance. Keep refrigerated.

If you make one of the nut variations below, add the toasted chopped nuts the same day you want to serve the sauce so they are nice and crunchy. They can be added to the sauce in advance but will eventually soften.

VARIATIONS

Toasted Almond Caramel Sauce: **Make the caramel sauce as directed above. When it is cold, stir in 1 to 2 tablespoons Amaretto di Saronno, to taste. Also stir in ⅓ cup (1½ ounces) whole natural almonds, toasted (254) and coarsely chopped.**

Toasted Pecan Caramel Sauce: **Follow the directions for toasted almond caramel sauce, substituting pecans for the almonds. If you like, substitute brandy or whiskey for the amaretto.**

Toasted Hazelnut Caramel Sauce: **Make the caramel sauce as directed above. When it is cold, stir in 1 to 2 tablespoons Frangelico, to taste. Also stir in ⅓ cup (1½ ounces) whole hazelnuts that have been toasted (227), peeled, and coarsely chopped.**

Pomegranate Dacquoise

serves 8

Dacquoise is a classic French dessert featuring two crispy meringue discs sandwiching a buttercream filling—crunchy, smooth, and rich at the same time. This recipe sends classic dacquoise into another dessert realm by layering pistachio meringues with the silkiest of buttercreams flavored with a Middle Eastern specialty called pomegranate molasses—a syrup made by boiling down fresh pomegranate juice to a thick liquid (see page 71). The bright, acidic fruit of the pomegranate molasses cuts through the richness of the buttercream. And while this dessert can be made year-round, it is especially nice in the fall, when fresh pomegranates are in season and a sprinkling of their beautiful crimson seeds can garnish each plate. Of all the desserts my mother gamely sampled (and sampled again) while I was writing this book, these individual cakes were her hands-down favorite.

EQUIPMENT AND ADVANCE PREPARATION: Two 16½ x 11½-inch baking sheets with sides • Cut 2 pieces of parchment paper to line the bottom of the pans. Use a pencil to trace eight 3-inch rounds on each piece of parchment (I use the top of a wide-mouth canning jar as a template). Turn the parchment over onto the sheet pans, pencil side down. • A candy thermometer (for the buttercream) • You will need to begin the pistachio meringues the day before you assemble the cakes, as they need to dry in the oven overnight. • If you find only pistachios in shells, buy double the weight given below and shell them by hand.

FOR THE PISTACHIO MERINGUE

½ cup (2¼ ounces) raw unsalted shelled pistachios, toasted (213)

⅓ cup (2¼ ounces) plus ½ cup (3½ ounces) sugar

2½ tablespoons (¾ ounce) sifted cornstarch

4 large egg whites

1 teaspoon pure vanilla extract

FOR THE POMEGRANATE BUTTERCREAM

2 large eggs, room temperature

⅔ cup (4¾ ounces) sugar

⅓ cup (2 ¾ ounces) water

¼ teaspoon cream of tartar

2 sticks (8 ounces) unsalted butter, very soft

3 tablespoons (1 ½ ounces) pomegranate molasses

FOR FINISHING

¾ cup (3 ¾ ounces) raw unsalted shelled pistachios, toasted (213) and
    coarsely chopped

FOR SERVING

Powdered sugar

¼ cup (1 ¼ ounces) raw unsalted shelled pistachios, toasted (213) and
    coarsely chopped

1 pomegranate (if available), seeded

Preheat the oven to 225°F. Position 2 oven racks in the center and top third of the oven.

To make the meringue, place the pistachios and ⅓ cup sugar in the bowl of a food processor and process until the nuts are finely ground, about 20 to 30 seconds. Transfer the mixture to a medium bowl and stir in the cornstarch until well blended.

    Place the egg whites and vanilla in the bowl of an electric mixer fitted with the whisk attachment and whip on medium-high speed until soft peaks form, about 1 ½ to 2 minutes (a handheld mixer is fine; just allow a little extra time to reach each stage in the recipe). With the mixer running, slowly add the remaining ½ cup sugar, tablespoon by table-spoon, then turn the speed to high and whip until the meringue is very stiff, about 30 to 45 seconds. Using a rubber spatula, gently fold in the nut mixture, then immediately transfer the meringue to a pastry bag fitted with a plain ½-inch tip.

    "Glue" the parchment paper to the sheet pans by piping a dot of meringue under each corner of the paper and pressing the paper down onto the pans. This will prevent the paper from moving while you are piping. Beginning in the center of each template, pipe the meringue in a circular pattern, spiraling out toward the edge of the circle as shown on the previous page. Keep the tip of the pastry bag about 1 inch from the surface—the meringue should fall to the paper in a thick ribbon. Bake for 1 hour, then turn off the oven and leave the meringues inside overnight to finish drying.

To make the buttercream, place the eggs in the bowl of an electric mixer fitted with the whisk attachment and whip on high speed until they are very thick and light in color, about 4 minutes. Place the sugar, water, and cream of tartar in a small saucepan over low heat and cook slowly, swirling the pan occasionally, until the sugar is melted and the liquid is clear. Place a candy thermometer in the liquid, then turn the heat to high and boil rapidly until the syrup registers 240°F (soft ball stage) on the thermometer.

When the syrup reaches the correct temperature, remove the pan immediately from the heat and, with the mixer on medium-high, slowly pour the syrup into the beaten eggs (pour it near the side of the bowl so it doesn't splatter). Continue beating on high until the mixture is cool to the touch, about 8 to 10 minutes. At this point, begin adding the softened butter, a couple of tablespoons at a time, blending well before each new addition, until all the butter has been incorporated. Add the pomegranate molasses and blend well.

To assemble the dacquoise, place the buttercream in a pastry bag fitted with a plain ½-inch tip. Place half (8) of the meringue discs, flat side down, on the table in front of you. Pipe a layer of buttercream on each disc, beginning in the center and spiraling outward, holding the pastry bag about an inch from the surface (you want the buttercream to fall onto the meringue in a thick ribbon, not be squashed onto it). Place the remaining discs on top of the filling, flat side up, pressing lightly to force the buttercream all the way to the edges of the meringue. Use an icing spatula or kitchen knife to smooth the filling around the sides, then lightly press the ¾ cup of chopped, toasted pistachios into the sides of the cakes. To press the nuts into the sides of the cake, put a small mound of nuts in the palm of your hand. With your other hand, tilt the cake toward the nuts as you gently press the nuts into the buttercream, letting the excess nuts fall onto your work surface. Proceed around each cake until all the sides are coated evenly with the chopped pistachios. Put the cakes on a sheet pan and wrap the pan in plastic (buttercream picks up any odors in the refrigerator very quickly). Refrigerate until serving time.

SERVING AND STORAGE NOTES: Remove the cakes from the refrigerator 15 to 20 minutes before serving to soften the buttercream. Dust each cake with powdered sugar. If you like, dust a bit of powdered sugar over each serving plate as well. Place a dacquoise in the center of each plate. Scatter the remaining ¼ cup of chopped pistachios and some fresh pomegranate seeds (if available) around the plates.

GETTING AHEAD: The pistachio meringues can be prepared up to 1 month in advance. Store them, with the parchment paper still attached to the bottom (this will help to prevent cracking), in an airtight container. If left out, they will absorb moisture in the air and gradually lose their crispness.

The buttercream may be prepared in advance. It will keep in the refrigerator for 1 week or in the freezer for up to 1 month. Store in an airtight container, as butter picks up odors easily. The buttercream must be at room temperature to finish the recipe.

The cakes may be assembled, then individually double-wrapped in plastic and stored in the refrigerator for 3 to 4 days, or they may be frozen for several weeks (thaw overnight in the refrigerator, still wrapped in plastic).

Pomegranate Molasses

Pomegranate molasses is a thick, intensely flavorful syrup made by boiling down fresh pomegranate juice. It packs a wollop of tartness, but the underlying caramelized sweetness of the cooked fruit juice adds complexity to the syrup. Its uses in the savory dishes of the Middle East are many—from meats and fish to vegetables and salads—but it is rarely seen in desserts. This is surprising, since its extraordinary flavor lends a burst of bright, acidic freshness to everything it touches. One reason may be the color, a deep brown-red, which is very appealing in savory dishes but, when blended with the yellows, creams, and whites of the pastry world, turns a rather unappetizing gray or pinkish brown. The key is to include it in desserts in which the color can be hidden. Color aside, once you taste pomegranate molasses, you'll be thinking up all kinds of uses for it in the pastry kitchen—adding a touch to caramel sauce, homemade candy, ice cream, pastry cream, curd, sabayon, sorbet—the list goes on. I like to keep a mixture of pomegranate molasses and sugar syrup on hand in the refrigerator to flavor mineral water—pure refreshment.

Pomegranate molasses is available in stores catering to a Middle Eastern clientele, though I've also found it in Italian markets and my local supermarket. My local Middle Eastern store carries three brands, and I've found the best and most reliable to be Cortas. If you can't find Cortas, buy a couple of brands and taste them to see which one you like best before adding it to a dessert—occasionally you may run across a brand that is bitter. Once you've opened the bottle, it will keep refrigerated for about a year. For the Cortas brand, see Mail-Order Sources, 327.

Tarts

What better way to frame the ripe, luscious fruits of the Mediterranean than in a crispy, buttery tart shell? Tarts can be found throughout the Mediterranean, though they are most closely associated with the countries of France, Italy, and Spain. And though pies are still more popular in this country, tarts are quickly gaining favor. The most important difference between a tart and a pie is the pans in which they are baked. In general, a tart pan is a flat ring with straight sides, about 1 inch high, usually sporting a fluted edge (pans with a removable bottom are the easiest to work with), while a pie pan is anywhere from 2 to 3 inches deep and has sloping sides. Tarts are almost always removed from the baking pan before serving, while pies must remain in their pans because their sides might collapse from the weight of the filling. In fact, some tarts use no pan at all and are made free-form style by simply shaping and filling the crust right on a sheet pan for baking. This difference between tart and pie pans translates to a dramatic difference in the final product; since the sides of the tart pan are so low, the ratio of crust to filling is much closer, which means the crust plays a more important part in the final dessert.

This closer partnership between crust and filling makes harmony between their flavors and textures all the more important. Most of the recipes in this chapter rely on two basic crust doughs—a flaky crust and a crumblier, cookie-like crust that I call shortcrust and is known as *pasta frolla* in Italy. Traditionally, a crisp, flaky dough is paired with meltingly sweet fruit like that in Apricot Tart with Shredded Filo and Pistachios, but it also enhances the confection-like filling of Caramel, Date, and Sesame Tart with Orange. And while a sweeter, more cookie-like dough is classically paired with the enchanting simplicity of sweet, fresh cheese in Goat Cheese and Ricotta Tart, it also marries well with the silken chocolate custard in Marbleized Chocolate Velvet Tart. There is even a fun stand-in for these traditional tart shells—a chewy macaroon-like crust that acts as a foil to pucker-up lime curd in Lime Brûlée Tartlets.

The great thing about the tarts in this chapter is that in addition to bursting with the flavors of the Mediterranean, they are very simple to make. The tart doughs can be made up to 3 months in advance and frozen, then baked on the day you want to finish the tart. When I have time, I make a double recipe of tart dough, roll it out and put it in the tart pans, then double-wrap the pans in plastic wrap, label, and freeze them. I always have at least one flaky tart shell and one shortcrust tart shell ready to bake in the freezer. With recipes this simple and tart shells in the freezer, dessert making is almost effortless.

Plum and Hazelnut Tart with Port Wine Glaze

serves 8 to 10

In this wine country variation of a favorite French bakery tart, sliced plums are nestled in a cake-like hazelnut filling and topped with a burgundy glistening of port wine that has been cooked to a syrupy glaze. The nut filling, known as frangipane to pastry makers, is traditionally made with almonds, but I've substituted hazelnuts here for their earthiness, which rounds out the sweet-tart flavor of the plums.

I first made this tart while living in the Napa Valley, with plums picked from abandoned trees laden with sweet purple jewels, but I've also made it with all manner of plums (a combination of several varieties can be beautiful), and it's always good. Just make sure the plums are firm ripe, for if they are very soft and juicy, they will exude too much liquid during the cooking process and make the tart soggy. My favorite varieties for this tart are Santa Rosa, Friar, and Casselman.

EQUIPMENT AND ADVANCE PREPARATION: 1 recipe Shortcrust Dough (114) to fill a 9- or 9½-inch fluted tart pan with removable bottom, partially baked and cooled

FOR THE HAZELNUT FILLING

¾ cup (4 ounces) hazelnuts, toasted and skinned (227)

½ cup (3½ ounces) sugar

4 tablespoons (2 ounces) unsalted butter, softened

2 large eggs

2 tablespoons unbleached all-purpose flour

4 large (16 ounces) firm-ripe plums

FOR THE PORT WINE GLAZE

1 cup (8 ounces) tawny port wine

⅓ cup (2⅓ ounces) sugar

½ teaspoon cornstarch

1 teaspoon water

Hazelnut Ice Cream (295), Lavender and Almond Praline Ice Cream (305), or Crème Fraîche Ice Cream (302) OR crème fraîche (303)

Preheat the oven to 375°F. Position an oven rack in the center of the oven.

To make the hazelnut filling, place the nuts and sugar in the bowl of a food processor and process until the nuts are finely ground, about 30 to 60 seconds. Add the butter and process until well blended, about 20 seconds. Add the eggs and flour and process to mix thoroughly, about 30 seconds, scraping down the bowl about halfway through. Pour the filling into the partially baked and cooled tart shell and use a small spatula or the back of a spoon to level and smooth the surface.

To prepare the plums, use a small, sharp knife and follow the natural line of the plums to cut the fruit in half. If the pit does not separate easily from the flesh, slice as close as possible to the pit, removing a large cheek from both sides of the plum. There will be a small piece of flesh left at the edges, and these can be sliced off and used in the tart. Cut each half into thirds. Place the plum slices, skin side down and close together, in a circular pattern on top of the filling, pressing them gently into the mixture. Bake the tart for 40 to 50 minutes, or until the filling is firm in the center and lightly browned. Remove from the oven and place on a rack to cool completely before glazing.

To make the port wine glaze, place the port wine and sugar in a small saucepan over medium heat and bring to a boil, stirring several times with a metal spoon to help dissolve the sugar. Continue boiling until the mixture is reduced to ½ cup. In a small bowl, whisk together the cornstarch and water, then add this mixture to the boiling wine, whisking constantly, and cook until the mixture has thickened slightly, about 30 seconds. Remove from the heat immediately (the glaze will thicken further as it cools). Brush the glaze lightly over the top of the tart, concentrating a little extra liquid on the plums. Reserve the remaining glaze.

To unmold, center the tart pan on top of a large can (I use a large can of tomatoes) so that it balances midair as the rim of the tart pan falls to the counter as shown. Leave the bottom of the pan under the tart for support, or slide the tart onto a serving plate by running a large spatula between the crust and the pan, using it to guide the tart onto the plate.

SERVING AND STORAGE NOTES: Drizzle each dessert plate with some of the reserved port wine glaze and serve the tart accompanied by your choice of Hazelnut, Lavender and Almond Praline, or Crème Fraîche Ice Cream. On the simpler side, a spoonful of crème fraîche topped with a bit of the port wine glaze is a silken accompaniment. Store the tart with plastic wrap pressed against the cut areas to prevent drying out. It will keep at room temperature for 2 days, refrigerated for 3 to 4 days (be sure to bring the tart to room temperature before serving).

GETTING AHEAD: The hazelnut filling can be prepared up to 4 days in advance—keep refrigerated in an airtight container. On the day you wish to make the tart, let it sit at room temperature for at least an hour before using, as it is difficult to spread in the tart shell when chilled (and the pressure you would have to use to spread it might break the tart shell).

The port wine glaze can be prepared up to 2 days in advance—keep refrigerated in an airtight container. If needed, warm slightly before using, just until it is liquid, so it is easier to brush on the fruit.

Wine Country Plums and Other Delights

Though best known for their grape plantings, Italian and Spanish settlers in the Napa Valley also cultivated a profusion of plum, fig, and olive trees. It is not unusual to happen upon plum trees nestled in the nooks and crannies of the valley in a wild-looking state, for much of their nurturing has been abandoned in favor of the almighty grape by succeeding landowners. But the plums, though small, are potent—juicy and flavorful and full of raisiny undertones that make them a perfect partner to port. Luckily, foraging in the land of the grape is not necessary. There are still a few farmers here and there who tend orchards and vegetable patches, and in the summer and early fall, homemade signs beckon from the sides of the two-lane road that traverses the center of the Napa Valley, enticing oenophiles to a local farmstand harvest. I've followed those signs often and have been rewarded with some of the best apples, pears, plums, quinces—and even eggs—I've ever eaten.

Louis and Ellie Fracchia have been farming in the valley for more than forty years, and if you follow the signs to Ellie's Apple Shack, you can savor the rewards of their labor. Summer into fall you'll find them knee deep in fragrant apples, from Gravensteins (the local favorite) to Pippins to Arkansas Blacks and more. Depending on the month, you'll also find juicy peaches, Black Mission figs from one of the most beautiful trees I've ever seen, sweet pears, persimmons, and even walnuts. Long retired from the grape-growing business, the Fracchias continue to cultivate their fruit trees out of a passion and commitment to their land. A few miles away a German man known only as Horse offers fresh-that-day eggs from his flock of free-roaming chickens—eggs with yolks of such a deep orange hue that one questions the comparatively sickly color of supermarket eggs. But don't visit him during the dog days of summer, when temperatures can reach well over 100°F, as chickens just stop laying when it gets too hot.

There are also a couple of weekly farmers' markets where flowers, baked goods, and local specialty foods can be found alongside the gorgeous produce. If you're planning a visit, contact the Napa Valley Chamber of Commerce for information on the days and times of the farmers' markets and enjoy a bit of Napa Valley flavor beyond the excellent wines.

Goat Cheese and Ricotta Tart

serves 8 to 10

Though its use in savory courses is well known, goat cheese rarely surfaces in desserts, which is a shame because its creamy acidity marries beautifully with the sweet, juicy fruits of summer. This simple tart may seem modest upon first glance, but its filling is a melt-in-your-mouth marriage of goat cheese with vanilla, orange zest, and ricotta, baked in a crumbly shortbread-like crust to form a dessert that I find irresistible . . . so much so that I keep slicing off little wedges ("Oh, just one more little taste") until I finish the whole thing. Surrounded by sweet farmstand berries, juicy summer peaches, or meltingly ripe figs, it is the perfect ending for a simple summer meal. I also enjoy it plain at breakfast or in the afternoon with a cup of tea all year long.

EQUIPMENT AND ADVANCE PREPARATION: 1 recipe Shortcrust Dough (114) to fill a 9- or 9½-inch fluted tart pan with removable bottom, fully baked and cooled

FOR THE FILLING

7 ounces fresh mild goat cheese (chèvre)

½ cup (3½ ounces) sugar

9 ounces whole-milk ricotta

2 large eggs

1½ teaspoons pure vanilla extract

1 teaspoon finely minced orange zest (145)

FOR SERVING

2 to 3 cups fresh sweet berries, such as raspberries, blackberries, strawberries, and/or blueberries OR 3 to 4 large ripe peaches, pitted and sliced into eighths OR 8 to 10 sweet ripe figs, cut into halves or quarters, depending on their size

Preheat the oven to 350°F. Position an oven rack in the center of the oven.

To make the filling, place the goat cheese and sugar in the bowl of a food processor and process until very smooth, about 10 to 15 seconds. Add the ricotta and process to combine thoroughly, another 8 to 10 seconds. Add the eggs, vanilla, and orange zest and process until well mixed, about 10 seconds. Pour the filling into the prebaked tart shell (the filling fits perfectly in a 9½-inch shell; if you use a smaller pan, you may have a little left over) and bake for about 25 to 30 minutes, or just until the center is set and firm, not jiggly, when the tart is gently shaken. If you notice a few little bubbles around the edge of the tart (resembling the bubbles on the top of a cooked pancake), the tart is probably done or very close to it, as they are a sign that the filling is just beginning to boil. Do not let the filling boil, or the eggs will scramble, resulting in a rough, cottage cheese–like texture rather than a smooth one. Remove from the oven and place on a rack to cool completely.

To unmold, when cool, center the tart pan on top of a large can (I use a large can of tomatoes) so that it balances midair as the rim of the tart pan falls to the counter (see illustration, 77). Leave the bottom of the pan under the tart for support, or slide the tart onto a serving plate by running a large metal spatula between the crust and the pan, using it to guide the tart onto the plate.

SERVING AND STORAGE NOTES: This tart is best served at room temperature the same day it is baked. Serve each slice surrounded by your choice of summer fruit. Wrapped in plastic, the tart can be stored in the refrigerator for 3 days. I like to bring the tart to room temperature before serving, but some friends swear the leftovers are best cold, so give it a taste and decide which you prefer.

Ricotta Tarts

Cheese tarts or pies can be found throughout much of the Mediterranean, though the ricotta *crostate* of Italy, upon which the Goat Cheese and Ricotta Tart recipe was based, are what first come to my mind. Popular in Rome and the surrounding area, as well as on the islands of Sicily, Calabria, and Sardinia, these tarts are based on a simple filling of eggs and sugar mixed with fresh ricotta cheese and are almost always made with a sweet, cookie-like crust. The thickness of the tart commonly grows to fill the depth of a springform pan, resulting in a dessert more reminiscent of a cheesecake than a tart, though I prefer the thinner version. These cheesecake-like *crostate* often include raisins, candied fruit, nuts, spices, and liquor or wine, such as rum or Marsala.

Historically, ricotta tarts are most closely associated with the celebration of Easter and the spring, for it was only during this season that villages had soft, fresh cheeses like ricotta. Spring is when farm animals give birth, and it was during this time that local herds of cows or ewes nursing their offspring provided the village with the milk required for cheese making. So it was natural that fresh, highly perishable cheeses were used to make celebratory foods for the season's religious festivals—though nowadays ricotta tarts are enjoyed at special occasions year-round.

Peach and Cornmeal Tart with Crème Fraîche Ice Cream

serves 8 to 10

It's not officially peach season for me until I've made this double-crusted tart and eaten a big slice, warm from the oven, with a generous scoop of Crème Fraîche Ice Cream alongside. The ice cream melts slightly and blends with the pie's juices, forming a luscious warm peach sauce. Based on a double-crusted tart from the Piedmont region of Italy, this pie features a nubby dough made with cornmeal, which is known as pasta melgun *in Italy. I have replaced the classic filling of pears poached in red wine with fresh summer peaches. I love the way the muted yellow of the cornmeal crust sandwiches the peachy-red streaked filling, like a slice of summer sunshine. Yes, the juices sprout from the tart like a leaky sprinkler, and yes, the juices soften the crust, and yes, it doesn't hold for days, but to me that's the whole point of a good summer pie—it should be an embodiment of the immediacy and pleasure of the season.*

Nectarines, though marketed as a separate fruit, are really just a fuzzless peach (albeit a tasty one) and may be used instead of peaches in this recipe. To choose the ripest peaches or nectarines, look for a creamy background color without any green—the blush or redness on the skin, though beautiful, has nothing to do with the ripeness or quality of the fruit.

EQUIPMENT AND ADVANCE PREPARATION: 1 recipe Cornmeal Shortcrust Dough (118) to fill and top a 9- or 9½-inch fluted tart pan with removable bottom • Follow the directions in the dough recipe under "To line the tart pan" (120) to prepare the top and bottom crusts.

FOR THE FILLING

1½ pounds (about 4 to 5 medium) ripe peaches, pitted and cut into
   ¾-inch cubes

3 to 4 tablespoons (about 1½ to 1¾ ounces) sugar

1 teaspoon tapioca flour, or 2 teaspoons unbleached all-purpose flour

1 teaspoon freshly squeezed lemon juice

Scant ¼ teaspoon ground nutmeg

1 large egg, lightly beaten

FOR SERVING

Vanilla Bean Crème Fraîche Ice Cream (303) or good-quality vanilla ice
cream

Preheat the oven to 375°F. Position an oven rack in the lower third of the
oven.

To prepare the filling, place the peaches, sugar, tapioca flour, lemon juice, and
nutmeg in a bowl and toss until the peaches are evenly coated. Transfer the filling
to the prepared tart shell, then place the circle of dough on top, pressing down
around the edges with the heel of your hand to remove the excess dough and to
seal the top and bottom layers of dough as shown. Brush the
surface of the pie lightly with the beaten egg.
With a thin, sharp knife, beginning in the center of the tart and moving toward the edge,
cut 3 evenly spaced 3-inch slits in the surface
as shown to allow steam to escape.

Bake for 40 to 45 minutes, or until the
crust is golden brown and the fruit is soft when
pierced with the tip of a sharp knife. The crust will crack and settle
around the fruit. Remove from the oven and place on a rack to cool
completely.

To unmold, when cool, center the tart pan
on top of a large can (I use a large can of
tomatoes) so that it balances midair as the
rim of the tart pan falls to the counter (see
illustration, 77). Leave the bottom of the pan
under the pie for support, or slide the pie onto a
serving plate by running a large spatula between the crust and the pan, using it to
guide the pie onto the plate.

SERVING AND STORAGE NOTES: Serve warm or at room temperature with ice
cream. Because the fruit juices will soften the crust, this pie is best served the
same day it is baked. Those who don't mind a softened crust will find the flavor

quite good the second day (I particularly like it for breakfast). Store, covered loosely with foil, at room temperature for 1 or 2 days.

Buying Cornmeal

Try to purchase cornmeal from the bulk section of a store that has a high turnover. Because cornmeal is a whole grain, the oils in it can go rancid when it is left on a store shelf for a long time. I've found that natural food stores usually carry a higher-quality product than the nationally packaged brands available at the supermarket. Buy small amounts and store any extra in the refrigerator.

Always try to buy stone-ground cornmeal. The ancient method of turning grain into flour between two huge rotating stone wheels retains much more of the corn's flavor and nutrients than more modern (and efficient) processing equipment. For pastry-making purposes, always sift stone-ground cornmeal before measuring it to remove the larger particles of dried corn.

Raspberry Mascarpone Tart
with Chocolate Crust

serves 8 to 10

This summer dessert takes advantage of fresh red raspberries' natural affinity for choco-late. A tart shell baked early in the day, before the heat rises, is filled with sweetened mascarpone and topped with fresh raspberries. A very thin layer of chocolate ganache, a silken mixture of melted chocolate and cream, on the bottom of the tart prevents mois-ture in the filling from softening the pastry.

EQUIPMENT AND ADVANCE PREPARATION: 1 recipe Chocolate Shortcrust Dough (122) to fill a 9- or 9½-inch fluted tart pan with removable bottom, fully baked • If you wish to make your own mascarpone (42), you will need to begin at least 3 days before you want to make the tart.

FOR THE GANACHE

1 ounce bittersweet or semisweet chocolate, finely chopped

1 tablespoon (½ ounce) heavy cream

FOR THE FILLING

1 pound mascarpone

2 to 3 tablespoons (1 to 1½ ounces) sugar, to taste

½ teaspoon pure vanilla extract

1½ teaspoons framboise eau-de-vie (raspberry brandy)

2½ half-pint baskets (about 15 ounces) raspberries

FOR THE GLAZE

1 tablespoon seedless raspberry jam

1 teaspoon water

FOR SERVING

Powdered sugar

To make the ganache, place the chocolate and heavy cream in a small bowl and set aside. Place an inch of water in a small sauté pan and bring to a boil. Remove the pan from the heat, set the bowl of chocolate into the hot water, and stir occasionally with a small metal spoon until the chocolate is melted and the mixture is smooth. Spread the ganache evenly in the bottom of the baked tart shell, using a small offset spatula or the back of a spoon. Place the tart shell in the freezer until the ganache is set, about 10 to 15 minutes.

To make the filling, in a medium bowl, stir together the mascarpone, sugar, vanilla, and framboise with a wooden spoon until they are well blended and the mixture is the consistency of thick pudding—dense enough to hold its shape when cut with a knife (this step can also be done in an electric mixer fitted with the paddle attachment on medium speed). With some brands of mascarpone, you may need to stir vigorously to thicken the filling; with others brands, just a few strokes will do the trick. On the other hand, if the filling seems too thick, stir in 1 or 2 tablespoons of heavy cream to achieve the proper consistency. Spoon the filling on top of the chilled ganache and use a small offset spatula or the back of a spoon to level and smooth the surface.

Sort through the raspberries and discard any debris or moldy berries (do not wash fresh raspberries, as they will absorb the water and disintegrate and are virtually impossible to dry, which leads to mushy berrries with watered-down flavor). Arrange the raspberries in concentric circles on top of the mascarpone, rounded end up, beginning at the outer edges and working toward the center, setting them very close together to hide the filling.

To make the glaze, in a small saucepan over low heat, gently warm the jam with the water, stirring with a teaspoon to blend—it should be the consistency of maple syrup. Dip a pastry brush in the heated glaze and lightly brush the tops of the raspberries with the jam—you want just enough to give them "sparkle," not a thick coating. Refrigerate the tart until ready to serve.

To unmold, center the tart pan on top of a large can (I use a large can of tomatoes) so that it balances midair as the rim of the tart pan falls to the counter (see illustration, 77). Leave the bottom of the pan under the tart for support, or slide the tart onto a serving plate by running a large spatula between the crust and the pan, using it to guide the tart onto the plate.

SERVING AND STORAGE NOTES: Dust each plate with powdered sugar and sprinkle a few extra raspberries around each slice of tart. Store the tart, covered in plastic wrap, in the refrigerator for 2 to 3 days. To keep the plastic wrap from sticking to the tart's glaze, inscrt 4 toothpicks at even intervals just inside the edge of the tart and gently wrap the plastic over them.

VARIATION

Double-Raspberry Mascarpone Tart: A layer of raspberry jam coupled with the fresh raspberry topping creates a raspberry "sandwich" for the mascarpone, adding another dimension of raspberries and a gentle sweetness as well. After you have spread the ganache in the tart shell and chilled it until firm, use the back of a spoon or a small offset spatula to spread 4 tablespoons of seedless raspberry jam in a thin layer over the hardened ganache. Proceed with the recipe as directed, spreading the mascarpone over the layer of jam.

Cherry, Red Wine, and Lavender Tart with Crème Fraîche

serves 8 to 10

This tart, though born in my kitchen in California, would be equally at home on the table of a farmhouse under the Provençal sun. The berry and herbal undertones in the local Provençal wines marry perfectly with the area's harvest of fat, juicy cherries and the dusty fragrance of lavender—and provide a lovely example of the dictum "those that grow together, go together."

Here, a flaky tart shell moistened with a thin layer of jam holds a glistening bounty of sweet cherries that have been cooked briefly in red wine infused with lavender. Though a Provençal wine would be very nice, I often use a California Cabernet or Merlot with lovely results (it needn't be an expensive bottle by any means, but keep in mind that if you wouldn't drink it, you shouldn't cook with it). If you're interested in exploring some inspiring wines from the south of France or Italy, Kermit Lynch Wine Merchant is a great place to start (see Mail-Order Sources, 327).

EQUIPMENT AND ADVANCE PREPARATION: 1 recipe Flaky Tart Dough (110) to fill a 9- or 9½-inch fluted tart pan with removable bottom, fully baked and cooled • A piece of cheese-cloth if using dried lavender

1¼ pounds (20 ounces) large, firm, sweet cherries, preferably Bing

1 cup (8 ounces) hearty red wine, such as Cabernet or Merlot

½ cup (3½ ounces) sugar

Three 3-inch sprigs fresh lavender (91), or 1 teaspoon dried lavender

1 teaspoon cornstarch

1 teaspoon water

3 to 4 tablespoons cherry, red currant, or seedless raspberry jam

FOR SERVING

Crème fraîche (303)

Fresh lavender sprigs

To cook the cherries, place the cherries in a colander, rinse under cold water, then gently pat the fruit dry. Remove the stems and pits. In a 10-inch nonaluminum sauté pan large enough to hold all the cherries in one layer, place the red wine, sugar, and lavender sprigs. If you are using dried lavender, wrap it in cheesecloth for easy removal later. Over medium heat, bring the mixture to a boil, stirring occasionally with a metal spoon to help dissolve the sugar. Once it begins to boil, turn the heat to low and simmer the wine for 2 minutes. Add the cherries, return to a simmer, and cook for 3 to 5 minutes, until softened but not falling apart. You should still feel some resistance when you pierce a cherry with the tip of a small, sharp knife. Remove the pan from the heat and, using a slotted spoon, lift the cherries from the liquid and place them in a single layer on a baking sheet with sides to cool.

To make a glaze for the tart, remove the lavender from the wine and bring the liquid back to a boil. Cook over medium heat for 3 to 5 minutes, or until reduced by half—you should have about ½ cup of liquid. In a small bowl, stir together the cornstarch and the water until smooth. Whisk this into the boiling wine and, stirring constantly, cook until the mixture has thickened somewhat and looks syrupy, about 30 seconds. Remove from the heat and cool until lukewarm.

To assemble the tart, spread the jam in a thin layer on the bottom of the baked and cooled tart shell. Arrange the cherries in a single layer on top of the jam, rounded side up, so that the pitting holes don't show. They should completely fill the shell, packed tightly together. Brush some of the red wine glaze lightly over the top of the cherries (you will not use all of it). Leftover glaze is delicious when warmed and poured over vanilla ice cream—store it in a covered container in the refrigerator for up to 2 weeks.

To unmold, center the tart pan on top of a large can (I use a large can of tomatoes) so that it balances midair as the rim of the tart pan falls to the counter (see illustration, 77). Leave the bottom of the pan under the tart for support, or slide the tart onto a serving plate by running a large spatula between the crust and the pan, using it to guide the tart onto the plate.

SERVING AND STORAGE NOTES: Serve at room temperature with a spoonful of crème fraîche and a sprig or two of fresh lavender. This tart is at its best the same day it is made, because the cherries tend to lose their liquid, causing the crust to become moist. Store the tart, covered loosely with foil, at room temperature for 1 or 2 days or refrigerated for up to 3 days. Bring the tart to room temperature before serving.

Lavender

Lavender is a highly aromatic member of the mint family. Though best known for its contribution to the scented world of soaps and potpourri, lavender can be found in recipes throughout the south of France, from roasted lamb to cookies. One of the most glorious sights in Provence, a major growing region for the herb, is the fields of lavender—row after row of dusty purple mounds extending over the tawny hills, the warmth of the sun releasing their familiar scent like a sachet in a hot bath. When cooking with lavender, always use organic flowers that have been grown specifically for eating, as those available in flower shops and craft stores have been treated with chemicals that can be dangerous if ingested. The best sources for chemical-free lavender are farmers' markets, herb and spice companies (see Mail-Order Sources, 327), or even your own backyard.

Lavender, often seen as an edging in gardens, is easy to grow as long as the plants receive full sun and are rooted in sandy (quick-draining) alkaline soil. If you live in a cold climate, look for the English lavender (*Lavandula spica*), which is the hardiest variety and bears flowers at the end of summer. In warmer climates, French lavender (*L. dentata*) may bloom all year long. Spanish lavender (*L. stoechas*), which blooms in early summer, sports flowers that are a dramatic dark purple color. Other varieties offer white or pink flowers. Whatever variety you choose, be sure to prune the plants directly after blooming so they keep their compact, rounded shape.

Lime Brûlée Tartlets with Coconut Macadamia Crust

serves 6

These little tartlets offer a bit of everything I crave in a dessert—a soft, mouth-puckering lime curd set in a sweet, chewy, macaroon-like crust and finished with a crisp, burnt sugar topping. I always encourage my guests to pick up the tartlets and eat them out of hand because the crust, while truly yummy, is also sticky, which makes it a challenge to cut with a fork. If protocol excludes hands as utensils, be sure to save your guests some frustration by serving these accompanied by a steak knife. They're delicious when served with slices of fresh mango alongside.

EQUIPMENT AND ADVANCE PREPARATION: Six 4½-inch fluted round tartlet pans with removable bottoms • Coat the inside of the pans with pan spray or a thin, even coat of melted butter. • A double boiler (or a medium saucepan coupled with a medium stainless-steel mixing bowl that will fit halfway into the saucepan when sitting on top of it) • A propane torch (see explanation, 168) to brûlée the tartlets.

FOR THE LIME CURD

3 large eggs

3 large egg yolks

1 cup minus 1 tablespoon (6½ ounces) sugar

¾ cup (6 ounces) freshly squeezed and strained lime juice

Zest of 3 limes, in strips

6 tablespoons (3 ounces) cold unsalted butter, cut into ½-inch pieces

FOR THE COCONUT MACADAMIA CRUST

1⅓ cups (6 ounces) unsalted macadamia nuts (see Notes)

1⅓ cups (4 ounces) finely shredded unsweetened coconut (see Notes)

½ cup (3½ ounces) sugar

2 large egg whites

FOR SERVING

1 tablespoon (scant ½ ounce) sugar

1 large mango, peeled and sliced (optional)

NOTES: If you must buy salted macadamia nuts, place the nuts in a strainer and rinse the salt off under a stream of cold water, turning the nuts with one hand while holding the strainer with the other. Pat the nuts dry with a kitchen towel, then transfer them to a baking sheet with sides. Finish drying the nuts by placing them in a 250°F oven for 10 minutes—they should feel dry and have a light golden color. Cool completely before continuing with the recipe.

The type of coconut I use in this recipe is very finely shredded (it looks almost ground) and is often available in the bulk section of natural food stores. If the coconut you find is a larger shred or even the "chip" style, don't worry. Just be sure to buy the correct weight and avoid measuring it in cups—it will eventually be ground to the correct consistency while you are making the crust in the food processor. If you must buy the coconut in a package and don't own a scale, open the package in the produce department of the grocery store and weigh out 4 ounces into a plastic produce bag. You'll pay for the whole bag, but at least you'll have the correct amount you need for the recipe set aside.

To make the lime curd, fill the bottom of the double boiler with 2 inches of water and bring it to a rolling boil—the water should be at least 2 inches away from the top portion of the double boiler.

Place the eggs, egg yolks, and sugar in the top of the double boiler and whisk until blended. Add the lime juice and zest and mix well. Place the top of the double boiler over the boiling water and turn the heat down until the water is at a gentle boil. Whisk constantly, scraping around the edges frequently so the eggs don't scramble there, until the curd is very thick, about 7 minutes. When the whisk is lifted and a bit of curd falls back into the bowl, it should hold its shape on the surface rather than just blending back into the mixture. Do not let the mixture boil, or you will have bits of scrambled egg in your curd (if this happens, quickly remove the bowl from the heat and continue to the next step).

Immediately pour the curd into a fine-mesh strainer set over a medium bowl. Push the curd through with a rubber spatula, then quickly add the butter pieces, burying them in the hot curd so they begin to melt. Wait 1 minute, then whisk until the butter is completely melted and blended with the mixture. Place a piece of plastic wrap directly on the surface of the curd to prevent a skin from forming. Refrigerate until cold.

Preheat the oven to 325°F. Position an oven rack in the center of the oven.

To make the tartlet shells, place the macadamia nuts, coconut, and sugar in the bowl of a food processor and process until the nuts are finely ground, about 20 seconds. Add the egg whites and pulse just until they are incorporated, about 5 to 10 seconds. Divide the mixture among the prepared tartlet pans (about 2½ ounces in each) and press it in with your hands to completely fill the bottom and sides of each pan in an even layer. Have a small bowl of cold water handy as you work, and lightly wet your hands occasionally to keep the coconut mixture from sticking to them. Place the tartlet pans on a baking sheet and bake for 25 to 28 minutes, or until set and lightly golden brown. Do not overbake, or they will become hard and crispy rather than chewy. Remove from the oven and place on a rack to cool completely.

To unmold, gently push the removable tart bottom upward with one hand while holding the rim steady with the other. If a shell sticks, gently pry loose the problem area with the tip of a small, sharp knife. Once the sides are free, run a small knife or metal spatula between the bottom of the tart shell and the pan. Fill the tartlets with lime curd, then smooth and level the top with a small offset spatula or the back of a spoon. You will not use all of the curd—save what is left (about ⅓ cup) to spread on toast in the morning, sandwich between butter cookies, or serve with fresh fruit. Refrigerate the tartlets until serving time.

SERVING AND STORAGE NOTES: To finish the tartlets, sprinkle the center of each one with ½ teaspoon sugar, leaving a ½-inch border around the edge so that the torch flame will not burn the crust. Use a propane torch to caramelize the sugar—keep the flame aimed at the center of the tart so it doesn't blacken the edges (see page 168). Refrigerate until serving time—the sugar may be caramelized up to 1 hour in advance. To serve, place a tartlet in the center of a plate and arrange several slices of mango to one side. Leftover tartlets may be covered loosely with plastic wrap and refrigerated for several days, though the brûlée will melt and the crust will soften (a new layer of sugar may be caramelized over the softened one).

GETTING AHEAD: The lime curd may be prepared up to 3 days in advance—keep refrigerated in an airtight container.

The tartlet shells may be prepared 1 day in advance—set the cooled shells on a clean piece of parchment on a sheet pan and wrap the entire pan tightly with plastic wrap. Leave at room temperature.

Assemble the tartlets the same day you want to serve them, up to 12 hours in advance.

Apricot Tart with Shredded Filo and Pistachios

serves 8 to 10

This is the tart that inspired this book. A crispy tart shell cradles a filling of fresh apricots scented with orange flower water, which is then topped with a crown of shredded filo. Dusted with powdered sugar and sprinkled with chopped pistachios, the orange of the apricots peeking through the lacy filo topping, this tart never fails to bring a gasp of delight.

It makes the perfect ending to a North African– or Middle Eastern–inspired meal, as three staples of those cuisines—apricots, filo, and orange flower water—form the trio of flavors that transport this dessert to the Mediterranean. The best apricot variety for dessert making is the Blenheim, also known as Royal, which has a wonderfully tart edge to it that I love. Other varieties are simply sweet and, while good, do not have the complexity of flavor that the Blenheim is famous for. If you cannot find Blenheims, add 2 to 3 teaspoons of lemon juice to the filling for a balance of flavor (depending upon your taste and the sweetness of the apricots).

EQUIPMENT AND ADVANCE PREPARATION: 1 recipe Flaky Tart Dough (110) to fill a 9- or 9½-inch fluted tart pan with removable bottom, fully baked and cooled • 4 ounces of shredded filo, or ¼ of a box (rewrap the remaining filo and return it to the refrigerator, where it will keep for several weeks). To thaw the frozen shredded filo, place it on the counter and let it come to room temperature (2 to 3 hours) or thaw overnight in the refrigerator.

FOR THE FRUIT FILLING

1¼ pounds firm-ripe apricots, preferably Blenheim, or Royal

⅓ cup (2½ ounces) sugar

2 teaspoons tapioca flour, or 4 teaspoons unbleached all-purpose flour

½ teaspoon orange flower water (260)

FOR THE TOPPING

4 ounces (¼ box) shredded filo (also called *kunafeh* or *kataifi*), room temperature (see Note)

4 tablespoons (1¾ ounces) sugar

½ teaspoon ground cinnamon

6 tablespoons (3 ounces) unsalted butter, melted

FOR SERVING

Powdered sugar

3 tablespoons pistachios, toasted (213) and coarsely chopped

Honey cream (53)

NOTE: Shredded filo can be found in the frozen section of the supermarket with the other filo products and is more commonly found in markets catering to a Middle Eastern clientele. For more information on shredded filo, see page 208, and for a mail-order source, see page 327. There is really no substitute for this light and crispy dough, which resembles shredded wheat. However, you can create a slightly different version of this tart's topping using regular filo dough—see the variation at the end of the recipe.

Preheat the oven to 375°F. Position an oven rack in the center of the oven.

To make the filling, slice the apricots in half and remove the pits. Cut each half into 4 slices and place in a medium bowl. Toss the apricots with the sugar, tapioca flour, and orange flower water until they are evenly coated. Transfer the filling to the cooled tart shell and pat into an even layer.

To make the topping, place the shredded filo in a medium bowl. Carefully toss the filo with your hands, gently pulling the strands apart, and remove and discard any hard clumps of dough. In a small bowl, blend the sugar and cinnamon. Pour the warm melted butter over the dough, then sprinkle with the cinnamon sugar. Toss the filo until the strands are evenly coated with the butter and sugar mixture. Arrange the filo in an even layer on top of the apricots.

Bake for 35 to 40 minutes, or until the fruit is tender when pierced with the tip of a small, sharp knife and the filo is golden brown. Remove from the oven and place on a rack to cool completely.

To unmold, when cool, center the tart pan on top of a large can (I use a large can of tomatoes) so that it balances midair as the rim of the tart pan falls to the counter (see illustration, 77). Leave the bottom of the pan under the tart for support, or slide the tart onto a serving plate by running a large spatula between the crust and the pan, using it to guide the tart onto the plate.

SERVING AND STORAGE NOTES: Dust the top of the tart with powdered sugar. Sprinkle 2 tablespoons of the chopped pistachios evenly over the surface of the tart. Serve with honey cream, sprinkling each serving plate with some of the remaining pistachios. This tart is at its best the same day it is baked—eventually the liquid in the apricots will soften both the crust and the filo topping. Store, covered loosely with foil, at room temperature for 1 or 2 days.

VARIATION

If you cannot find shredded filo, try this version of the topping—it will not be as crispy or as high as the shredded filo but is quite delicious and beautiful. Regular filo absorbs moisture more quickly than the shredded filo, so bake this tart as close to serving time as possible. To make the topping, you will need 5 tablespoons sugar, ½ teaspoon ground cinnamon, 5 sheets of filo from a package that has been thawed overnight in the refrigerator (see Working with Filo, 207), and 4 tablespoons melted unsalted butter.

Place the sugar and cinnamon in a small bowl and mix well. Place a sheet of filo on your work surface, with the long side parallel to the edge of the counter. Brush the surface with melted butter and sprinkle evenly with a tablespoon of the sugar mixture. Place the second sheet of filo on top of the first and repeat with the melted butter and sugar. Repeat the process with each of the remaining 3 sheets of filo. Then, beginning with the long edge nearest you, roll the stack of filo into a tight cylinder. Using a sharp knife, cut the cylinder into ⅛-inch-wide slices. Toss the slices so they unroll into long strands of filo. Gently cover the top of the apricots with the filo strands, fluffing them so they have a bit of height. Bake as directed above.

Apricots

I grew up with a graceful old apricot tree in my backyard, and though it bore a prodigious amount of fruit each summer, I remember it most fondly as the site of our coveted treehouse. Through the eyes of a child, the fruit was a sweet bonus, though an elusive one. It seemed that the birds had the inside scoop on the moment the fruit turned ripe and sweet, for on that very day they would swoop in and devour the best, leaving the green apricots for children's battles.

That tree, now long gone, was a Blenheim apricot tree, which bears the best sweet-tart fruit for eating, cooking, and drying. Until recently Blenheim was the most widely planted variety in California, and many brands of dried apricots still proudly bear its varietal name on the package. The Patterson apricot, introduced in 1969, is now the most dominant variety. Big, orange, and firm fleshed, it was developed mainly for the canning industry but has taken over in sales of fresh apricots as well. Whatever the variety, apricots, like figs, do not develop their true complexity of flavors or their best texture unless allowed to ripen fully on the tree, which is why it is so hard to buy a good one at the supermarket; ripe fruit, which is soft, just doesn't ship well. Underripe fruit is best used in recipes like this tart, for baking helps to bring latent flavors to the foreground. Always taste a piece of the fruit before cooking with it, and if it seems very tart or astringent, add an extra tablespoon or two of sugar.

When choosing fresh apricots, look for fruit that seems heavy for its size and has a good orange color—avoid those that are a very pale orange or yellow or those that have a greenish cast to the skin. Fruit that is hard as a rock can never deliver the flavor you want. If that is your only option, choose another recipe or look for a recipe that utilizes dried apricots, which are generally of very high quality and excellent flavor. The California season for fresh apricots (which accounts for almost all fresh apricots sold in the United States) runs from May through August. Like most fruit, the best will be found in season at a farmers' market, where the farmers know that their soft, tree-ripened fruit will be appreciated.

Caramel, Date, and Sesame Tart with Orange

serves 8 to 10

This caramel tart, dense with dates and sesame seeds and laced with orange, has a chewy, almost candy bar texture. Although it is gloriously rich, the slightly bitter edge of the caramel keeps it from becoming cloying. Dates can be found throughout the Mediterranean, but are nowhere more entwined in the cuisine and in the lives of the people than in the Middle East and North Africa, where their presence in sweets is delightfully predictable.

EQUIPMENT AND ADVANCE PREPARATION: 1 recipe Flaky Tart Dough (110) to fill a 9- or 9½-inch fluted tart pan with removable bottom, fully baked and cooled

FOR THE FILLING

9 ounces Medjool dates (about 11 large dates)

⅓ cup (2¾ ounces) water

¾ cup (5¼ ounces) sugar

¾ cup (6 ounces) heavy cream

1 large egg

1 large egg yolk

6 tablespoons (1¾ ounces) sesame seeds, lightly toasted (101)

1 tablespoon finely minced orange zest (145), about 1 large orange

FOR SERVING

Softly whipped cream (54), unsweetened, OR crème fraîche (303)

Preheat the oven to 350°F. Position an oven rack in the center of the oven.

To pit the dates, make a slit in one side and pull out the seed. Using a thin, sharp knife that has been lightly coated with a flavorless vegetable oil to prevent the fruit from sticking to it, slice each date in half lengthwise, then cut it crosswise into ¼- to ½-inch pieces. Place in a small bowl and set aside.

To make the caramel filling, pour the water into a medium saucepan, add the sugar, and set the pan over medium heat. Stir constantly with a wooden spoon or swirl the pan frequently until the sugar is dissolved and the liquid is clear. Turn the heat to high and boil rapidly, swirling the pan occasionally (do not stir at this point) so that the sugar cooks evenly, until it turns a golden brown. Remove the pan from the heat and immediately add the cream—be careful, the mixture will rise dramatically in the pan and sputter; you may want to wear an oven mitt on the hand holding the pan. Stir with the wooden spoon to blend. If the caramel has solidified, set the pan back over low heat and stir until it melts again. Remove from the heat and cool until the caramel is lukewarm.

When the caramel has cooled, whisk in the egg and egg yolk, then stir in the chopped dates, gently breaking up any clumps of fruit that have formed. Add the toasted sesame seeds and orange zest and stir to blend. Pour the filling into the prebaked tart shell, making sure the dates are evenly distributed. Bake for 20 to 25 minutes, or until the filling is just set in the center. Remove from the oven and place on a rack to cool completely.

To unmold, when cool, center the tart pan on top of a large can (I use a large can of tomatoes) so that it balances midair as the rim of the tart pan falls to the counter (see illustration, 77). Leave the bottom of the pan under the tart for support, or slide the tart onto a serving plate by running a large spatula between the crust and the pan, using it to guide the tart onto the plate.

SERVING AND STORAGE NOTES: Serve at room temperature with a spoonful of unsweetened softly whipped cream or crème fraîche. Because the filling is rather sticky, I find it easiest to cut this tart with a thin, sharp knife that has been lightly coated with a flavorless vegetable oil. Store, covered with foil, at room temperature for up to 3 days.

Sesame Seeds

Sesame seeds are native to the Mediterranean area, and records of their cultivation in the Tigris and Euphrates valleys of Mesopotamia date back to 1600 B.C. The Egyptians used sesame oil for cooking, and as with other herbs and spices, they believed the seeds contained medicinal qualities and therefore also used them for perfumes, ointments, and even embalming. Sesame seeds were introduced to America in the seventeenth century by African slaves, who called them benne (in the South, they are often still referred to by this name), and are currently grown throughout the Southwest, including California.

Sesame seeds are available either hulled or unhulled and may be used interchangeably. Unhulled seeds come in a range of colors, from red to yellow to brown or black, but once hulled, the seeds are always a creamy white, the style most Americans are familiar with. Their high oil content means they become rancid quickly when stored in a warm environment, so always store sesame seeds in an airtight container in the freezer, where they will last for about 6 months. Their sweet, nutty flavor is intensified by lightly toasting them.

To toast sesame seeds: Place a dry 8-inch heavy skillet over medium heat. When the pan is hot, add the sesame seeds and cook, stirring frequently, until they are lightly browned, about 2½ to 3 minutes. They will not brown evenly but will be a mixture of beige and brown—this is fine. Remove the pan from the heat and immediately pour the seeds onto a plate or a baking sheet to cool. If left in the skillet, they will continue to cook from the residual heat and could burn. Set aside until needed. Sesame seeds may be toasted several days in advance and stored at room temperature. Since their flavor is best when freshly toasted, do not toast seeds you will be storing in the freezer.

Pear Brown Butter Tart with Vanilla Bean

serves 8 to 10

The sweet nectar of softly perfumed winter pears blends beautifully here with the nutti-ness of brown butter and the floral essence of a real vanilla bean. As the tart bakes, the brown butter filling separates into a creamy custard surrounding the pears and a cracked, rustic, crunchy topping reminiscent of a thin meringue. I especially love pears in this tart, but in the summer give fresh cherries or blueberries a try. You'll need just enough fruit to cover the tart shell in a single layer.

EQUIPMENT AND ADVANCE PREPARATION: 1 recipe Flaky Tart Dough (110) to fill a 9- or 9½-inch fluted tart pan with removable bottom, fully baked and cooled

    2 medium (about 1 pound) winter pears, such as Bosc or Anjou

    1 teaspoon tapioca flour, or 2 teaspoons unbleached all-purpose flour

    1 large egg, room temperature

    ⅓ cup (2¼ ounces) sugar

    4 tablespoons (2 ounces) unsalted butter

    ½ vanilla bean

    1½ teaspoons freshly squeezed lemon juice

    2 tablespoons (1 ounce) unbleached all-purpose flour

    Pinch of salt

    FOR SERVING
    Softly whipped cream (54) flavored with Poire William, optional

Preheat the oven to 350°F. Position an oven rack in the center of the oven.

To prepare the fruit, peel, core, and cut the pears into slices ⅜ inch to ½ inch thick. Place the slices in a medium bowl and toss with the tapioca flour until the pears are evenly coated. Arrange the pear slices in a single layer in the bottom of the baked and cooled tart shell.

To make the filling, place the egg and sugar in the bowl of an electric mixer fitted with the whisk attachment and beat on high speed until the egg is very thick and light in color, about 2 to 3 minutes. Stop the mixer while you prepare the brown butter.

Cut the butter into ½-inch pieces and place in a small saucepan. Use a small, sharp knife to split the vanilla bean in half and scrape out the small black seeds inside. Add the seeds and the vanilla pod to the pan with the butter. Place the pan over low heat until the butter is melted, then raise the heat to medium and cook until the solids floating in the butter turn a dark brown color (do not let them blacken, or they will be bitter). Immediately remove the pan from the heat and add the lemon juice to keep the butter from cooking any further. Remove and discard the vanilla pod.

Turn the mixer on medium-low and pour the brown butter slowly down the side of the bowl into the beaten egg. Stop the mixer and use a rubber spatula to scrape down the bowl and to scrape any remaining bits of butter or vanilla seeds from the pan into the bowl. Continue to beat until well blended, another 20 to 30 seconds. Add the flour and salt and continue to mix another 15 to 30 seconds. Remove the bowl from the mixer and stir with the rubber spatula several times to make sure the batter is well blended.

Slowly pour the filling over the pears in a thin stream, being careful to cover all the pears and any spaces between them with the filling—there is just enough batter to cover everything in a thin layer. Bake for 45 to 55 minutes, or until the filling is a deep golden brown and the pears are tender when pierced with the tip of a sharp knife. Remove from the oven and place on a rack to cool completely.

To unmold, when cool, center the tart pan on top of a large can (I use a large can of tomatoes) so that it balances midair as the rim of the tart pan falls to the counter (see illustration, 77). Leave the bottom of the pan under the tart for support, or slide the tart onto a serving plate by running a large spatula between the crust and the pan, using it to guide the tart onto the plate.

SERVING AND STORAGE NOTES: Serve at room temperature, plain or with a spoonful of softly whipped cream laced with a few drops of Poire William eau-de-vie (pear brandy). This tart is at its best the same day it is baked, for the juice of the pears will eventually soften the crust and the meringue-like topping of the filling. Store at room temperature for 1 day; for longer storage, cover with plastic and refrigerate for up to 2 days. Bring to room temperature before serving.

Marbleized Chocolate Velvet Tart

serves 10 to 12

With a surface that resembles the elegant Italian marbled papers of Florence, and a velvety-soft texture that melts into a warm pool of chocolate in your mouth, this tart is the one I serve most often to chocolate-loving friends. The best part is that it is so utterly simple and foolproof to prepare—just heavy cream combined with melted chocolate and a bit of egg to set the mixture—yet it looks (and tastes) sublime. Splurge on the finest chocolate possible, for its flavor is the very heart of this dessert.

EQUIPMENT AND ADVANCE PREPARATION: 1 recipe Chocolate Shortcrust Dough (122) to fill a 9- or 9½-inch fluted tart pan with removable bottom, fully baked and cooled

> ½ ounce white chocolate, finely chopped
>
> ½ ounce milk chocolate, finely chopped
>
> **FOR THE FILLING**
> 10 ounces bittersweet chocolate, finely chopped
>
> 1¼ cups (10 ounces) heavy cream
>
> 1 large egg
>
> 1 large egg yolk
>
> **FOR SERVING**
> Softly whipped cream (54)
>
> Miniature chocolate curls (106)

Preheat the oven to 350°F. Position an oven rack in the center of the oven.

To melt the white and milk chocolates (to be used for marbleizing the surface of the tart), fill a sauté pan with 1 to 2 inches of water. Over high heat, bring the water to a boil. Remove the pan from the heat (you want the water hot but not boiling). Place the white chocolate in a small stainless-steel bowl and set the bowl into the hot water. Stir constantly with a rubber spatula until the chocolate is melted and smooth (don't walk away—this will happen very quickly). Remove the bowl from the water and wipe the bottom dry.

Place an unpleated plastic sandwich bag in a cup and fold the top of the bag over the rim of the cup to hold the bag in place. Use the spatula to scrape the melted chocolate into the bag, then use your hand to squeeze the chocolate into one corner of the bag. Set it on a plate in a warm place where the chocolate will stay melted. Repeat this procedure in a clean, dry bowl with the milk chocolate and place it next to the white chocolate while you finish the filling. (I like to set the bags directly on the griddle portion of my stove, where the heat of the oven underneath keeps the chocolate warm and liquid, but you could also reheat the water in the sauté pan, remove it from the heat, then set both bags of chocolate into a clean bowl in the water.)

To make the filling, place the bittersweet chocolate in a medium bowl. Pour the cream into a small saucepan and place over medium heat. When the cream begins to boil, immediately pour it over the chocolate. Let it sit for 2 minutes, then gently whisk until the mixture is smooth and blended. Add the egg and the egg yolk, mix well, then pour the mixture through a strainer into the baked and cooled tart shell.

To marbleize the top, use a pair of scissors to snip off and discard the very tip of the corner holding the white chocolate, making a small hole in the bag. Pipe the white chocolate over the entire surface of the tart in any pattern you like as shown. Repeat with the milk chocolate. Drag the tip of a small, sharp knife in small circles through the mixture to create a marbled effect as shown—do not overmix the chocolates, or you will lose the marbled pattern.

Place the tart in the oven and bake for 10 to 12 minutes, or just until the filling is set. If the tart is gently shaken, the filling will be firm for about an inch around the edges, and the center portion will move as one piece. Bubbles on the surface indicate it is getting over-baked—you do not want the filling to boil. Remove from the oven and place on a rack to cool completely.

To unmold, when cool, center the tart pan on top of a large can (I use a large can of tomatoes) so that it balances midair as the rim of the tart pan falls to the counter (see illustration, 77). Leave the bottom of the pan under the tart for support, or slide the tart onto a serving plate by running a large spatula between the crust and the pan, using it to guide the tart onto the plate.

SERVING AND STORAGE NOTES: Serve the tart at room temperature with a spoonful of softly whipped cream. I like to sprinkle each serving plate with miniature chocolate curls. This tart is at its best the same day you bake it but will keep refrigerated for 4 days. If you are serving the tart the same day you bake it, leave it at room temperature. For longer storage, refrigerate the tart until cold, then gently wrap it with plastic wrap (at serving time, remove the wrap before bringing the tart to room temperature—this will ensure the surface stays smooth and shiny). Allow 1 hour for the tart to come to room temperature before serving. Cut the tart with a thin, sharp knife that has been warmed under a stream of hot water and wiped dry.

Miniature Chocolate Curls

These quick, easy-to-make curls are a fun garnish for almost any chocolate dessert. The only equipment you will need is a sharp vegetable peeler (a dull peeler results in too-thick curls with rough edges that tend to break in the center). Use a high-quality chocolate bar (such as Lindt or Tobler) or a hand-sized block of bulk chocolate (such as Callebaut, Scharffen Berger, or Valhrona) at warm room temperature. Hold the chocolate in a paper towel (to keep your body heat from melting the chocolate) over a plate to catch the curls, then run the vegetable peeler along the edge of the chocolate as shown. If the curls are very tiny or resemble shavings instead of curls, the chocolate is too cool. Warm it very slightly by placing it on a plate in a gas oven with the heat turned off—the pilot is warm enough. Check the chocolate every few minutes by running the peeler along the edge until you get the curls you want.

The curls can be stored in an airtight container at cool room temperature until needed (if it is very warm, keep them in the refrigerator). Because of their small size, the curls will melt quickly if you touch them, so be sure to use a small spoon (a tiny demitasse spoon is perfect) rather than your fingers when sprinkling them over a plate or dessert.

Siena Tart with Almonds, Cherries, Honey, and Spices

serves 8 to 10

Siena is a charming medieval city just south of Florence that is best known for its famous horse race, called the Palio, in which riders wearing the bright, traditional colors and insignia of each of the city's time-honored neighborhoods vie for first place in a thunderous free-for-all around the beautiful piazza. It is a place that takes tradition seriously, in food as well as horse races, which is evident in its dedication to panforte. Every store in the city seems to have its own "best" version of this honey-based cross between a fruitcake and a candy, with a chewy, dense, caramel-like texture packed with almonds and hazelnuts, spices, and candied citrus peels. It is an enchanting descendant of the Middle Ages, when spices and sugar were exotic and used as much for medicinal purposes as they were for flavoring.

Some panforte are light in color, and others are dark (scuro) due to the addition of a little cocoa. While in Siena, I tasted many versions—all for research purposes, you understand—and my favorites were those that contained the cocoa, which tempers the sweetness and adds complexity to the flavor. I couldn't help thinking that panforte would be even better packed with those addictive dried sour cherries from Michigan that I adore. This tart is very reminiscent in flavor to a scuro panforte, although it is not the classic cake-like confection. Instead, a crisp tart shell is filled with almonds (both sliced and whole for a contrast of textures) and dried sour cherries coated with just enough honey, spices, and citrus zest to sweeten them. The tart is a gorgeous, rustic sight, the sensuous curves of the nuts and cherries a glistening medley of browns. I serve it during the winter months, when its spicy flavors and chewy crunchiness are most appreciated.

EQUIPMENT AND ADVANCE PREPARATION: 1 recipe Shortcrust Dough (114) to fill a 9- or 9½-inch fluted tart pan with removable bottom, partially baked and cooled

FOR THE FILLING

1½ cups (4½ ounces) sliced almonds

¾ cup (3¾ ounces) whole natural almonds

¾ cup (3½ ounces) dried sour cherries

4 tablespoons (¾ ounce) powdered sugar

2 teaspoons unsweetened Dutch-process cocoa powder (262)

½ teaspoon ground cinnamon

¼ teaspoon ground cloves

⅛ teaspoon ground coriander

Pinch of ground white pepper

½ cup (6 ounces) honey, preferably orange blossom or wildflower

1 tablespoon finely minced orange zest (145), about 1 large orange

1 teaspoon finely minced lemon zest (145)

FOR SERVING

Powdered sugar

Honey cream (53) flavored with brandy or dark rum OR Hazelnut Ice
    Cream (295)

Preheat the oven to 350°F. Position an oven rack in the center of the oven.

To make the filling, place the sliced almonds, whole almonds, and cherries in a medium mixing bowl. Sift the powdered sugar, cocoa powder, and spices over them and stir with a rubber spatula until they are evenly coated. Place the honey, orange zest, and lemon zest in a small saucepan and cook over low heat just until the honey is hot to the touch and very liquid—do not let it boil. Remove from the heat and let the mixture sit for 5 minutes, so that the honey is flavored with the citrus zests. Then pour the honey over the nuts and cherries, scraping every bit out of the pan with the rubber spatula. Stir until everything is evenly coated with the honey. At first, it will seem that there is not enough honey, but continue to stir gently (trying not to break the sliced almonds) and eventually the nuts will be thoroughly coated. Be sure to scrape up from the bottom of the bowl as you stir, as pockets of dry cocoa powder and spices tend to form there.

Scrape the filling into the prebaked tart shell and use the spatula or your hands to pat it into an even layer. Bake for 25 to 30 minutes, or until a deep golden brown. Remove from the oven and place on a rack to cool completely.

To unmold, when cool, center the tart pan on top of a large can (I use a large can of tomatoes) so that it balances midair as the rim of the tart pan falls to the counter (see illustration, 77). Leave the bottom of the pan under the tart for support, or slide the tart onto a serving plate by running a large spatula between the crust and the pan, using it to guide the tart onto the plate.

SERVING AND STORAGE NOTES: If desired, dust the surface of the tart with a bit of powdered sugar. Serve at room temperature with a spoonful of honey cream flavored with brandy or dark rum. Hazelnut Ice Cream is also a good accompaniment. Because the filling is rather sticky, I find it easiest to cut this tart with a thin, sharp knife that has been lightly coated with a flavorless vegetable oil. Store, covered loosely with foil, at room temperature for up to 5 days.

VARIATION

Siena Tart with Hazelnuts, Almonds, Cherries, Honey, and Spices: For an additional layer of flavor, add some hazelnuts to the mixture. Follow the recipe exactly as directed above, reducing the whole natural almonds to 1 cup (5¼ ounces) and adding ½ cup (2½ ounces) whole, skinned hazelnuts (227), each nut sliced in half.

Flaky Tart Dough

This recipe produces a crisp, flaky, and flavorful crust. When it comes to making flaky pastry, there are a few basic precepts: use very cold butter and work quickly so it doesn't warm and blend with the remaining ingredients; add only enough water to bring the dough together (excess liquid causes toughening and shrinking); and don't overwork the dough by mixing or kneading it for too long.

In addition, I add a little lemon juice with the water, because its acidity helps to keep the dough tender by retarding the formation of toughening gluten strands. When using a mixer, I also always freeze the butter, cut into ½-inch pieces, for several hours before beginning the recipe, which reduces any chance of it becoming too warm during the mixing process—this creates a flakier dough. Just remember to cut it up before you freeze it, because once frozen, the butter is much more difficult, and dangerous to cut. There are no instructions here for making this dough in a food processor, because this efficient machine can miniaturize the butter pieces too quickly and overwork the dough.

EQUIPMENT AND ADVANCE PREPARATION: One 9- or 9½-inch fluted tart pan with removable bottom • A piece of heavy-duty foil and enough pie weights to fill the tart shell to the top for prebaking • Rice and/or dried beans may be used instead of metal pie weights, but note that rice and beans used in this manner are no longer suitable for eating (though they may be used over and over again to prebake tart shells).

- **1 cup (5 ounces) unbleached all-purpose or pastry flour**
- **1 teaspoon sugar**
- **¼ teaspoon salt**
- **7 tablespoons (3½ ounces) unsalted butter, cut into ½-inch pieces and frozen if using a mixer**
- **2 to 3 tablespoons ice water**
- **1 teaspoon freshly squeezed lemon juice**

TO PREPARE THE DOUGH

To mix using a mixer: Place the flour, sugar, and salt in the bowl of a standing mixer fitted with the paddle attachment. Mix on low for 1 minute to blend the ingredients. Add the frozen butter pieces and mix on medium speed just until the mixture resembles small peas and cornmeal, about 4 to 5 minutes. Combine 2 tablespoons of the ice water with the lemon juice and, with the mixer running on low, add it to the bowl. Mix just until the dough begins to form shaggy clumps. Test the dough by squeezing several clumps in your hand—they should hold together. If not, add the remaining tablespoon of water. Remove the dough from the bowl and knead it gently 2 or 3 times, just to finish bringing it together. Shape it into a round disc about ¾ inch thick and 5½ inches in diameter. Wrap in plastic wrap and refrigerate for 1 hour.

To mix by hand: Place the flour, sugar, and salt in a medium bowl and blend well with a whisk. Add the cold butter pieces (do not freeze the butter for this technique) and toss until they are lightly coated with the flour. Use your fingertips, 2 knives, or a pastry blender to cut the butter into the flour until the mixture resembles small peas and cornmeal. If at any time during this process the butter softens and becomes warm, place the bowl in the freezer for 10 minutes before continuing. Combine 2 tablespoons of the cold water with the lemon juice and sprinkle over the mixture. Toss between your fingertips 10 to 12 times to evenly distribute the moisture. The dough should begin to form shaggy clumps. Test the dough by squeezing several clumps in your hand—they should hold together. If not, add the remaining tablespoon of water, 1 teaspoon at a time, until the dough coheres. Turn the dough out of the bowl onto your work surface and knead it gently 5 or 6 times, just to finish bringing it together. Shape it into a round disc about ¾ inch thick and 5½ inches in diameter. Wrap in plastic wrap and refrigerate for 1 hour.

TO LINE THE TART PAN

To roll out the dough: It is easiest to roll this dough when it is at cool room temperature. This means that you should let it sit on the counter for 10 to 15 minutes before rolling it out (if it is too cold, the dough will crack as you attempt to roll it).

On a lightly floured surface, roll out the dough into a 12-inch round. Lightly dust the surface of the dough with flour as needed to keep the rolling pin from sticking. If the dough cracks, piece it back together using a tiny bit of water as "glue." And if the dough becomes warm at any time during this process, transfer it to a cookie sheet and refrigerate until cold before continuing.

Fold the 12-inch round in half and then into quarters, brushing off any excess flour as you go. Set the point of the dough in the center of the tart pan, then unfold the dough as shown. Ease the dough into the corners of the pan by lifting the dough, then gently pressing it into place using your fingertips. Trim any overhanging dough to about 1 inch. Fold the excess dough inward and press it against the side of the tart pan to create a double-sided edge as shown, then build the edge slightly above the rim of the pan by reinforcing each flute. To do this, press the index finger of one hand against the dough inside the curve of each flute to push the dough upward while at the same time pressing the dough from the outside of each flute with the thumb and index finger of your other hand in a pinching position as shown. The dough should rise about ¼ inch above the rim of the pan all the way around. Place the tart pan, uncovered, in the refrigerator for 1 hour or in the freezer for 30 minutes.

TO BAKE THE TART SHELL

To prebake the tart shell: Preheat the oven to 375°F. Position an oven rack in the lower third of the oven. Line the chilled tart shell with heavy-duty foil, pressing the foil firmly into the corners of the pan. Fill the pan with metal pie weights, dried beans, or rice. The center layer of weights may be thinner, but be sure to push the weights all the way up the sides of the pan to reduce shrinkage and to ensure the edges are straight.

To partially bake the shell: Bake for about 20 minutes, or until the edges and center are set and no longer stick to the foil when you try to remove it. Remove the foil and weights and return the pan to the oven for another 10 to 12 minutes, or until the crust is lightly browned. Place on a rack to cool completely before filling the shell.

To fully bake the shell: Bake for about 20 minutes, or until the edges and center are set and no longer stick to the foil when you try to remove it. Remove the foil and weights and return the pan to the oven for another 20 to 25 minutes, or until the crust is golden brown all over. Place on a rack to cool completely before filling the shell.

GETTING AHEAD: The dough can be made ahead, wrapped tightly in plastic wrap, and held in the refrigerator for up to 3 days or in the freezer for up to 1 month. If frozen, thaw overnight in the refrigerator before proceeding.

The dough may also be rolled out and placed in the tart pan as directed, then the whole pan can be wrapped tightly with plastic wrap and frozen for up to 1 month. Frozen dough will need to prebake an additional 3 to 5 minutes.

Shortcrust Dough

This dough has a higher butter and sugar content than a classic flaky dough, resulting in a sweet, crisp, yet crumbly tart shell reminiscent of a butter cookie (known as pâte sablée *in France or* pasta frolla *in Italy). The dough can be rolled out or simply pressed into the tart pan. In my experience, rolling the dough between sheets of plastic wrap results in a more uniformly thick tart shell than does pressing the dough into the pan, and it's faster. The extra butter and sugar can sometimes cause the dough to crack when it is transferred from the counter to the tart pan—just press the crack back together with your fingertips to seal it up.*

EQUIPMENT AND ADVANCE PREPARATION: One 9- or 9½-inch fluted tart pan with removable bottom • A piece of heavy-duty foil and enough pie weights to fill the tart shell to the top for prebaking • Rice and/or dried beans may be used instead of metal pie weights, but note that rice and beans used in this manner are no longer suitable for eating (though they may be used over and over again to prebake tart shells).

> 1¼ cups (6¼ ounces) unbleached all-purpose flour
>
> ¼ cup (1¾ ounces) sugar
>
> ¼ teaspoon salt
>
> 1 stick (4 ounces) cold (*not* frozen) unsalted butter, cut into ½-inch pieces
>
> 2 large egg yolks
>
> 1½ teaspoons pure vanilla extract
>
> 1 to 3 teaspoons water (as needed)

TO PREPARE THE DOUGH

To mix using a mixer: Place the flour, sugar, and salt in the bowl of a standing mixer fitted with the paddle attachment. Mix on low for 1 minute to blend the ingredients. Add the butter pieces and mix on medium speed just until the mixture resembles breadcrumbs, about 3 to 4 minutes. In a separate bowl, whisk together the yolks, vanilla, and 1 teaspoon of water. Add this to the dry ingredients and blend just until the dough begins to form large clumps. Test the dough by squeezing several clumps in your hand—they should hold together. If not, add the remaining water, 1 teaspoon at a time, until the dough coheres. Remove the dough from the bowl and knead it gently 2 or 3 times, just to finish bringing it together. Shape the dough into a round disc about ¾ inch thick and 5½ inches in diameter. Wrap tightly in plastic wrap and refrigerate for 30 minutes before proceeding.

To mix using a food processor: Place the flour, sugar, and salt in the bowl of a food processor fitted with the metal blade. Pulse 5 times to blend the ingredients. Add the cold butter pieces and pulse 6 to 8 times, just until the butter is the size of large peas. In a separate bowl, whisk together the yolks, vanilla, and 1 teaspoon of water. Add this to the bowl of the processor, then process just until the dough begins to form small clumps—do not let it form a ball. Test the dough by squeezing a handful of clumps—they should hold together. If not, add the remaining water, 1 teaspoon at a time, until the dough coheres. Remove the dough from the bowl and knead it gently 2 or 3 times, just to finish bringing it together. Shape it into a round disc about ¾ inch thick and 5½ inches in diameter. Wrap tightly in plastic wrap and refrigerate for 30 minutes before proceeding.

To mix by hand: Place the flour, sugar, and salt in a medium bowl and blend well with a whisk. Add the cold butter pieces and toss until they are lightly coated with the flour. Use your fingertips, 2 knives, or a pastry blender to cut the butter into the flour until the mixture resembles breadcrumbs. If at any time during this process the butter softens and becomes warm, place the bowl in the freezer for 10 minutes before continuing. In a separate bowl, whisk together the yolks, vanilla, and 2 teaspoons of water. Add this to the dry ingredients and toss between your fingertips 20 to 30 times to evenly distribute the moisture. The dough will still look very crumbly, but if the mixture is squeezed in your hand, it should hold together. If not, add the remaining teaspoon of water and toss to blend. Turn the dough out of the bowl onto your work surface and knead it gently 5 or 6 times, just to finish bringing it together. Shape it into a round disc about ¾ inch thick and 5½ inches in diameter. Wrap tightly in plastic wrap and refrigerate for 30 minutes before proceeding.

TO LINE THE TART PAN
To roll out the dough: It is easiest to roll this dough when it is at cool room temperature. This means that if it has been refrigerated for longer than 30 minutes, let it sit on the counter for 10 to 15 minutes before rolling it out (if it is too cold, the dough will crack as you attempt to roll it).

Place the disc of dough between two 12-inch pieces of plastic wrap. Roll the dough into an 11-inch round as shown, rotating it clockwise slightly after each roll to create an even round. Remember to roll from the center outward and to lift the rolling pin at the edge rather than smashing the edge down. As you roll, the plastic wrap will wrinkle and resist. When this happens, peel it off and replace it smoothly, then flip the dough over and repeat with the plastic on the other side before you continue rolling. You may need to do this several times during the rolling process. (Experienced pastry makers may wish to roll the dough out on a lightly floured work surface, turning the dough as you roll and dusting the work surface and dough with extra flour as needed to keep it from sticking. Before transferring the dough to the tart pan, brush any excess flour from the surface, then flip it over and brush the flour from the bottom as well. Transfer the dough to the tart pan by rolling it around your rolling pin, then unrolling it into the pan.)

Transfer the dough to the tart pan by removing the top piece of plastic wrap. Leave the bottom piece on to hold the dough together while you lift it and flip it over into the tart pan (remaining plastic side should be up), centering it as best you can as shown. Remove the top layer of plastic wrap and press the dough into the corners of the pan using your fingertips. Patch any tears by simply pressing the dough together, then build the edge of the tart slightly above the rim of the pan by reinforcing each flute. To do this, press the index finger of one hand against the dough inside the curve of each flute to push the dough upward while at the same time pressing the dough from the outside of each flute with the thumb and index finger of your other hand in a pinching position (see illustration, 112). The dough should rise about ¼ inch above the rim of the pan all the way around. Place the tart pan, uncovered, in the refrigerator for 1 hour or in the freezer for 30 minutes.

To press the dough into the tart pan: Break the chilled dough into small pieces, roughly an inch or two in diameter, and scatter them evenly over the bottom of the tart pan. Use the heel of your hand to press the pieces of dough flat, connecting them into a smooth, even layer as shown on the following page. Then press from the center outward, building up some extra dough around the base at the edge of the tart. Using your thumbs, press this excess up the sides of the pan to form the walls, making sure that they are the same thickness as the dough on the bottom of the pan. Build the top edge of the tart slightly above the rim of the pan by reinforcing each flute. To do this, press the index finger of one hand against the dough  inside the curve of each flute to push the dough upward while at the same time pressing the dough from the outside of each flute with the thumb and index finger of your other hand in a pinching position (see illustration, 112). The dough should rise about ¼ inch above the rim of the pan all the way around. Place the tart pan, uncovered, in the refrigerator for 1 hour or in the freezer for 30 minutes.

TO BAKE THE TART SHELL

To prebake the tart shell: Preheat the oven to 375°F. Position an oven rack in the lower third of the oven. Line the chilled tart shell with heavy-duty foil, pressing the foil firmly into the corners of the pan. Fill the pan with metal pie weights, dried beans, or rice. The center layer of weights may be thinner, but be sure to push the weights all the way up the sides of the pan to reduce shrinkage and to ensure the edges are straight.

To partially bake the shell: Bake for about 20 to 22 minutes, or until the edges and center are set and no longer stick to the foil when you try to remove it. Remove the foil and weights and return the pan to the oven for another 8 to 12 minutes, or until the crust is a pale tan color. Place on a rack to cool completely before filling the shell.

To fully bake the shell: Bake for about 20 to 22 minutes, or until the edges and center are set and no longer stick to the foil when you try to remove it. Remove the foil and weights and return the pan to the oven for another 15 to 20 minutes, or until the crust is golden brown all over. Place on a rack to cool completely before filling the shell.

GETTING AHEAD: The dough can be made ahead, wrapped tightly in plastic wrap, and held in the refrigerator for up to 3 days or in the freezer for up to 1 month. If frozen, thaw overnight in the refrigerator before proceeding.

The dough may also be rolled out, placed in the tart pan as directed, then the whole pan can be wrapped tightly with plastic wrap and frozen for up to 1 month. Frozen dough will need to prebake an additional 3 to 5 minutes.

Cornmeal Shortcrust Dough

**enough dough for one double-crusted tart in a
pan up to 10 inches in diameter**

*A variation on the basic shortcrust pastry, this recipe substitutes yellow cornmeal or
corn flour for part of the all-purpose flour, resulting in a sunny yellow, slightly nubby
crust. Always sift the cornmeal before measuring—especially if it's stone-ground—to
make sure the texture is very fine. Toasting the cornmeal intensifies its wonderfully
sweet, nut-like flavor.*

EQUIPMENT AND ADVANCE PREPARATION: One 9- or 9½-inch fluted tart pan with
removable bottom

> ½ cup (1¾ ounces) fine cornmeal or corn flour (85), sifted, then spooned
> lightly into the cup for measuring
>
> 1½ cups (7½ ounces) unbleached all-purpose flour
>
> 6 tablespoons (2¾ ounces) sugar
>
> ¼ teaspoon salt
>
> 1½ sticks (6 ounces) cold (*not* frozen), unsalted butter, cut into ½-inch
> pieces
>
> 3 large egg yolks
>
> 2 teaspoons pure vanilla extract
>
> 1½ tablespoons (¾ ounce) water

To toast the cornmeal: Place a dry 8-inch skillet over high heat. When the
pan is hot, add the cornmeal and toss or stir frequently until the cornmeal is very
fragrant and has a golden toasted look (it should not brown), about 4 to 5 minutes. Remove from the heat immediately and pour the cornmeal onto a plate or
a baking sheet to cool. If left in the skillet, the cornmeal will continue to cook
from the residual heat and could burn. Cool completely before continuing with
the recipe.

TO PREPARE THE DOUGH

To mix using a mixer: Place the cornmeal, flour, sugar, and salt in the bowl
of a standing mixer fitted with the paddle attachment. Mix on low for 1 minute
to blend the ingredients. Add the butter pieces and mix on medium speed just

until the mixture resembles breadcrumbs, about 5 to 6 minutes. In a separate bowl, whisk together the yolks, vanilla, and 1 tablespoon of water. Add this to the dry ingredients and blend just until the dough begins to form large clumps. Test the dough by squeezing several clumps in your hand—they should hold together. If not, add the remaining water, 1 teaspoon at a time, until the dough coheres. Remove the dough from the bowl and knead it gently 2 or 3 times, just to finish bringing it together. Divide the dough into 2 pieces, one weighing about 12 ounces, the other about 8½ ounces. Shape both portions into discs about ¾ inch thick. If you don't have a scale, the larger portion of dough should form a 5½-inch disc, and the smaller portion should form a 4½-inch disc. Wrap tightly in plastic wrap and refrigerate for 30 minutes before proceeding.

To mix using a food processor: Place the cornmeal, flour, sugar, and salt in the bowl of a food processor fitted with the metal blade. Pulse 5 times to blend the ingredients. Add the cold butter pieces and pulse 6 to 8 times, just until the butter is the size of large peas. In a separate bowl, whisk together the yolks, vanilla, and 1 tablespoon of water. Add this to the bowl of the processor, then process just until the dough begins to form small clumps—do not let it form a ball. Test the dough by squeezing a handful of clumps—they should hold together. If not, add the remaining water, 1 teaspoon at a time, until the dough coheres. Remove the dough from the bowl and knead it gently 2 or 3 times, just to finish bringing it together. Divide the dough into 2 pieces, one weighing about 12 ounces, the other about 8½ ounces. Shape both portions into discs about ¾ inch thick. If you don't have a scale, the larger portion should form a 5½-inch disc, and the smaller portion should form a 4½-inch disc. Wrap tightly in plastic wrap and refrigerate for 30 minutes before proceeding.

To mix by hand: Place the cornmeal, flour, sugar, and salt in a medium bowl and blend well with a whisk. Add the cold butter pieces and toss until they are lightly coated with the flour. Use your fingertips, 2 knives, or a pastry blender to cut the butter into the flour until the mixture resembles breadcrumbs. If at any time during this process the butter softens and becomes warm, place the bowl in the freezer for 10 minutes before continuing. In a separate bowl, whisk together the yolks, vanilla, and 1 tablespoon of water. Add this to the dry ingredients and toss between your fingertips 20 to 30 times to evenly distribute the moisture. The dough will still look very crumbly, but if the mixture is squeezed in your hand, it should hold together. If not, add the remaining water, 1 teaspoon at a time, and toss to blend. Turn the dough out of the bowl onto your work surface and knead it gently 5 or 6 times, just to bring it together. Divide the dough into 2 pieces, one weighing about 12 ounces, the other about 8½ ounces. Shape both portions into discs about ¾ inch thick. If you don't have a scale, the larger portion of dough should form a 5½-inch disc, and the smaller portion should form a 4½-inch disc. Wrap tightly in plastic wrap and refrigerate for 30 minutes before proceeding.

TO LINE THE TART PAN

To roll out the dough: It is easiest to roll this dough when it is at cool room temperature. This means that if it has been refrigerated for longer than 30 minutes, let it sit on the counter for 10 to 15 minutes before rolling it out (if it is too cold, the dough will crack as you attempt to roll it). Place the larger disc of dough between two 12-inch pieces of plastic wrap. Roll it into an 11-inch round (see illustration, 116), rotating it clockwise slightly after each roll to create an even round. Remember to roll from the center outward and to lift the rolling pin at the edge rather than smashing the edge down. As you roll, the plastic wrap will wrinkle and resist. When this happens, peel it off and replace it smoothly, then flip the dough over and repeat with the plastic on the other side before you continue rolling. You may need to do this several times during the rolling process. (Experienced pastry makers may wish to roll the dough out on a lightly floured work surface, turning the dough as you roll and dusting the work surface and dough with extra flour as needed to keep it from sticking. Before transferring the dough to the tart pan, brush any excess flour from the surface, then flip it over and brush the flour from the bottom as well. Transfer the dough to the tart pan by rolling it around your rolling pin, then unrolling it into the pan.)

Transfer the dough to the tart pan by removing the top piece of plastic wrap. Leave the bottom piece on to hold the dough together while you lift it and flip it over into the tart pan (remaining plastic side should be up), centering it as best you can (see illustration, 116). Remove the top layer of plastic wrap and press the dough into the corners of the pan using your fingertips. Patch any tears by simply pressing the dough together. Level the top of the tart shell by pressing your thumb against the top edge of the tart pan and rolling it from the inside outward to cut off any excess dough.

To press the dough into the tart pan: Follow the directions on page 116 of the Shortcrust Dough recipe.

To shape the top portion of the tart: Roll out the smaller piece of dough by placing it between two new 12-inch pieces of plastic wrap. Following the directions above, roll it into a 10-inch round. Leave the plastic in place and transfer the round to a sheet pan. Refrigerate both the tart pan and the top of the tart for 1 hour or freeze for 30 minutes. For longer storage, wrap the tart pan in plastic wrap so the dough won't absorb any odors.

TO BAKE THE TART SHELL

Follow the directions in the recipe for Peach and Cornmeal Tart on page 83.

GETTING AHEAD: The dough can be made ahead, wrapped tightly in plastic wrap, and held in the refrigerator for up to 3 days or in the freezer for up to 1 month. If frozen, thaw overnight in the refrigerator before proceeding.

The dough may also be rolled out and placed in the tart pan as directed, then both the tart pan and the rolled-out top layer of dough can be wrapped tightly with plastic wrap and frozen for up to 1 month.

Chocolate Shortcrust Dough

enough dough to line a tart pan up to 10 inches in diameter

Another variation on the basic shortcrust recipe, this chocolate version has a deep, almost bitter chocolate flavor and a crisp, cookie-like texture.

EQUIPMENT AND ADVANCE PREPARATION: One 9- or 9½-inch fluted tart pan with removable bottom • A piece of heavy-duty foil and enough pie weights to fill the tart shell to the top for prebaking • Rice and/or dried beans may be used instead of metal pie weights, but note that rice and beans used in this manner are no longer suitable for eating (though they may be used over and over again to prebake tart shells).

> 1¼ cups (6¼ ounces) unbleached all-purpose flour
>
> 2 tablespoons unsweetened Dutch-process cocoa powder (262)
>
> ⅓ cup plus 1 tablespoon (2¾ ounces) sugar
>
> ¼ teaspoon salt
>
> 1 stick (4 ounces) cold (*not* frozen) unsalted butter, cut into ½-inch pieces
>
> 2 large egg yolks
>
> 1 teaspoon pure vanilla extract
>
> 1 to 3 teaspoons water, as needed

TO PREPARE THE DOUGH

To mix using a mixer: Place the flour, cocoa powder, sugar, and salt in the bowl of a standing mixer fitted with the paddle attachment. Mix on low for 1 minute to blend the ingredients. Add the butter pieces and mix on medium speed just until the mixture resembles breadcrumbs, about 5 to 6 minutes. In a separate bowl, whisk together the yolks, vanilla, and 1 teaspoon of water. Add this to the dry ingredients and blend just until the dough begins to form large clumps. Test the dough by squeezing several clumps in your hand—they should hold together. If not, add the remaining water, 1 teaspoon at a time, until the dough coheres. Remove the dough from the bowl and knead it gently 2 or 3 times, just to finish bringing it together. Shape the dough into a disc about ¾ inch thick and 5½ inches in diameter. Wrap tightly in plastic wrap and refrigerate for 30 minutes before proceeding.

To mix using a food processor: Place the flour, cocoa powder, sugar, and salt in the bowl of a food processor fitted with the metal blade. Pulse 5 times to blend the ingredients. Add the cold butter pieces and pulse 6 to 8 times, just until the butter is the size of large peas. In a separate bowl, whisk together the yolks, vanilla, and 1 teaspoon of water. Add this to the bowl of the processor, then process just until the dough begins to form small clumps—do not let it form a ball. Test the dough by squeezing a handful of clumps—they should hold together. If not, add the remaining water, 1 teaspoon at a time, until the dough coheres. Remove the dough from the bowl and knead it gently 2 or 3 times, just to finish bringing it together. Shape it into a disc about ¾ inch thick and 5½ inches in diameter. Wrap tightly in plastic wrap and refrigerate for 30 minutes before proceeding.

To mix by hand: Place the flour, cocoa powder, sugar, and salt in a medium bowl and blend well with a whisk. Add the cold butter pieces and toss until they are lightly coated with the flour. Use your fingertips, 2 knives, or a pastry blender to cut the butter into the flour until the mixture resembles breadcrumbs. If at any time during this process the butter softens and becomes warm, place the bowl in the freezer for 10 minutes before continuing. In a separate bowl, whisk together the yolks, vanilla, and 2 teaspoons of water. Add this to the dry ingredients and toss between your fingertips 20 to 30 times to evenly distribute the moisture. The dough will still look very crumbly, but if the mixture is squeezed in your hand, it should hold together. If not, add the remaining teaspoon of water and toss to blend. Turn the dough out of the bowl onto your work surface and knead it gently 5 or 6 times, just to bring it together. Shape it into a round disc about ¾ inch thick and 5½ inches in diameter. Wrap tightly in plastic wrap and refrigerate for 30 minutes before proceeding.

TO LINE THE TART PAN

To roll out the dough: It is easiest to roll this dough when it is at cool room temperature. This means that if it has been refrigerated for longer than 30 minutes, let it sit on the counter for 10 to 15 minutes before rolling it out (if it is too cold, the dough will crack as you attempt to roll it).

Place the disc of dough between two 12-inch pieces of plastic wrap. Roll the dough into an 11-inch round (see illustration, 116), rotating it clockwise slightly after each roll to create an even round. Remember to roll from the center outward and to lift the rolling pin at the edge rather than smashing the edge down. As you roll, the plastic wrap will wrinkle and resist. When this happens, peel it off and replace it smoothly, then flip the dough over and repeat with the plastic on the other side before you continue rolling. You may need to do this several times during the rolling process. (Experienced pastry makers may wish to roll the dough out on a lightly floured work surface, turning the dough as you roll and dusting the work surface and dough with extra flour as needed to keep it from sticking. Before transferring the dough to the tart pan, brush any excess flour from the surface, then flip it over and brush the flour from the bottom as well. Transfer the dough to the tart pan by rolling it around your rolling pin, then unrolling it into the pan.)

Transfer the dough to the tart pan by removing the top piece of plastic wrap. Leave the bottom piece on to hold the dough together while you lift it and flip it over into the tart pan (remaining plastic side should be up), centering it as best you can (see illustration, 116). Remove the top layer of plastic wrap and press the dough into the corners of the pan using your fingertips. Patch any tears by pressing the dough together, then build the edge of the tart slightly above the rim of the pan by reinforcing each flute. To do this, press the index finger of one hand against the dough inside the curve of each flute to push the dough upward while at the same time pressing the dough from the outside of each flute with the thumb and index finger of your other hand in a pinching position (see illustration, 112). The dough should rise about ¼ inch above the rim of the pan all the way around. Place the tart pan, uncovered, in the refrigerator for 1 hour or in the freezer for 30 minutes.

To press the dough into the tart pan: Follow the directions on page 116 of the Shortcrust Dough recipe.

TO BAKE THE TART SHELL
Follow the directions on page 116 of the Shortcrust Dough recipe.

GETTING AHEAD: The dough can be made ahead, wrapped tightly in plastic wrap, and held in the refrigerator for up to 3 days or in the freezer for up to 1 month. If frozen, thaw overnight in the refrigerator before proceeding.

The dough may also be rolled out and placed in the tart pan as directed, then the whole pan can be wrapped tightly with plastic wrap and frozen for up to 1 month. Frozen dough will need to prebake an additional 3 to 5 minutes.

Fruit Desserts

There is no more authentic ending to a Mediterranean meal than a piece of fresh ripe fruit. Sometimes the fruit is accompanied by nuts or cheese, but there is always fruit, often piled in a bowl and set in the middle of the table so guests can help themselves. This penchant for simple, healthful endings is one of the reasons people in the Mediterranean live such long lives—one of the others is their healthy attitude toward enjoying good food. They do eat sweets, often and with gusto, but they tend to enjoy their sweets between meals with a cup of coffee or tea, reserving their after-dinner extravaganzas for holidays and special occasions.

Our lifestyle includes dinner as a social time, a period to relax and catch up with family and friends, and we like to end our evening meal with a luscious little something. The recipes in this chapter combine the best of both worlds by featuring fruit as the main focus, but for American tastes and with entertaining in mind, they transform simple fruit into elegant endings. Some recipes here are the essence of simplicity, such as Roasted Pears with Spiced Sabayon or Raspberry and Cannoli Cream Parfaits. Others venture into a more complex presentation, though each element is quite easy, such as Mascarpone-Stuffed Dates with Spiced Blood Orange Caramel Sauce and Seeded Praline or the Figs Stuffed with Goat Cheese Served with Raspberry and Caramel Sauces.

There are even a couple of recipes for poached fruit, a popular Mediterranean method of preparing fruit. Poached fruit deserves another look. It's light, healthful (well, compared to other dessert choices), and simple to prepare—one need only pluck the fruit from the syrup at its moment of doneness. And as the flavor of the poaching ingredients meld, the end result is always more than the sum of its parts. Want further proof? Try Poached Quinces with Fromage Blanc, Plums in Port with Clove Cream, or Cherries Poached in Red Wine with Rose Geranium and Blackberries.

Please note that these recipes rely on great-tasting fruit, so before you choose a recipe, see what fruit is in season where you live. A farmers' market or a roadside farmstand are the best places to find ripe, in-season, locally grown fruit. The natural food store can also be a good source for produce. If the supermarket is your only choice, you can still find fruit that is flavorful by making friends with the produce clerks and being vigilant in asking questions: what's good today? what just came in? where is it from? and most important, may I have a taste?

Roasted Pears with Spiced Sabayon

serves 4

In this simple dessert, warm, glistening, caramelized pears are topped with a sensuously rich port sabayon, fragrant with cinnamon and cloves. Sabayon is a delicate sauce and must be served as soon as it has finished cooking, so if you are entertaining, you will be in the kitchen for about 15 minutes while you finish the dessert. The sabayon can be made ahead of time if it is served cold—see the variation at the end of the recipe.

EQUIPMENT AND ADVANCE PREPARATION: One 10-inch ovenproof sauté pan or skillet (if you use very large pears, you may need a larger skillet—you want to cook all the pear halves at one time, in a single layer) • A double boiler (or a medium saucepan coupled with a medium stainless-steel mixing bowl that will fit about halfway into the saucepan when sitting on top of it) • A pear corer (130), optional (you can certainly core pears without one, but this device gives an especially elegant result)

FOR THE PEARS

4 medium (about 8 ounces each) firm-ripe winter pears, such as Bosc or Winter Nelis

1 lemon

3 tablespoons (1½ ounces) unsalted butter, cut into small pieces

¼ cup (1¾ ounces) sugar

2 tablespoons Poire William eau-de-vie (pear brandy)

FOR THE SPICED SABAYON

4 large egg yolks

¼ cup (1¾ ounces) sugar

½ cup (4 ounces) tawny port

⅛ teaspoon ground cinnamon

⅛ teaspoon ground cloves

Preheat the oven to 400°F. Position an oven rack in the center of the oven.

To prepare the pears, peel the pears, then cut them in half. Use the rounded end of a pear corer or a melon baller to carefully remove the core and the bit of blossom at the bottom of the pear. Then use the narrow end of the corer or the tip of a small, sharp knife to remove the fibrous line of flesh extending from the core to the stem. I like to leave the stems on one-half of each pear for a pretty presentation, but you may remove the stems as well. Slice the lemon in half and rub it all over the pears, squeezing the lemon slightly as you work to coat the fruit with juice.

To cook the pears, place the butter and sugar in a large ovenproof skillet and warm over low heat until the butter is melted. Add the Poire William and swirl the pan to blend and to distribute the mixture evenly. Place the pear halves in the skillet, cut side down, in a single layer. Turn the heat to high and cook until the sugar begins to caramelize and turns a light golden brown color, about 5 to 7 minutes. Swirl the pan every few minutes to help the sugar caramelize as evenly as possible. Place the pan in the oven and roast the pears for 15 to 20 minutes, or until they are easily pierced with the tip of a small, sharp knife and the cut sides are nicely browned. Remove the pan from the oven and place it on the stovetop. Leave the pears in the pan to keep warm while you prepare the sauce.

To prepare the sabayon, place 2 inches of water in the bottom of the double boiler and bring to a gentle boil. The water should be at least 2 inches from the top of the double boiler. Place the egg yolks and sugar in the top of the double boiler and whisk briefly, just until they are well blended and slightly lightened in color. Add the port and blend well.

Place the top of the double boiler over the simmering water and whisk constantly. As the sauce cooks, it will become very light and fluffy, resembling softly whipped cream in texture. This will take about 5 minutes. Be careful that the mixture does not get too hot, or the eggs will scramble. If you see the sauce beginning to scramble, remove the top of the double boiler from the heat and whisk furiously. This will usually save the mixture, but if it still looks flat and broken or there are large pieces of scrambled egg in the sauce, there is no recourse but to begin again. As soon as the sauce is finished, remove it from the heat. Whisk in the cinnamon and cloves.

SERVING AND STORAGE NOTES: Place 2 warm pear halves on each plate or in individual compote bowls, then divide any remaining pan juices among them. Spoon the sabayon over the pears. Serve immediately.

Cold Sabayon: If you wish to make the sabayon ahead and serve it cold, you will need to stabilize it with whipped cream—otherwise, it will collapse. To do this, follow the recipe above, and when the sauce is finished, immediately set the top of the double boiler into a large bowl filled halfway with a mixture of ice and water; whisk until the sauce is cold. Place ½ cup heavy cream in the bowl of an electric mixer fitted with the whisk attachment and whip on medium speed to firm peaks. Be careful not to overwhip the cream, or it will begin to separate and look curdled. If this happens, remove the bowl from the mixer and use a rubber spatula to gently stir in 1 or 2 tablespoons of cream, just until the whipped cream has smoothed out again. Use a rubber spatula to gently fold the cream into the cooled sauce. Cover with plastic wrap and refrigerate until needed.

GETTING AHEAD: The pears may be peeled, halved, cored, and coated with a bit of lemon juice early in the day. Cover and refrigerate until needed.

The cold sabayon may be prepared up to 12 hours ahead, but it must be made the same day it is to be served.

Pear Corer

This is a recipe in which you want the pear halves to look as beautiful as possible. The perfect tool for this job is a pear corer, basically a handle with an exaggerated egg-shaped strip of metal on one end. Use the larger, rounded side to lift out both the center core and the little blossom end at the bottom of each pear half, and use the narrow side to remove the tough, stringy line of flesh extending from the core to the stem. (I've also seen a double-ended model that has a half-circle metal strip to take out the center and a long, narrow strip of metal with a bent tip to take out the line of core extending to the stem. This model, while more cumbersome, also does the job.) I'm not a big collector of kitchen gadgets, but this one is in constant use in my kitchen—I also use it for apples. You can find pear corers in well-stocked kitchen supply stores or order one from a source like Sur La Table (see Mail-Order Sources, 327).

Poached Quinces with Fromage Blanc

serves 6

Quinces are one of the few proud fruits that stubbornly refuse to have their season artificially extended or to be included in that pricy display in the produce section that should be called "tired, tasteless fruit flown at great expense from a country currently experiencing the season you wish you were in." Granted, part of their problem is a complete lack of promotion by quince growers, and it is true that they can be difficult to find (though during the fall and early winter, they can sometimes be found at farmers' markets or in the specialty fruits section of the produce department). But I promise that once you have tried this gorgeous Old World fruit, cooked to a soft, glistening deep rose to pink-orange color, and experienced its apple-pineapple-citrus flavor, you will add it to your list of eagerly anticipated seasonal items. Here, beautiful sliced quinces surround a creamy mound of orange-scented goat cheese, looking like an old master painting yet tasting like the perfect ending that it is for a blustery evening filled with the soul-warming foods of fall.

EQUIPMENT AND ADVANCE PREPARATION: Six 12-ounce compote dishes or bowls

FOR THE POACHED QUINCES

2 pounds quinces

4 cups water

¾ cup (5¼ ounces) sugar

½ vanilla bean, split lengthwise in half

Zest of ½ orange, in strips

Zest of ½ lemon, in strips

One 3- to 4-inch stick cinnamon

3 nickel-size slices of fresh ginger

2 tablespoons (1 ounce) freshly squeezed lemon juice

FOR THE FROMAGE BLANC

8 ounces fromage blanc (a very fresh goat cheese, similar in texture to ricotta but with a lightly acidic flavor)

6 tablespoons (3 ounces) heavy cream

2 tablespoons plus 2 teaspoons (1¼ ounces) sugar, or to taste

½ teaspoon orange liqueur, such as Grand Marnier or Cointreau

FOR SERVING
Candied orange zest (236), optional

To prepare the fruit, wash the quinces and pat dry. Peel, halve, and core the fruit (217), reserving the peels and cores. Use a large, sharp knife to cut the fruit into ½-inch-thick slices. Place the slices in a medium bowl, cover with plastic wrap, and set aside until needed. The fruit will turn brown but will turn pink when cooked.

Place the peels and cores in a saucepan with the water and sugar. Use a small, sharp knife to scrape the tiny black seeds from inside the vanilla bean, then add both the seeds and the bean to the pan, as well as the orange and lemon zests, cinnamon stick, ginger slices, and fresh lemon juice. Warm over medium heat until the mixture begins to simmer and the sugar is dissolved, then cover the pan, lower the heat, and cook at a gentle boil for 30 minutes (the peels and cores are very flavorful and, with the other flavorings, will make a quince "stock" in which to poach the fruit). Strain the mixture and return the liquid to the pan, along with the vanilla bean and cinnamon stick.

To poach the quinces, add the prepared quince slices to the pan and bring the mixture back to a boil over medium heat. Once it has reached a boil, turn the heat down to very low, cover the pan, and cook at the lowest possible simmer (lift the lid and check occasionally to see that the liquid is not boiling rapidly—this can cause the fruit to fall apart) for 1½ to 2 hours, or until the fruit is very tender and a stunning deep rose to orange color. Gently stir the fruit once or twice during this time to ensure that the pieces cook evenly. The fruit will be tender long before it has turned the beautiful color you want, so don't be tempted to remove it from the heat too early. Quinces have the amazing ability to hold their shape long after they are cooked through (unlike apples, which turn to applesauce), so be patient, keep the liquid at a low simmer, and you will be rewarded with a dessert of striking color and flavor.

When the quinces have finished cooking, gently pour the contents of the pan into a large bowl and set aside to cool. If you would like the broth to be a bit thicker and deeper in color, return the liquid to the pan, place over medium heat, and boil until it is reduced to about 1¼ to 1½ cups. Cool the reduced broth and pour it over the quince slices. Refrigerate, covered, until serving time.

To prepare the fromage blanc, in a medium bowl, use a wooden spoon to gently blend the fromage blanc with the cream and sugar. Add just enough cream to smooth the cheese—too much will liquefy the mixture, and it should still have plenty of body. Stir in the orange liqueur to taste. Refrigerate until needed.

SERVING AND STORAGE NOTES: Spoon some quince slices and broth into each compote bowl or serving dish and top with a spoonful of fromage blanc. Garnish, if you wish, by topping the fromage blanc with strands of candied orange zest.

GETTING AHEAD: The poached quinces can be prepared up to 4 days in advance and held in an airtight container in the refrigerator.

The fromage blanc can be prepared 1 day ahead—keep refrigerated in an airtight container.

Mascarpone-Stuffed Dates with Spiced Blood Orange Caramel Sauce and Seeded Praline

serves 6

It is not unusual to see fruit and cheese served at the end of a meal in the Mediterranean, though this particular combination shows the playfulness of California cooking. Big soft dates are stuffed with a spoonful of mascarpone, then partnered with warmly spiced, brilliantly colored blood orange caramel sauce. A seeded praline, striking with its blend of sesame and poppy seeds in a network of deep amber caramel, is broken into irregular pieces and scattered around the plates for a pleasing contrast in texture and flavor.

EQUIPMENT AND ADVANCE PREPARATION: A baking sheet with sides, brushed with a thin coat of melted butter or flavorless vegetable oil • If you wish to make your own mascarpone (42), you will need to begin a least 3 days in advance.

FOR THE DATES
18 moist Medjool dates

4½ ounces mascarpone

FOR THE SEEDED PRALINE
½ cup water

1 cup (7 ounces) sugar

½ cup (2½ ounces) sesame seeds, lightly toasted (101) and cooled to
  room temperature

¼ cup (1¼ ounces) poppy seeds, room temperature

FOR SERVING
Spiced blood orange caramel sauce (231)

To pit the dates, make a slice in one side and pull out the seed. Then pinch the ends together to loosen the slit where the pit was removed and use a small spoon to place about 1½ teaspoons of mascarpone in the date (the cheese should be a visible mound). Cover with plastic wrap and refrigerate until needed.

To make the seeded praline, place the water in a medium saucepan, add the sugar, and set the pan over medium heat. Stir constantly with a wooden spoon or swirl the pan frequently until the sugar is dissolved and the liquid is clear. Turn the heat to high and boil rapidly, swirling the pan occasionally (do not stir at this point) so the sugar cooks evenly, until it turns a deep golden brown. Remove the pan from the heat, add the sesame and poppy seeds, and stir the mixture with the wooden spoon just until blended. If the caramel has solidified, set the pan back over low heat and stir until it melts again. Pour the praline onto the sheet pan and use a lightly oiled offset spatula or kitchen knife to spread it into a thin layer about ⅛ inch thick. Cool completely. Use a meat pounder or the blunt end of a large knife to break the praline into pieces. I like pieces no larger than about ½ inch, but the size is up to you—just keep in mind that they are an accent on the dessert plate, not the focus.

NOTE: It can be fun to cut the praline into shapes. Wait until the praline on the pan is warm and pliable but not liquid, about 2 minutes. Lightly oil a miniature cookie cutter and press it into the praline, but do not attempt to free the shapes from the sheet pan. Wait until the praline has completely cooled, then pop the shapes off the pan by sliding a spatula under the hardened caramel and pressing upward. You will need to pull off the surrounding excess praline with your fingers.

SERVING AND STORAGE NOTES: Place 3 stuffed dates on each dessert plate. Drizzle the dates and the plates with the caramel sauce. Garnish with the praline pieces.

GETTING AHEAD: The dates may be stuffed up to 2 days in advance. Store in an airtight container in the refrigerator.

The spiced blood orange caramel sauce may be made up to 5 days in advance. Store in an airtight container in the refrigerator.

The seeded praline may be prepared up to 1 month in advance. Store in a dry, airtight jar or storage container, layered with pieces of parchment or wax paper, at room temperature. If the weather is very warm or humid, place the container in the refrigerator, but be sure to let the praline come to room temperature, still in the container, for several hours before serving.

Dates

The Coachella Valley in southern California is perhaps best known for the city of Palm Springs, the star-studded golf and suntan getaway of Los Angeleans. Those who make the drive into the blistering heat in this subtropical low desert will find that the valley has another side—an agricultural area second only to Iraq in date production.

For many years the only contact I had with dates was the tiny, hard, ultra-sweet bits contained in granola, which I always picked out and threw away. I hated dates . . . or so I thought. Then one day at a farmers' market in Los Angeles, I stopped at the table of a date farmer, intrigued by the seven or eight varieties available. As I tasted my way down the table, I gained a whole new appreciation for the range of textures and tastes and vowed to give dates another chance. Since then I've included them in all sorts of desserts, from cakes and tarts to biscotti and ice cream, always pairing them with an ingredient that is either bitter (like caramel) or acidic (like orange) to temper their intense sweetness.

The date has been cultivated since ancient times in the Middle East and North Africa and features prominently in their cuisines. In many areas it sustains the poor in both nourishment and materials, for the stems, leaves, and trunk of the date palm are used for everyday necessities such as baskets, hats, floor coverings, and even firewood for cooking. Though there are many varieties of dates, there are only a few that are available commercially, and the most popular by far is the Deglet Noor, accounting for 95 percent of dates sold. I prefer the Medjool, a large, soft, mahogany-colored date with wrinkled skin and a custard-like interior (see Mail-Order Sources, 327). Though dates are really a fresh fruit, most often they can be found packaged in the dried fruit section of the supermarket, except for Medjools, which are usually sold loose in the fresh produce section.

When choosing dates, try to taste one before purchasing because sometimes, due to either the variety or poor storage, they are just too dry and tough to be of value in dessert making. Store them in an airtight container at cool room temperature for a few weeks; for longer storage, place them in the refrigerator, where they will keep for up to 1 year. If a whitish bloom appears on the surface, do not be alarmed—it is only sugar crystals. They will not affect the flavor, but if you are concerned about the appearance of the fruit, wipe the crystals off with a damp cloth.

Figs with Espresso-Sambuca Sabayon with Shaved Chocolate

serves 4

If you can find only a few ripe figs each year, you'll probably want to enjoy them unadorned. On the other hand, if you are lucky enough to have a couple of trees, as I am, you can enjoy your fill of fruit and still have plenty left for experimenting in the kitchen. This recipe pairs fresh figs with a silky sabayon gently flavored with espresso and anise. The anise, or licorice, flavor comes from sambuca, an Italian liqueur infused with elderflowers. Figs often have an almost anise-like note to their sweet, complex flavor, and the sambuca accentuates this quality. The flavor of the espresso rounds out the sweetness with earthy, savory tones, accenting the sweetness with a touch of bitterness.

EQUIPMENT AND ADVANCE PREPARATION: A double boiler (or a medium saucepan coupled with a medium stainless-steel mixing bowl that will fit about halfway into the saucepan when sitting on top of it) • A large bowl filled halfway with a mixture of ice and water

FOR THE SABAYON

6 large egg yolks

¼ cup (1 ¾ ounces) sugar

¼ cup plus 2 tablespoons (3 ounces) sambuca

1½ tablespoons instant espresso granules, preferably Medaglia d'Oro

1 cup (8 ounces) heavy cream

FOR SERVING

10 small to medium figs, stems trimmed, each fig cut in half through the stem end

Miniature chocolate curls (106)

To make the sabayon, place 2 inches of water in the bottom of the double boiler and bring to a gentle boil. Place the egg yolks and sugar in the top of the double boiler and whisk briefly, just until they are well blended and slightly lightened in color. Add the sambuca and espresso granules and blend well.

Place the top of the double boiler over the simmering water and whisk constantly. As the sauce cooks, it will become very light and fluffy, resembling softly whipped cream in texture. This will take about 5 minutes. Be careful that the mixture does not get too hot, or the eggs will scramble. If you see the sauce beginning to scramble, remove the top of the double boiler from the heat and whisk furiously. This will usually save the mixture, but if it still looks flat and broken or there are large pieces of scrambled egg in the sauce, there is no recourse but to begin again.

As soon as the sauce is finished, remove the top of the double boiler from the heat and immediately set it into the large bowl of ice and water. Whisk constantly until the sauce is cold. In the bowl of an electric mixer fitted with the whisk attachment, whip the cream on medium speed to firm peaks. Be careful not to overwhip the cream, or it will begin to separate and look curdled. If this happens, remove the bowl from the mixer and use a rubber spatula to gently stir in several tablespoons of cream, just until the whipped cream has smoothed out again. Use a rubber spatula to gently fold the whipped cream into the cooled sauce. Cover and refrigerate until needed.

SERVING AND STORAGE NOTES: Place 5 fig halves on each dessert plate or in each compote bowl. If you have large figs, serve 3 halves per person instead of 5—an odd number on the plate is much more pleasing to the eyes than an even number. Spoon the sabayon over and around the figs but do not completely hide the fruit. Sprinkle with miniature chocolate curls.

GETTING AHEAD: The cold sabayon may be prepared up to 12 hours ahead, but it must be made the same day it is to be served.

La Mosca

Whenever I think of sambuca, the bracing elderflower-infused liqueur of Italy, I think of coffee beans. The first time I tasted sambuca, which tastes of anise, my host slipped a coffee bean into the glass, teasing me that a fly, *la mosca*, had landed in my drink. I finished the sambuca, then chewed on the bean, delighting in the flavor combination. Later, when I traveled to Italy, I realized *sambuca con la mosca* was a popular drink after an evening on the town. When I questioned a bartender about it, he winked and explained that if you chew the bean after you finish the drink, your breath will smell of coffee, and the wife at home will be none the wiser for your night of drinking. I think the wife would have to be pretty naive to fall for that one, but it is an intriguing pairing, for the deep, round, earthy flavors of the coffee, with its bitterness and acidity, blend well with the lighter, sweeter, almost candy-like notes of anise. Both notes are strong and assertive, but like a yin and yang pairing, they bring opposite qualities into harmony.

Citrus Compote in Spiced Champagne Broth

serves 6

This is a light and refreshing dessert, especially welcome after a hearty winter meal. A beautiful array of citrus fruits is served in a broth scented with vanilla, anise, cloves, and cinnamon. Just before serving, a splash of champagne is added to the mixture, giving it a surprising fizz and a pleasant hint of yeast. Sectioning the citrus does take a little time, but it can be done early in the day, and your guests will appreciate your effort—with no membranes to deal with, the dessert is all about pleasure. Feel free to include more or less of each of the citrus fruits suggested and to add any other varieties that you enjoy. Do not use your best champagne—an inexpensive to moderately priced bottle will serve the purpose well, just so long as it is drinkable.

For an exciting contrast of temperatures and textures, warm the compote briefly in a large skillet, then spoon it into small bowls and place a scoop of Tangerine (317) or Blood Orange Sorbet (318) in the center.

EQUIPMENT AND ADVANCE PREPARATION: Six 12-ounce wineglasses or compote bowls

FOR THE FRUIT

6 (about 1½ pounds) medium blood oranges

3 (about 2½ pounds) medium to large ruby grapefruit

3 (about 12 ounces) lavender gems (see Note)

3 (about 1 pound) medium navel oranges

FOR THE BROTH

1¼ cups (10 ounces) freshly squeezed and strained orange juice

1 tablespoon freshly squeezed lemon juice, or more if needed

4 to 6 tablespoons sugar, or more, depending on your taste and the sweetness of the fruit

1 vanilla bean, split lengthwise in half

One 3-inch stick cinnamon, lightly crushed

2 whole cloves

¼ teaspoon anise seeds

FOR SERVING

6 to 12 tablespoons champagne

Orange Cornmeal Rosettes with Apricot Jam (264)

NOTE: A lavender gem is a cross between a grapefruit and a mandarin. It has lovely sunset-colored flesh and an invigorating sweet-tart flavor. If lavender gems are not available in your area, feel free to substitute more navel oranges or another citrus fruit you like.

To prepare the fruit, peel and section the citrus (see page 145), working over a bowl to catch any juices. When you have finished sectioning each fruit, squeeze the membranes and add their juices to the work bowl. Place the fruit sections in a separate bowl. Refrigerate until needed.

To make the broth, place the reserved citrus juices, orange juice, lemon juice, sugar, and vanilla bean in a medium nonaluminum saucepan. To toast the spices, place a dry skillet over high heat. When it is hot, add the cinnamon stick, cloves, and anise seeds. Shake the pan gently to toast them evenly. When the spices are hot to the touch and very fragrant (do not let them brown), about 30 to 90 seconds, immediately transfer them to the saucepan and place it over medium heat.

Bring the liquid just to a boil, then remove from the heat, cover, and allow the mixture to steep for 5 minutes. Immediately pour the liquid through a fine-mesh strainer or a double thickness of cheesecloth into a bowl. Rinse the vanilla bean under water briefly, then return it to the broth—discard the remaining spices. Allow the broth to cool completely, then taste and adjust for sweetness by adding a little sugar if it is too tart or a bit of lemon juice if it seems too sweet. Add the citrus sections to the cooled broth and let the fruit sit, refrigerated, for at least an hour before serving to allow the flavors to blend.

SERVING AND STORAGE NOTES: Divide the compote and its broth among the wineglasses or compote bowls. Splash a little champagne into each glass right before serving—this is done to taste, about 1 to 2 tablespoons per glass. Serve accompanied by Orange Cornmeal Rosettes. This dessert can be made early in the day but is at its best the same day it is made. After that, the acidity of the broth starts to break down the citrus sections, causing them to become mushy.

Citrus Fruits

Palates can sail into the doldrums during the colder months, saturated with the rich, fatty foods of winter. It is then that the refreshing flavors of citrus are especially welcome as they tingle, torture, and delight us. From sweet to sour, ruby red to blushing pink to sunshine yellow, citrus fruits are a joyous staple of winter dessert making. Here is a brief overview of the most popular citrus available in the United States. Check for more obscure—and often more flavorful—specialty citrus, which are grown on a small scale, at your farmers' market.

When choosing citrus, look for fruit that feels heavy for its size (indicating juiciness), is smooth skinned with small pores, and is brightly colored. If you will be using the fruit within a few days, store it at room temperature; otherwise, keep it in a plastic bag in the refrigerator. Always try to buy organic fruit, and remember to wash the fruit before use to remove any coloring, dirt, or pesticide residue.

VARIETIES

Oranges

Originally from China, oranges traveled to Europe with Arab traders, spread quickly across the continent, and soon became a sign of wealth and prestige. These early oranges were the bitter variety, prized for their aromatic skin. By the mid-1600s, the sweet orange had arrived and was flourishing, but the bitter variety was still favored in cooking for many years. Today the bitter orange, also known as the Seville, is grown almost solely for marmalade, while the sweet orange has permeated our lives to the point where its juice is often the first thing that crosses our lips in the morning.

There are many varieties of oranges, but the two most common are the Valencia and the navel. Valencias are considered to be the best juice orange, while the seedless navels are great for eating out of hand or sectioning for cakes and compotes. We had a large navel tree in our backyard while I was growing up, and I can remember the skin around my lips peeling and tender from the acid of eating too many juicy and flavorful oranges.

Blood oranges are a relative newcomer on the citrus scene in this country, but they have been enjoyed for centuries in the Mediterranean, where the hot, dry summers and cold winters provide prime conditions for this beautiful fruit. Smaller than navel or Valencia oranges, blood oranges nonetheless pack a wallop of flavor into their petite package. With flesh that ranges from rosy orange to deep burgundy and a flavor that combines the rich sweetness of orange juice with deep berry undertones and a sprightly nip of acidity, blood oranges are an exciting addition to the dessert maker's citrus repertoire.

The three varieties grown here in California are the Moro, Sanguinelli, and Tarocco. The Moro usually has the deepest-colored flesh, from blood red to an almost purple color, and is the most popular of the three—it is also the easiest to peel. The Sanguinelli often has an enticing red-blush peel, though the color of its flesh is not as dramatic or as deep as that of the Moro. The Tarocco may not have any color on the rind at all, but it is the largest of the three varieties and, when grown under perfect conditions, is the best tasting—sweet and rich with a strong undercurrent of berries. The color of its flesh varies—some years it is barely colored; other years it's a beautiful deep red. Unfortunately, the strain of Tarocco grown currently in the United States is unpredictable. If you run across a batch of Taroccos, ask for a sample taste if you can.

Choose blood oranges as you would any other citrus, looking for fruit that seems heavy for its size, is firm, and has small pores in the skin. If possible, ask for a sample before buying so you can see the internal color and test the flavor. The flesh color can vary in intensity, depending on the variety of blood orange, the location of the orchard, and the age of the fruit. The color of their rind (or lack thereof) is no indication of the color inside the fruit and is thought to be caused simply by sunlight exposure. Blood oranges are in season from December to as late as May or June, depending upon the variety.

Mandarins

Mandarin is the group of citrus with loose, easy-to-peel skins and easy-to-separate segments. Tangerines are the most popular member of the Mandarin family. Seedless Japanese satsumas are my favorite eating tangerine, small and bursting with juicy sweetness, while I prefer the bright, fresh flavor of the honey tangerine for juicing (its segments do not pull apart easily like other tangerines).

Tangelos, a cross between a tangerine and a grapefruit, are recognizable by the protruding bump at the stem end. The most common variety is the Minneola.

The small clementine, a cross between a mandarin and a bitter orange, is a favorite in England at Christmas, where it can often be found wrapped in gold paper. It is popular in southern France as well, though in a dramatically different form. While shopping at the outdoor market in Nice, I noticed a local penchant for whole candied fruits called *comfits*. There were several stalls with glistening piles of these exquisitely translucent jewels, which ranged in variety from lemons to cactus prickly pears to figs. I felt it my professional duty to taste as wide a variety as possible and found the whole candied clementine to be one of the most beautiful and flavorful.

Lemons

Almost all of the commercially grown lemons in this country are the Eureka variety, but I prefer the Meyer lemon, which is most often found in home gardens here in California. Sometimes growing on a tree, sometimes on more of a bush, the Meyer lemon is soft and smooth, with skin that ranges from deep yellow to an egg-yolk orange color. It was once shunned by commercial growers because of its susceptibility to disease, but the introduction of a disease-resistant stock means that it is beginning to turn up in "gourmet" markets across the country during the winter months. It offers a wonderful perfume and a distinctive sweet-sour flavor that is assertive yet seductively inviting.

Limes

The most common variety of lime available is the Persian—a big round fruit with a deep green color. The much smaller Mexican lime has a thin green and yellow mottled skin and a more complex and interesting flavor. Lime juice tends to be less acidic than lemon, so if you are substituting, you may need to add a little extra lime juice to reach the same level of tang as with lemon juice.

Grapefruits

My aunt and uncle owned a grapefruit ranch when I was a child, and I vividly remember one day walking under a canopy of grapefruit branches so thick it virtually blocked out the sunlight. I glanced up and was startled to see what at first I thought were Christmas ornaments and which turned out to be golden orbs of grapefruit. These, like almost all yellow grapefruit, were the Marsh variety. Ruby grapefruit have a much sweeter and more complex flavor, as well as a lovely blush-pink flesh, which makes them a lovely addition to citrus desserts.

My favorite relative of the grapefruit is the lavender gem, a cross between a grapefruit and a mandarin. Its flesh is sunset colored, and its flavor is clean, sweet-tart refreshment.

The pomelo, thought to be the genetic forebear of grapefruit, is a huge caricature of its descendant and has a sweeter taste and a drier texture. It can be found in Asian food markets.

PREPARING CITRUS

To Zest

There are two ways to zest a piece of citrus, either with a grater or with a small tool called a zester. I do not advise grating zest, because a significant portion of the zest is either left on the grater or on the skin of the citrus, which can make a dramatic difference in the flavor of a dessert. It takes only an extra minute or two to zest and chop rather than grate, but the difference in flavor is immense.

A zester is a small, slightly angled, squarish piece of metal punched with a row of holes across the top and set into a handle. This tool does the amazing job of removing the colored, highly flavorful portion of the skin known as the zest while leaving the bitter white pith behind. To use, press the angled head of the zester firmly against the skin of the citrus at the top of the fruit. Place the thumb of the hand holding the zester against the bottom of the fruit and press upward with your thumb while firmly pulling the zester downward with your index finger as shown. If you do not have a zester, use a vegetable peeler to remove the zest, being careful not to remove any of the white pith beneath. You can use the zest as is, in strips, or chopped very finely with a large knife, which is best for most uses in cooking.

The zester is in constant use in my kitchen, and I've tried many kinds over the years. The best zester I've found is made by Victorinox of Switzerland. It is sharp, easy to hold, and made to last a lifetime—all for under $20. It is available in good knife stores. For a mail-order source, see page 327.

To Section

"Section" is a term describing the removal of the citrus flesh, leaving behind the tough white membranes and skin. Fruit served in this manner is a pleasure to eat, and without the membranes, the citrus flavor practically explodes in your mouth.

To section a citrus fruit, use a thin, sharp knife to slice a round off each end of the fruit, so that it will

stand without rolling. Then cut the peel off in pieces by placing the knife between the pith and the flesh and cutting
from top to bottom, following the curve of the fruit
as shown on the previous page. Make sure you
remove all the bitter white pith. When the fruit is
cleaned, hold it in your hand over a bowl to catch the
juices and the sections. Make a slice down one of the vertical white
membrane lines marking a section as shown. Stop at the center of the
fruit. Remove your knife and repeat the step starting inside the line of
the next membrane. The cleaned section of fruit should pull away easily.
Continue until all the flesh has been sectioned, then squeeze the membrane
mass and allow the juice to run into the bowl. Discard the skin and membranes
and use the fruit and juice as desired.

Caramelized Apricots
with Pistachio Ice Cream

serves 6

Here sweet and tart warm apricots are paired with an orange and honey sauce and topped with tiny scoops of pistachio ice cream that sit in the fruit-pit hollows, melting from the heat and adding a contrast of sweet coldness to the warm fruit.

2 tablespoons (1 ounce) unsalted butter, cut into small pieces

2 tablespoons (1½ ounces) mild honey, such as orange blossom or clover

1 tablespoon sugar

6 large firm-ripe apricots, halved and pitted

¼ cup (2 ounces) freshly squeezed and strained orange juice

2 tablespoons (1 ounce) heavy cream

FOR SERVING
Pistachio Ice Cream (294) or good-quality vanilla ice cream

To cook the apricots, place the butter, honey, and sugar in a 10-inch skillet over medium heat. When the butter is melted, swirl the pan to coat it evenly, then turn the heat to high. When the mixture is bubbling vigorously, add the apricot halves, cut side down. Cook for 1 minute. Use a pair of tongs or 2 spoons to turn the fruit over and cook for another minute. Then turn the apricots over, so they are cut side down again, and continue to cook over high heat for 2 to 3 minutes, or until they are easily pierced with the tip of a small, sharp knife and the cut side is nicely browned. Remove the pan from the heat and place 2 apricot halves, cut side up, on each serving plate. Return the pan to medium heat and bring the liquid remaining in the pan to a boil. Add the orange juice and heavy cream and cook for 1 to 2 minutes, or until it has reduced to a thick sauce.

SERVING AND STORAGE NOTES: Immediately spoon the sauce over and around the apricots. Place a small scoop of ice cream in each apricot half. Serve immediately.

GETTING AHEAD: You can make the Pistachio Ice Cream several days ahead. Homemade ice cream may get very hard after several days in the freezer. If so, let it soften in the refrigerator for 15 to 30 minutes before serving.

Figs Stuffed with Goat Cheese Served with Raspberry and Caramel Sauces

serves 4

When I was the pastry chef at Oliveto Restaurant and Cafe in Oakland, California, we always had a fruit and cheese pairing on the dessert menu. Some were exceedingly simple, like local Gravenstein apples paired with gorgonzola, while others were more complex. This fruit and cheese combination is admittedly on the more complex end, but it is also the most popular one I ever offered. Perfect for a special summer or early fall dinner, this beautiful dessert features ripe, luscious figs cut open like flowers and filled with creamy goat cheese. Raspberry and caramel sauces pick up on those same flavor undertones in the figs and add both sweet and bitter counterpoints to the fresh acidity of the cheese. Caramel-coated walnuts are a perfect match for the fruit and provide a crunchy contrast in texture. Not to worry—all the components can be made ahead, which means the dessert can be ready for serving in about 5 minutes.

EQUIPMENT AND ADVANCE PREPARATION: A thin wooden skewer • A baking sheet with sides and a fork, both lightly coated with butter or flavorless vegetable oil • 1 recipe sugar syrup (318)

FOR THE CARAMEL-COATED WALNUT GARNISH

3 tablespoons water

1 cup (7 ounces) sugar

16 walnut halves, toasted (follow directions for toasting whole almonds, 254)

FOR THE CARAMEL SAUCE

¼ cup (2 ounces) water

1 cup (7 ounces) sugar

1 ¾ cups (14 ounces) heavy cream, room temperature

1 half-pint basket (about 6 ounces) fresh raspberries

2 to 3 tablespoons sugar syrup (318), to taste

1 teaspoon freshly squeezed lemon juice

FOR THE FIGS

12 small ripe figs

4 ounces fresh, soft goat cheese (chèvre)

1 to 2 tablespoons (½ to 1 ounce) heavy cream

To make the caramel-coated walnuts, have ready a medium bowl filled with a couple inches of cold water. Place the 3 tablespoons water in a small saucepan, then add the sugar and set the pan over medium heat. Stir constantly with a wooden spoon or swirl the pan frequently, until the sugar is dissolved and the liquid is clear. Turn the heat to high and boil rapidly, swirling the pan occasionally (do not stir at this point) so the sugar cooks evenly, until it turns a golden brown. Immediately remove from the heat and touch the pan down briefly in the bowl of cold water (this will stop the darkening of the sugar)—be careful as you do this, because the water in the bowl will sputter when the pan touches it.

Gently insert the tip of the wooden skewer into a walnut half, dip it into the caramel, then use the oiled fork to nudge it off the skewer and onto the prepared baking sheet. Repeat with each of the remaining nuts (this process goes quickly). If the caramel begins to harden, place the pan back over low heat until it returns to a dipping consistency. Let the nuts cool completely.

To make the caramel sauce, place the water in a medium saucepan, then add the sugar and set the pan over medium heat. Stir constantly with a wooden spoon or swirl the pan frequently, until the sugar is dissolved and the liquid is clear. Turn the heat to high and boil rapidly, swirling the pan occasionally (do not stir at this point) so the sugar cooks evenly, until it turns a golden brown. Remove the pan from the heat and immediately add the heavy cream—be careful, the mixture will rise dramatically in the pan and sputter; you may want to wear an oven mitt on the hand holding the pan. Stir with the wooden spoon to blend. If the caramel has solidified, set the pan back over low heat and stir until it melts again. Cool. Store in a covered container in the refrigerator until needed.

To make the raspberry sauce, sort through the raspberries and discard any debris or moldy berries. Place the raspberries, 2 tablespoons of the sugar syrup, and the lemon juice in the bowl of a food processor or blender and puree until smooth. Pour the sauce into a fine-mesh strainer set over a medium bowl and use a rubber spatula to press the sauce through the strainer, extracting as much juice as possible. Taste the sauce and adjust the sweetness, if needed, with additional sugar syrup or lemon juice. Store in a covered container in the refrigerator until needed.

To prepare the figs, slice the figs into quarters through the stem end, but leave the fruit connected at the bottom, then gently press the quarters apart so that each fruit opens up like a flower. Place the goat cheese in a small bowl and gently stir until it is smooth, adding the cream, if necessary, to loosen the cheese and make the texture creamier but still able to hold its shape (this step can also be done in an electric mixer fitted with the paddle attachment on medium speed). Cover and refrigerate until needed.

SERVING AND STORAGE NOTES: Drizzle the dessert plates with caramel sauce. Place 3 figs on each plate, opened like flowers. Place a spoonful of goat cheese in the center of each fig. Spoon a little raspberry sauce over the cheese in each fig and drizzle a little more around the plate. Scatter 4 walnut halves around each plate.

GETTING AHEAD: The caramel-coated walnuts may be prepared up to 1 week in advance. Store in an airtight container, layered between pieces of parchment or wax paper, at room temperature.

The caramel sauce may be prepared up to 1 week in advance. Keep refrigerated.

The raspberry sauce may be prepared up to 12 hours ahead, but it is best when made the same day it is to be served.

Goat Cheese

Goats and their by-products can be found throughout the Mediterranean in areas historically unsuitable for the cow—mountainous or hilly regions and places with sparse grass or vegetation—areas in France, Italy, Greece, and Spain. Provence is perhaps the best-known region for goat cheese—so much so that the fresh soft goat cheese known as chèvre is one of the backbones of its cuisine. California cuisine, taking many of its cues from southern France, has also embraced goat cheese—so much so that it is considered an essential ingredient on most California menus. It was Alice Waters at Chez Panisse who began the goat cheese revolution with a warm, breadcrumb-crusted goat cheese medallion atop a salad of baby lettuces. Years later, with goat cheese in every supermarket, the war is won and food lovers are clearly the winners as America's love affair with this wonderfully flavorful and versatile cheese continues.

Every open-air market I visited in the south of France had at least one table offering locally made goat cheese, and this is mostly true of the large farmers' markets around California, as artisan goat-cheese makers have sprung up around the state to keep our passion fueled. The best way to purchase chèvre is from one of these tables, where pride and personal attention combine to ensure a high-quality, fresh cheese.

When buying chèvre to use in dessert, choose a fresh (packaged less than one week prior), soft, mild-flavored variety. The cheese should be a beautiful pure white color, because goat's milk, unlike cow's milk, does not contain carotene. Goat cheese comes in a variety of shapes, which may be confusing. Look for the *chabis,* a small cylindrical cheese; the plain log (avoid those coated with ash); the plain *pyramide,* a small, charming pyramid shape (again, avoid those coated with ash); or the round, flattened-disc shape (avoid those coated with herbs) commonly associated with the well-loved warm goat cheese and mesclun salad. These are the most traditional shapes for fresh chèvre, though there are a great many other shapes for aged and dried goat cheeses. If possible, ask for a sample—it should have a clean, creamy, lightly acidic flavor, with no hints of ammonia, a sure sign that it is past its prime. To store leftover chèvre, wrap the cheese in plastic, refrigerate, and eat it as soon as possible.

Plums in Port with Clove Cream

serves 4

Plums and port are one of those perfect, and classic, matches. In this variation on a theme, plums are poached in a spiced port, the liquid is then reduced to a thick, heady syrup, and the compote is topped with clove-flavored whipped cream. Use your favorite type of plum here, or mix a variety of plums when the markets are flush with the fruit, late summer into early fall. Enjoy this dessert after a hearty barbecue or on the first cool nights of fall, when the warmer spices are especially welcome.

EQUIPMENT AND ADVANCE PREPARATION: Four 12-ounce compote dishes or bowls

FOR THE POACHED PLUMS

2 cups (16 ounces) tawny port

²/₃ cup (4½ ounces) sugar

¼ teaspoon ground cinnamon

⅛ teaspoon ground cloves

½ vanilla bean, split lengthwise in half

1¾ pounds firm-ripe plums

FOR THE CLOVE CREAM

1 cup (8 ounces) heavy cream

1 tablespoon sugar

¼ teaspoon ground cloves

To poach the plums, place the port, sugar, spices, and vanilla bean in a medium saucepan over medium heat and bring to a low boil. Simmer for 5 minutes. To prepare the plums, halve and pit each fruit. If the plums are very small, leave in halves; otherwise, cut each half into 3 or 4 wedges, depending on the size of the fruit and your particular preference. Add the plums to the liquid, bring the mixture back to a boil, then turn the heat to low and poach the plums at a simmer for 6 to 12 minutes, or just until they have softened and are easily pierced with the tip of a small, sharp knife. Remove the pan from the heat, lift out the plums with a slotted spoon, and place them in a bowl to cool. Return the pan to medium heat, bring the liquid back to a boil, and cook until it has reduced by half (you should have about 1 cup of liquid). Cool the liquid to room temperature, then pour it over the plums. Store in a covered container in the refrigerator until needed.

To make the clove cream, in the bowl of an electric mixer fitted with the whisk attachment, whip the cream, sugar, and ground cloves on medium speed to soft peaks. Be careful not to overwhip the cream, or it will begin to separate and look curdled. If this happens, remove the bowl from the mixer and use a rubber spatula to gently stir in several tablespoons of cream, just until the whipped cream has smoothed out again.

SERVING AND STORAGE NOTES: Divide the plums and their poaching liquid among the compote bowls or serving dishes, then top with a generous spoonful of cream.

GETTING AHEAD: The plums may be poached up to 1 day in advance. After that, the acidity of the wine starts to break down the plums, causing them to become mushy.

Plum Crazy

Plums generally fall into one of two categories—European or Japanese. The European, also known as prune plums, are the "blue" varieties that are either blue or purple in color, often freestone (the pit separates easily from the flesh), and very, very sweet. This ultrasweetness, combined with their somewhat dry texture, is what allows them to dry as a whole fruit without fermenting at the pit, a problem in other fruits with more moisture, such as peaches, pears, and apricots. This extra moisture, which means extra drying time, also means more time for bacteria to develop during the drying process, which is why you rarely, if ever, see fruits other than prune plums dried "on the pit." While the majority of prune plums are dried, occasionally they can be found fresh at farmers' markets or specialty stores. Several varieties to look for include French Prune, Sugar, Italian Prune, and Brooks.

Japanese plums, on the other hand, span a range of colors and shapes, from green to yellow to red to black, and instead of pure sweetness, there is a lovely balance of acidic skin contrasting with the sweet flesh within, making them perfect for either eating fresh or cooking. These are the summer to fall plums you are probably familiar with, and there are literally hundreds of varieties, some freestone, others more tenacious. Grown mainly in California, these plums bear names like Elephant Heart, Friar, Santa Rosa, Satsuma, Shiro, and Wickson. My favorites include Santa Rosa, with its deep red skin and yellow flesh tinged with pink, whose flavor is an exquisite blend of sweet and acid; Elephant Heart, which has a purple-red skin, beautiful fuchsia flesh, and a sweet, juicy flavor (the Friar is similar); and Casselman, with its acidic apple-cheek red skin and yellow-orange flesh, which is delightful to eat out of hand and even better in preserves.

A ripe plum should feel heavy for its size and have a slight give at the blossom end (this is the end opposite the stem). While hard plums can be softened in a closed paper bag at room temperature over several days (the ethylene gas from their skins accumulates and speeds the ripening process—check the fruit twice a day to determine its progress and refrigerate when ripe), their sugar content does not increase after picking. So, if possible, taste the plums before making a purchase.

Raspberry and Cannoli Cream Parfaits

serves 4

I love cannoli filling—smooth, creamy, barely sweetened ricotta scented with orange and flecked with tiny chunks of bittersweet chocolate and toasted pistachios—and have been known to eat it by the spoonful, cannoli shells be damned. It is a good accompaniment to fresh fruit, and guests are always surprised at its voluptuousness. The secret? Use the food processor to combine the sugar and ricotta. Its whirling action, which incorporates almost no air, makes a dense, creamy, velvety-smooth cream that no mixer can match. And be sure to use only whole-milk ricotta. Once the mixture is smooth, remove it from the processor and stir in your favorite additions by hand so they retain their distinct flavors and textures. I usually leave out the nuts for this recipe, but feel free to add a couple tablespoons of coarsely chopped toasted pistachios if you like. Truth be told, you could make this recipe simpler by serving the berries in small bowls, topped with a luscious mound of the cannoli cream, but it's infinitely sexier layered in a tall champagne flute, so choose your presentation depending on your mood.

EQUIPMENT AND ADVANCE PREPARATION: Four 8-ounce champagne flutes • 1 recipe candied orange zest (236), optional • A large pastry bag fitted with a large plain tip, or a gallon-sized zip-top bag

FOR THE PARFAITS

One 15-ounce container whole-milk ricotta

6 tablespoons (about 1¼ ounces) unsifted powdered sugar

2 teaspoons candied orange zest (236), rinsed of excess sugar, patted dry on paper towels, then packed into the teaspoon for measuring (optional)

1 to 2 teaspoons orange liqueur, such as Grand Marnier or Cointreau, to taste

1 ounce bittersweet chocolate, finely chopped

2 half-pint baskets (about 12 ounces) fresh raspberries

FOR SERVING

Toasted Almond and Dried Sour Cherry Biscotti (274) or other light, crispy cookies

To prepare the cannoli cream, place the ricotta and powdered sugar in the bowl of a food processor and process until the mixture is well blended and very smooth, about 30 to 60 seconds. Use a rubber spatula to scrape the ricotta into a medium bowl. If using, chop the candied orange zest very, very finely and add it to the ricotta along with the orange liqueur and chopped chocolate. Stir gently with a spoon until the mixture is thoroughly blended.

To prepare the raspberries, sort through them and discard any debris or moldy berries (do not wash fresh raspberries, as they will absorb the water and disintegrate and are virtually impossible to dry, which leads to mushy berries with watered-down flavor).

To assemble the parfaits, place about 10 to 12 berries in the bottom of each champagne flute. Spoon half of the cannoli cream into a pastry bag fitted with a large plain tip (or use an unpleated zip-top bag, squeezing the cream into one corner and snipping off the corner to simulate a pastry bag) and divide the cream evenly among the 4 glasses. Top the cream with another 12 to 15 berries in each flute, then spoon the remaining cream into the pastry bag and pipe it evenly among the flutes. Top the last layer of cannoli cream with another mound of fresh berries.

SERVING AND STORAGE NOTES: Serve the parfaits immediately, accompanied by crisp cookies, such as Toasted Almond and Dried Sour Cherry Biscotti.

GETTING AHEAD: The cannoli cream can be made up to 3 days in advance and held in an airtight container in the refrigerator.

Cherries Poached in Red Wine
with Rose Geranium
and Blackberries

serves 4

Cherries are abundant in southern France, and this recipe celebrates that summer harvest with a nod to the Provençal talent for blending fruit with herbs. Sweet summer cherries are lightly poached in red wine, then the poaching liquid is combined with rose geranium leaves and reduced to a luscious syrup, and finally fresh blackberries are gently stirred in. The cherries highlight the underlying berry flavors in the wine, and the rose geranium leaves add a subtle taste of garden roses that is simply exquisite.

EQUIPMENT AND ADVANCE PREPARATION: Four 12-ounce compote dishes or bowls

FOR THE POACHED CHERRIES

1½ cups (12 ounces) fruity red wine, such as **Merlot** or a light **Cabernet**

¾ cup (5¼ ounces) sugar

1 pound firm-ripe, sweet cherries, preferably Bing, pitted

1 half-pint basket (about 6 ounces) sweet, ripe blackberries

4 medium rose geranium leaves, about 2 inches at their widest point (see Note)

FOR SERVING

Softly whipped cream (54) or crème fraîche (303), optional

NOTE: There is really no substitute for the quietly enchanting presence of rose geranium. However, if you cannot find it (see Mail-Order Sources, 327), you can flavor the dish with a few drops of rose water. Beguiling in its own right, rose water is not known for its subtlety and can quickly become overpowering. So add the rose water carefully and slowly—1 or 2 drops at a time—to the cooled poaching liquid, tasting after each addition.

To poach the cherries, place the wine and sugar in a medium nonaluminum saucepan over medium heat and bring to a boil. Add the cherries, return to a low boil, and simmer until the fruit is tender but still holds its shape and gives a bit of resistance when pierced with the tip of a small, sharp knife, about 3 to 5 minutes. Remove the pan from the heat, lift out the cherries with a slotted spoon and place them in a medium bowl. Add the blackberries to the bowl. Return the pan to medium heat, add the rose geranium leaves, and bring the liquid back to a boil. Cook until it has reduced to 1 cup. Pour the wine through a medium strainer over the cherries and berries and discard the leaves. Stir once or twice to coat the fruit with the syrup. Cool at room temperature, then store in a covered container in the refrigerator until needed.

SERVING AND STORAGE NOTES: Spoon some of the fruit and poaching liquid into each compote bowl or serving dish. Top with a spoonful of softly whipped cream or crème fraîche, if desired. This dessert is best the same day it is made.

Rose Geranium

Rose geranium (*Pelargonium graveolens*) is but one member of the large scented-geranium family, which also includes geraniums whose leaves carry the scent of lemon, lime, orange, nutmeg, ginger, peppermint, coconut, or chocolate, among others. The flowers tend to be smaller than those of window-box geranium varieties, but the prize here is the leaves, textured and fragrant, which not only lend beauty to the garden but also a lovely essence to dishes in the kitchen. Rose geranium in particular has long been prized in the kitchen, especially for use in flavoring jellies and custards or other dishes in which its leaves can infuse a hot liquid with their subtle perfume. You can also gently flavor a pound cake by lining the cake pan with fresh leaves before adding the batter; infuse the custard for ice cream or the sugar syrup for sorbet with their scent; or add a hint of rose to all manner of poaching broths for fruit simply by including a few leaves. Rose geraniums are easy to grow and thrive in full sun or partial shade in well-drained soil; they need little water or fertilizer. They are a perennial in warm climates, but if you live in a cold-winter area, you will need to bring them indoors, where they will flourish if provided a sunny windowsill. Don't discount the flowers. Most of the scented geraniums have charming little blossoms that are delightful when eaten fresh but are best when preserved under a glittering coating of egg white and fine sugar (known as crystallization) and used to decorate desserts.

Summer Peaches and Raspberries with Essencia Sabayon

serves 4

Here, the essence of summer simplicity is found in a glass, in which the ripest, sweetest, juiciest, and most tender summer peaches are sliced, sprinkled with tart-sweet raspberries, and enveloped with a smooth sabayon redolent of orange muscat. It doesn't get better than this on a sultry summer evening.

EQUIPMENT AND ADVANCE PREPARATION: Four 12- to 16-ounce balloon wineglasses or compote dishes • A double boiler (or a medium saucepan coupled with a medium stainless-steel mixing bowl that will fit about halfway into the saucepan when sitting on top of it) • A large bowl filled halfway with a mixture of ice and water

FOR THE SABAYON

4 large egg yolks

¼ cup (1 ¾ ounces) sugar

¼ cup (2 ounces) Essencia dessert wine (see Note)

¼ cup (2 ounces) freshly squeezed and strained orange juice

½ cup (4 ounces) heavy cream

FOR THE FRUIT

4 medium (6 to 7 ounces each) peaches or nectarines

1 half-pint basket (about 6 ounces) raspberries

FOR SERVING

Orange Cornmeal Rosettes with Apricot Jam (264), Lacy Sesame Crisps (267), or any crispy cookie or biscotti

NOTE: Essencia is an orange muscat dessert wine from Quady Winery in California, made in the style of the French Muscat de Beaumes de Venise. It can be found nationwide in fine liquor stores. If unavailable, substitute a French or Italian orange muscat wine.

To make the sabayon, place 2 inches of water in the bottom of the double boiler and bring to a gentle boil. Place the egg yolks and sugar in the top of the double boiler and whisk briefly, just until they are well blended and slightly lightened in color. Add the Essencia and orange juice and whisk until well blended.

Place the top of the double boiler over the simmering water and whisk constantly. As the sauce cooks, it will become very light and fluffy, resembling softly whipped cream in texture. This will take about 5 minutes. Be careful that the mixture does not get too hot, or the eggs will scramble. If you see the sauce beginning to scramble, remove the top of the double boiler from the heat and whisk furiously. This will usually save the mixture, but if it still looks flat and broken or there are large pieces of scrambled egg in the sauce, there is no recourse but to begin again.

As soon as the sauce is finished, remove the top of the double boiler from the heat and immediately set it into the large bowl of ice and water. Whisk constantly until the sauce is cold. In the bowl of an electric mixer fitted with the whisk attachment, whip the cream on medium speed to firm peaks. Be careful not to overwhip the cream, or it will begin to separate and look curdled. If this happens, remove the bowl from the mixer and use a rubber spatula to gently stir in several tablespoons of cream, just until the whipped cream has smoothed out again. Use a rubber spatula to gently fold the whipped cream into the cooled sauce. Cover and refrigerate until needed.

To prepare the peaches and raspberries, halve and pit the peaches and slice each half into 4 pieces. (Since most peaches are fuzzless nowadays, I don't bother to remove the skins, but if you prefer them skinned, drop the peaches into boiling water for 30 to 60 seconds, remove to an ice bath, then blot dry and peel.) Sort through the raspberries and discard any debris or moldy berries (do not wash fresh raspberries, as they will absorb the water and disintegrate and are virtually impossible to dry, which leads to mushy berries with watered-down flavor).

SERVING AND STORAGE NOTES: Place 1 sliced peach in each wineglass, then top with a scattering of raspberries. Divide the sabayon among the glasses, spooning it gently over the fruit. Serve immediately. If you like, serve cookies alongside the dessert—Orange Cornmeal Rosettes or Lacy Sesame Crisps are particularly good choices. Pour a glass of Essencia dessert wine for each guest.

GETTING AHEAD: The cold sabayon may be prepared up to 12 hours ahead, but it must be made the same day it is to be served.

Just Peachy

Al Courchesne grows the sweetest, juiciest peaches I've ever had the pleasure of eating at his Frog Hollow Farm in Brentwood, about an hour east of San Francisco. Named with a nod to both his favorite childhood book, *Wind in the Willows,* and also to the local frogs who serenade him every spring from their home in the nearby irrigation channel, his farm sports twenty-three varieties of peaches and nectarines, with fruit ready to harvest from mid-May to early September. When I visited him at the farm one summer, the fruit hung heavy in the trees, filling the air with a fragrance so thick and sweet that breathing was like taking a bite of a peach.

During the season, Al can be found at farmers' markets in the Bay Area with a line of customers, me included, eagerly waiting for their bagful of organic peaches and nectarines. Tall, tan, and ruggedly handsome, he could be the poster boy for organic farming, and his passion for his work is contagious—it's hard to resist the call of the land when he speaks so eloquently of "working in the beauty of nature every day of your life." Al's philosophy? Grow the foods you love to eat. Well, it's not hard to guess what *he* enjoys snacking on. Though the best peach varieties vary from region to region and state to state, Al highly recommends Cal Red, Suncrest, O'Henry, and Summer Lady. If it's nectarines you crave, try Flavor Top, June Red, Ruby Grand, or Summer Fire. Al's peaches and nectarines are available through the mail (see Mail-Order Sources, 327).

Custards and Puddings

One of my long-time fascinations with pastry and baking is the almost limitless number of products that can be made with just a few simple ingredients, and there is no better example of this than custard. The basic components are eggs, sugar, and milk or cream, yet the variety of flavors, textures, and presentations possible is staggering. Members of this family range from custard sauce (which can also be the basis of ice cream) to flan (a custard usually made with whole eggs, which is turned out of its baking dish) to bavarian (a freestanding gelatin dessert). But it is the pot de crème, silken in texture and the base for crème brûlée, that is my favorite. Most of the baked custards in this chapter are modeled on this style. Yolks only and a greater percentage of cream account for the meltingly sensuous texture they posses.

The name *pots de crème* refers to the little ceramic baking cups with tight-fitting lids crafted expressly for these custards (as shown). Any number of containers can be used, as long as they hold the amount of custard stipulated in the recipe—anything from Pyrex custard cups or ceramic ramekins to small soufflé molds or even tea or espresso cups.

Note: The recipes for baked custards and flans in this chapter call for 6-ounce custard cups. If you do not know the size of your custard cups, here's how to figure it out. Fill a 1-cup liquid measuring cup with water and then pour the water into one of your custard cups, just until the water reaches the rim. Then check to see how much water is remaining in the measuring cup and subtract the amount left from the original amount (which was 1 cup, or 8 ounces). If you have ¼ cup water (2 ounces) left, you know you have a 6-ounce custard cup.

Making a good custard means understanding eggs, for they are responsible for the thickening and binding that occur during the cooking process. Eggs must be heated slowly and at a low temperature for the smoothest texture. Those cooked at too high a temperature or for too long have an unpleasant rubbery quality and can curdle or scramble, resulting in a grainy texture. The best way to achieve the tender, trembling texture associated with the best custards is to keep the oven low (325°F) and to surround the baking cups with a water bath.

Also known as a *bain-marie,* a water bath insulates the custards from fluctuating temperatures and moderates the exchange of heat between the oven and the eggs. To make a *bain-marie,* choose a baking or roasting pan that will accommodate your custard cups. Place the filled dishes in the pan and then add enough hot water to come halfway up the sides of the dishes. Cover the pan loosely with a piece of foil, which traps steam, creates a moist environment, and prevents a leathery skin from forming on top of the custards.

The category of puddings includes baked custards and more, running the gamut from a classic American stovetop custard like butterscotch pudding to bread pudding, which is custard poured over bread and baked in the oven, rice pudding, or even mousse, which may or may not contain eggs but is loved for its lightness, which comes from a good quantity of whipped cream. And whether or not whipped cream is a part of the dessert, it is almost always the perfect accompaniment. It seems strange, doesn't it, that a rich, voluptuous dessert can be made to seem lighter when topped with additional richness? The key is in the contrast of textures—puddings are luxuriously dense, and whipped cream provides an airy contrast when the two are combined on your tongue.

Whether custard or pudding, the desserts in this chapter are filled with flavor . . . and a few surprises. For pure pleasure, try the Crema Catalana, a Spanish-flavored crème brûlée, or Apricot Fool with Almond Cream, in which the vibrancy of fresh apricots is blended with the softness of almond-scented whipped cream. For something with a bit of a kick, try Bonet, a delicate flan with a punch of amaretto and an intriguing crust of crushed amaretti cookies, or the sensuously rich Chocolate Espresso Pots de Crème. Looking for excitement? Black and White Mascarpone Parfait, with its layers of deep chocolate and vanilla cream alternating with crushed bitter chocolate cookies, is a knock-out, while the Coconut Rice Pudding Brûlée, with its hidden filling of mangoes in lime caramel sauce, will leave your guests wishing it was served in soup bowls rather than custard cups. For dessert with a surprise, Mint and Chocolate Pots de Crème offers a luscious creamy white mint custard disguised with a thin layer of dark chocolate ganache on top, and Champagne Jelly with Raspberries is a fun, potent, and effervescent ending. Soothing, comforting, invigorating, exciting—the many facets of custards and puddings await you.

Crema Catalana

Traditionally this custard is infused with lemon and cinnamon, a flavor combination so common in milk-and-egg-based desserts in Spain that it is comparable to our nationwide love of vanilla. Never one to shy from gilding the lily where appropriate, I have added a beloved vanilla bean to the mixture as well, because its deep, floral fragrance brings this dessert to a whole new level of goodness. Crema Catalana, also sometimes called crema cremada *("burnt cream") is served like crème brûlée, topped with a thin, glass-like layer of caramelized sugar—a perfect foil to the rich custard beneath. The Catalans claim to have "invented" this style of dessert, but whatever its origins, in Spain, as everywhere else, it is extremely popular.*

EQUIPMENT AND ADVANCE PREPARATION: Six 6-ounce custard cups (I use Pyrex) or ceramic ramekins • If you do not know the size of your custard cups, see note on page 164 to figure it out. • A roasting or baking pan large enough to hold all the cups without touching each other or the sides of the roasting pan • A propane torch (see explanation, 168) to brûlée the custards

FOR THE CUSTARD
1⅓ cups (10¾ ounces) whole milk

1⅓ cups (10¾ ounces) heavy cream

¼ cup (1¾ ounces) sugar

1 whole vanilla bean

Zest of 1 lemon, in strips

One 3-inch stick cinnamon

6 large egg yolks

FOR THE BURNT SUGAR CRUST
4 tablespoons (1¾ ounces) sugar

To flavor the custard, place the milk, cream, sugar, vanilla bean, lemon zest, and cinnamon stick in a medium saucepan over medium-low heat. Cook, stirring several times to dissolve the sugar, just until the mixture begins to simmer. Remove the pan from the heat, cover with a lid, and allow the mixture to steep for 30 minutes.

Preheat the oven to 325°F. Position an oven rack in the center of the oven.

To finish the custard, place the pan back over medium heat, remove the lid, and reheat the mixture just until it begins to simmer. In a medium bowl, whisk together the egg yolks. Slowly whisk the hot milk into the egg yolks. Pour the mixture through a fine-mesh strainer into a pitcher or large measuring cup with a spout. Discard the lemon zest and cinnamon stick but save the vanilla bean. (Rinse it under water and let it dry, then save it for use in another recipe, as it is still very flavorful and the seeds inside are still intact.)

Place the custard cups in the roasting pan. Divide the warm custard among the custard cups. Place the pan in the oven, then pour enough hot tap water into the pan to come halfway up the sides of the cups. Cover the pan with foil and crimp it loosely around the edges (in about 4 places—do not make it airtight). Bake until the edges of the custards are set but there is still a small liquid area in the center of the custard about the size of a dime (test by gently shaking one of the cups), about 40 to 60 minutes.

Use a pair of tongs (or your hand protected with a kitchen towel) to immediately remove the cups from the pan and place them on a rack to cool, about 40 minutes. Refrigerate, covered with plastic wrap, until cold.

SERVING AND STORAGE NOTES: To brûlée the custards, sprinkle the surface of each one evenly with 2 teaspoons of sugar. Use a propane torch to caramelize the sugar (below). Refrigerate for 5 minutes before serving. The burnt sugar topping can be done up to 1 hour in advance—keep refrigerated.

GETTING AHEAD: The custards may be baked 1 or 2 days in advance. Store in the refrigerator, covered with plastic wrap. Brûlée them just before serving.

The Propane Torch: Treasured Tool of the Pastry Chef

One of the most valuable tools in the pantry of the professional pastry chef is the propane torch, and unlike other professional tools and molds that may be hard to find, the propane torch is accessible to any enthusiastic home baker who ventures to the hardware store. You may even have one tucked away in your garage, never guessing that its presence in the kitchen could make your dessert life so much easier.

Its uses in the pastry kitchen seem almost endless, from browning meringue to quickly warming the outside of a mold to loosen a chilled mousse, from warming the bottom of a cake pan to loosen a cake to caramelizing the top of a fruit tart, but its most frequent use currently is for caramelizing sugar on top of custard for the most popular dessert of our time—crème brûlée. Here's how to turn grainy sugar to a glass-like, deep golden brown caramel in mere seconds.

To brûlée a custard, cover the surface of the cooled custard with a thin layer of sugar. Light the torch and, with the tip of the flame just touching the surface as shown, move the flame over the sugar in a gentle circular motion until the sugar is melted. When melted, the sugar turns from white and grainy to clear droplets of liquid. Ideally, all the sugar should be melted before caramelizing begins, but in reality, some areas will always cook faster than others. Continue to use a circular motion, keeping the flame moving at all times, until the sugar begins to brown. At this point you will probably need to focus the flame on certain areas to bring them "up to color" with other areas that have caramelized more quickly. The sugar should be a deep golden brown color—do not let it blacken, or it will be unpleasantly bitter. As soon as the correct color is reached, remove the flame from the surface and move on to the next custard. The molten caramel will bubble and smoke, then harden as it begins to cool. In about a minute it will solidify into a crisp surface.

When buying a propane torch, look for a model that works well when turned upside (flame end) down, as this is the position in which it will be held when making crème brûlée. If you have a little extra money to spend, spring for the automatic lighting attachment, which will light the torch with the flick of a switch. Otherwise, you will need to coordinate a lit match with running propane fuel, which is not nearly as scary as it sounds but can intimidate the novice user. The hardware store models are large and will supply you with enough caramelizing power to satisfy even the most ardent fan, but they can be cumbersome to maneuver and store. You may want to opt for a more manageable model like the kitchen-sized butane torches now being offered through fine cookware catalogs, such as Sur La Table and Williams-Sonoma (see Mail-Order Sources, 327). The palm-fitting dimensions of these torches are great for ease of use, and their small size means they fit unobtrusively into a kitchen cupboard.

Mint and Chocolate
Pots de Crème

serves 6

A delicate mint custard is hidden under a thin layer of warm chocolate ganache, creating a seamless illusion of chocolate custard. It may be a surprise when the spoon comes up with a light custard, but one bite and you'll see that the layering of flavors gives a whole new sensation to this classic pairing. First the silken mint custard cools and refreshes your mouth, then the deep, bittersweet chocolate warms against your tongue and gently blends into the mint. This gradual mingling heightens the appreciation of each flavor and their combination in a way that chocolate custard flavored with mint just can't do.

EQUIPMENT AND ADVANCE PREPARATION: Six 6-ounce custard cups or ramekins (for the element of surprise do not use glass cups) • If you do not know the size of your custard cups, see note on page 164 to figure it out. • A roasting or baking pan large enough to hold all the cups without touching each other or the sides of the roasting pan

FOR THE CUSTARD

1½ cups (12 ounces) heavy cream

1 cup (8 ounces) whole milk

40 medium to large fresh mint leaves, rinsed under cold water and patted dry

6 large egg yolks

⅓ cup plus 1 tablespoon (3¼ ounces) sugar

FOR THE CHOCOLATE GANACHE

1 ounce bittersweet chocolate, finely chopped

5 tablespoons (2½ ounces) heavy cream

FOR SERVING

Softly whipped cream (54)

Fresh mint sprigs

To flavor the custard, place the cream, milk, and cleaned mint in a medium saucepan over medium-low heat. Stir to cover the mint leaves with the liquid.

Heat just until the mixture begins to simmer. Remove the pan from the heat, cover with a lid, and allow the mixture to steep for 20 minutes.

Preheat the oven to 325°F. Position an oven rack in the center of the oven.

To finish the custard, place the pan back over medium heat, remove the lid, and reheat the mixture just until it begins to simmer. In a medium bowl, whisk together the egg yolks and sugar. Slowly whisk the hot milk into the egg yolks. Pour the mixture through a fine-mesh strainer into a pitcher or large measuring cup with a spout, pressing firmly against the leaves with a rubber spatula to remove all the liquid. Discard the mint leaves.

Place the custard cups in the roasting pan. Divide the warm custard among the custard cups. Place the pan in the oven, then pour enough hot tap water into the pan to come halfway up the sides of the cups. Cover the pan with foil and crimp it loosely around the edges (in about 4 places—do not make it airtight). Bake until the edges of the custards are set but there is still a small liquid area in the center of the custard about the size of a dime (test by gently shaking one of the cups), about 40 to 60 minutes.

Use a pair of tongs (or your hand protected with a kitchen towel) to immediately remove the cups from the pan and place them on a rack to cool, about 40 minutes. Refrigerate, covered with plastic wrap, until cold.

To make the ganache, place the chocolate in a small bowl. Place the cream in a small saucepan over medium heat and cook just until it begins to simmer. Immediately pour the cream over the chocolate. Allow the mixture to sit undisturbed for 1 minute, then gently stir until it is thoroughly blended and smooth. Spoon a tablespoon of ganache onto the surface of each custard, then gently swirl each cup until the chocolate completely covers the custard.

SERVING AND STORAGE NOTES: Serve immediately, while the ganache is still warm, or refrigerate until serving time, but not more than 1 hour, because as it chills, the chocolate begins to harden and pull away from the sides of the cup, exposing the custard beneath and thereby spoiling the surprise. Serve with a spoonful of softly whipped cream and a sprig of mint.

GETTING AHEAD: The custards may be baked 1 or 2 days in advance. Store in the refrigerator, covered with plastic wrap. Cover with ganache just before serving.

Mint

Well loved for its bright, refreshing flavor, mint is found in cooking across America and in western Europe, though it is particularly prized in the Near East (Greece, Turkey, and Armenia) and the Middle East. While we tend to think of mint as a "sweet" or dessert herb (even the mint jelly that accompanies lamb is sweet), in the Mediterranean it is used most frequently as an accent in savory dishes, lending its assertive flavor to everything from soup and salad to stuffed peppers and meatballs to marinades for meat and seafood.

Mentha is a large and varied genus, with species ranging from orange (or bergamot) mint, golden apple mint, and pineapple mint to the more common spearmint (*M. spicata*) and peppermint (*M. piperita*). For dessert purposes I prefer spearmint, which has a softer, rounder, and more delicate flavor than peppermint. It is easy to tell the difference between the two, once you know what to look for. Peppermint has red-purple stems and pointed leaves that are serrated at the edges, and it smells just like the red-and-white penny candies of childhood. Spearmint, on the other hand, has smaller, rounder, dark to bright green crinkly leaves sprouting from sturdy green stems. Mints are notoriously easy to grow and can quickly spread through the garden with their underground runners, so they are a good candidate for pots or window boxes. They prefer a good, moist soil and partial shade, though it seems as if they can grow almost anywhere. Pinch back the leaves to keep them bushy, and for goodness' sake, don't let them go to seed, or you'll find mint popping up all over the place.

Chocolate Espresso Pots de Crème

serves 6

Like edible velvet that melts on your tongue, this softly sensuous, intensely bittersweet chocolate custard comes with a kick—the deep, rich flavor of espresso beans. I bake the custard in coffee cups, then serve each one with a spoonful of whipped cream and a dusting of cinnamon—a mocha cappuccino for dessert.

EQUIPMENT AND ADVANCE PREPARATION: Six 6-ounce custard cups (I use Pyrex), ramekins, or coffee cups • If you do not know the size of your custard cups, see note on page 164 to figure it out. • A roasting or baking pan large enough to hold all the cups without touching each other or the sides of the roasting pan

> 1½ cups (12 ounces) heavy cream
>
> 1 cup (8 ounces) whole milk
>
> ¼ cup (1¾ ounces) sugar
>
> ⅓ cup (¾ ounce) whole espresso beans (decaffeinated beans may be substituted)
>
> 5 ounces bittersweet chocolate, finely chopped
>
> 7 large egg yolks
>
> **FOR SERVING**
>
> Softly whipped cream (54)
>
> Miniature chocolate curls (106) or ground cinnamon, optional

To flavor the custard, place the cream, milk, sugar, and espresso beans in a medium saucepan over medium-low heat. Warm, stirring several times to dissolve the sugar, to just below the boiling point. Do not allow the mixture to boil, or the acids in the espresso beans could cause it to curdle. Remove the pan from the heat, cover with a lid, and allow the mixture to steep for 15 minutes.

Preheat the oven to 325°F. Position an oven rack in the center of the oven.

To finish the custard, place the pan back over medium heat, remove the lid, and reheat the mixture just until it begins to simmer. Remove from the heat and immediately add the chopped chocolate to the pan. Let the mixture sit undisturbed for 2 minutes, then gently whisk until the chocolate is smooth and thoroughly blended with the cream. In a medium bowl, whisk the egg yolks. Slowly whisk the chocolate cream into the egg yolks. Pour the mixture through a fine-mesh strainer into a pitcher or large measuring cup with a spout. Discard the espresso beans.

Place the custard cups in the roasting pan. Divide the warm custard among the custard cups. Place the pan in the oven, then pour enough hot tap water into the pan to come halfway up the sides of the cups. Cover the pan with foil and crimp it loosely around the edges (in about 4 places—do not make it airtight). Bake until the edges of the custards are set but there is still a small liquid area in the center of the custard about the size of a dime (test by gently shaking one of the cups), about 40 to 60 minutes.

Use a pair of tongs (or your hand protected with a kitchen towel) to immediately remove the cups from the pan and place them on a rack to cool, about 40 minutes. Refrigerate, covered with plastic wrap, until cold.

SERVING AND STORAGE NOTES: Serve with a spoonful of softly whipped cream. Garnish with miniature chocolate curls or a light dusting of cinnamon, if desired. The custards are at their best the first day or two after baking—as they sit, the texture becomes more dense.

GETTING AHEAD: The custards may be baked 1 or 2 days in advance. Store in the refrigerator, covered with plastic wrap.

serves 8

This is one of my very favorite spoon desserts—a classic caramel-coated custard from the Piedmont region of Italy that is flavored with crushed amaretti cookies. The crushed cookies soften during the cooking process, both flavoring the satiny custard and forming a tiny "crust" along the bottom—two of many reasons that I find Bonet absolutely addictive. Others include a contrast between the sweet custard and the slightly bitter caramel that coats the pan; the rich cocoa that gives it just the slightest hint of chocolate; and the bracing flavor of amaretto, which makes this particular version lusciously refreshing. For best results, use the good stuff here—deep, dark, Dutch-process cocoa and real Amaretto di Saronno.

EQUIPMENT AND ADVANCE PREPARATION: Eight 6-ounce custard cups (I use Pyrex) or ramekins • If you do not know the size of your custard cups, see note on page 164 to figure it out. • A roasting or baking pan large enough to hold all the cups without touching each other or the sides of the roasting pan

FOR THE CARAMEL
½ cup (4 ounces) water

1½ cups (10½ ounces) sugar

FOR THE CUSTARD
8 (about 1¾ ounces) amaretti cookies

2¼ cups (18 ounces) heavy cream

¾ cup (6 ounces) whole milk

4 large egg yolks

2 large eggs

½ cup (3½ ounces) sugar

1½ tablespoons unsweetened Dutch-process cocoa powder (262)

4 tablespoons (2 ounces) Amaretto di Saronno

To caramelize the custard cups, place the water in a medium saucepan, add the sugar, and set the pan over medium heat. Stir constantly with a wooden spoon or swirl the pan frequently until the sugar has dissolved and the liquid is clear. Turn the heat to high and boil rapidly, swirling the pan occasionally (do not stir at this point) so the sugar cooks evenly, until it turns a deep golden brown. Remove the pan from the heat and immediately divide the caramel among the custard cups. Working quickly, swirl each cup to distribute the caramel evenly around the sides, about an inch from the bottom—be careful, the caramel is very hot (you may want to keep a small bowl of ice water nearby in case a bit of caramel escapes onto a finger during the swirling process). Set the cups in the roasting pan.

To crush the amaretti cookies, place them in a small zip-top bag and press them with a meat pounder or the bottom edge of a heavy saucepan. Do not use the food processor—you want crumbs, not powder. You should have ½ cup of cookie crumbs. Set aside until needed.

Preheat the oven to 350°F. Position an oven rack in the center of the oven.

To make the custard, place the cream and milk in a small saucepan over medium-low heat. Bring to just below the boiling point. In a medium bowl, whisk together the egg yolks, whole eggs, and sugar. Sift the cocoa powder over the top and whisk until well blended. Slowly whisk the hot cream into the yolk mixture and blend well. Pour the mixture through a fine strainer into a pitcher or large measuring cup with a spout. Stir in the crushed amaretti cookies and the amaretto liqueur.

Divide the warm custard among the caramelized custard cups. Place the pan in the oven, then pour enough hot tap water into the pan to come halfway up the sides of the cups. Cover the pan with foil and crimp it loosely around the edges (in about 4 places—do not make it airtight). Bake just until the centers of the custards are barely set, about 35 to 45 minutes.

Use a pair of tongs (or your hand protected with a kitchen towel) to immediately remove the cups from the pan and place them on a rack to cool, about 40 minutes. Refrigerate, covered with plastic wrap, for at least 6 hours or overnight before serving.

SERVING AND STORAGE NOTES: Unmold just before serving. To unmold the custards, run a thin, sharp, flexible knife around the edges of each cup, pressing the knife into the cup rather than gouging the custard. Place a serving plate upside down on top of the cup, then, holding the two together, flip the plate right side up—the custard should slide out of the cup and onto the plate. If the custard is a bit hesitant, pick up the plate, hold the cup in place on the plate, and give the two a firm but gentle shake once or twice. The custards are at their best the first day or 2 after baking—as they sit, the texture becomes more dense and less delicate.

GETTING AHEAD: The custards may be baked up to 2 days in advance. Store in the refrigerator, covered with plastic wrap. Unmold just before serving.

CLEANING TIP: Place the custard cups in a large pot and fill with water. Bring to a gentle boil and cook until the caramel remaining in the cups dissolves.

Amaretto di Saronno

This sweet, almond-flavored liqueur from Italy is named for both a small town near Milan (Saronno) and the famous local cookies made of almonds (amaretti). Though adding crushed amaretti to a bottle of alcohol had been done for centuries in the area, the producers of Amaretto di Saronno deepened the complexity of flavor by substituting apricot kernels. If you were to break open an apricot pit with a hammer, you would find hidden inside a small kernel resembling a miniature almond. These kernels have an intriguing bitter almond flavor due to the presence of hydrogen cyanide in their composition (don't worry, it's not dangerous ingested at this level in liqueur). No one knows exactly who came up with the idea of infusing alcohol with apricot pits, but the first reference to the resulting liqueur was in 1807.

Amaretto di Saronno is composed of a neutral alcohol combined with a distillate of apricot pits and a few herbs. The result is a dark, caramel-colored liqueur that tastes like a silky smooth parade of almonds. A bit of this luxuriantly potent liquid can enhance desserts of all kinds—from cakes (either mixed into the batter or added later in the form of a soaking syrup, as in Strawberry Mascarpone Layer Cake, 38) to cookies (such as Dried Sour Cherry and Bittersweet Chocolate Chip Biscotti, 272) to filo desserts (such as Sour Cherry and Almond Baklava, 219, or Tiropetes with Chocolate and Apricot Filling, 244), to ice creams (such as Pistachio, 294, or Almond Ice Cream, 295) to custards (such as Bonet, 175).

Pumpkin Flan with Spiced Pecans

serves 6

Winter squashes are popular throughout much of the Mediterranean, though their use in cooking is almost always savory. So while this spiced pumpkin flan seems like it might be served in a Spanish restaurant, it is really more at home on an American table. This flan is like the most delicious of pumpkin pies without a crust and is made even more special with a topping of bittersweet caramel and a garnish of pecans that have been roasted with a coating of sugar and spices.

EQUIPMENT AND ADVANCE PREPARATION: Six 6-ounce custard cups (I use Pyrex) or ramekins • If you do not know the size of your custard cups, see note on page 164 to figure it out. • A roasting or baking pan large enough to hold all the cups without touching each other or the sides of the roasting pan

FOR THE CARAMEL

⅓ cup (2½ ounces) water

1 cup (7 ounces) sugar

FOR THE CUSTARD

3 large eggs

2 tablespoons (1 ounce) granulated sugar

3 tablespoons (1½ ounces) packed light brown sugar

¼ teaspoon ground cinnamon

¼ teaspoon ground ginger

⅛ teaspoon ground allspice

⅛ teaspoon salt

1 cup (8 ounces) heavy cream

1 cup (8 ounces) canned pumpkin puree (do not use the canned pumpkin pie filling flavored with spices)

FOR SERVING

Softly whipped cream (54)

18 spiced pecans (180)

To caramelize the custard cups, place the water in a medium saucepan, add the sugar, and set the pan over medium heat. Stir constantly with a wooden spoon or swirl the pan frequently until the sugar has dissolved and the liquid is clear. Turn the heat to high and boil rapidly, swirling the pan occasionally (do not stir at this point) so the sugar cooks evenly, until it turns a deep golden brown. Remove the pan from the heat and immediately divide the caramel among the custard cups. Working quickly, swirl each cup to distribute the caramel evenly around the sides, to about an inch up from the bottom—be careful, the caramel is very hot (you may want to keep a small bowl of ice water nearby in case a bit of caramel escapes onto a finger during the swirling process). Set the cups in the roasting pan.

Preheat the oven to 325°F. Position an oven rack in the center of the oven.

To make the custard, place the eggs, granulated sugar, and brown sugar in a large bowl and whisk until thoroughly blended. Whisk in the spices and the heavy cream. Pour the mixture through a fine-mesh strainer into a pitcher or large measuring cup with a spout, pressing firmly with a rubber spatula to force through any lumps of brown sugar. Stir in the pumpkin puree until well blended.

Divide the custard among the caramelized custard cups. Place the pan in the oven, then pour enough hot tap water into the pan to come halfway up the sides of the cups. Cover the pan with foil and crimp it loosely around the edges (in about 4 places—do not make it airtight). Bake just until the centers of the custards are barely set, about 45 to 60 minutes.

Use a pair of tongs (or your hand protected with a kitchen towel) to immediately remove the cups from the pan and place them on a rack to cool, about 40 minutes. Refrigerate, covered with plastic wrap, for at least 6 hours, preferably overnight, before serving.

SERVING AND STORAGE NOTES: To unmold the custards, run a thin, sharp, flexible knife around the edges of each cup, pressing the knife into the cup rather than gouging the custard. Place a serving plate upside down on top of the cup, then holding the two together, flip them over so that the plate is right side up—the custard should slide out of the cup and onto the plate. If the custard is a bit hesitant, pick up the plate, hold the cup in place on the plate, and give the two a firm but gentle shake once or twice. Serve each custard with a small spoonful of softly whipped cream in the center surrounded by 3 spiced pecan halves. The custards are at their best the first day or two after baking—as they sit, the texture becomes more dense and less delicate

GETTING AHEAD: The custards may be baked 1 or 2 days in advance. Store in the refrigerator, covered with plastic wrap. Unmold just before serving.

CLEANING TIP: Place the empty custard cups in a large pot and fill with water. Bring to a gentle boil and cook until the caramel remaining in the cups dissolves.

Spiced Pecans

makes about ½ pound

Spicy, crunchy, and irresistible, these nuts are great as an accompaniment to Pumpkin Flan or simply as a snack. The black pepper adds just a hint of heat. You can add ⅛ to ¼ teaspoon cayenne pepper (depending on your heat tolerance) to the mixture and either serve them with cocktails or use them as an accent in salads. I often give these nuts as holiday gifts, nestled in decorated Chinese take-out boxes. This recipe can easily be doubled, tripled, or more until you have spiced nuts to your heart's desire. While pecans are my favorites, walnuts or almonds may be substituted. Leftover nuts can be chopped and sprinkled over ice cream, or ground and used to decorate the sides of cakes or to substitute for plain ground nuts in your favorite torte recipe. This recipe is adapted from one by talented chef and vegetarian cookbook writer Deborah Madison.

EQUIPMENT AND ADVANCE PREPARATION: A baking sheet with sides • Line the bottom of the pan with parchment paper.

> **1 large egg white**
>
> **1 teaspoon pure vanilla extract**
>
> **2 tablespoons (1 ounce) granulated sugar**
>
> **2 tablespoons (1 ounce) tightly packed light brown sugar**
>
> **1½ teaspoons ground cinnamon**
>
> **¾ teaspoon ground ginger**
>
> **¼ teaspoon ground allspice**

¼ teaspoon ground black pepper

⅛ teaspoon ground cardamom

8 ounces pecan halves

Preheat the oven to 275°F.

Place the egg white and vanilla in a medium bowl and beat lightly with a whisk just until frothy. In a separate bowl, stir together the sugars and spices until well blended.

Add the pecan halves to the egg white and use your hands to toss the nuts until they are thoroughly coated. Add the sugar and spices and blend well, again using your hands to toss the nuts until the coating is distributed evenly.

Spread the nuts on the prepared pan, using 2 forks to separate them as much as possible from each other. This can be a little time-consuming, but it's much easier now than after they have dried and stuck to each other in the oven. Place the pan in the oven and bake for 35 to 50 minutes, or until the nuts are very dry and toasted. Rotate the pan in the oven halfway through the cooking time.

To test whether they are done, remove a nut from the oven and cool it quickly in the refrigerator or freezer. If the spice coating is dry and the nut tastes toasted, they are finished. Do not let the nuts brown all the way through, as they become bitter at this point. Remove the nuts from the oven and place on a rack to cool completely before transferring to an airtight storage container or gift boxes.

GETTING AHEAD: Fresh pecans prepared in this manner keep well stored in an airtight container in a cool, dry location for 2 months. If it is warm, they tend to go rancid within a few weeks.

The spiced pecans can be frozen for 3 to 4 months. Thaw, still inside the container, to room temperature, then toast the nuts again for 10 to 15 minutes to recrisp them.

Chestnut Honey Flan

serves 6

Though flan makes me think of Spain, custards baked in caramel-coated molds are popular throughout France, Italy, and Greece as well. Flavor the custard with honey, and you could be almost anywhere in the Mediterranean, though the type of honey might give you a clue as to your location. I love chestnut honey, with its strong, bitter, slightly herbal flavor and its dark, mysterious color of deep caramel tinged with green and yellow. Chestnut honey is one of the special prides of beekeepers in Italy, where forests of chestnut trees provide their bees with the nectar they require. Interestingly, though most of the chestnut honey we can buy here comes from Tuscany, it is produced in many areas throughout Europe where the Roman legions spread this beautiful tree. The French island of Corsica in particular has been covered with the trees for centuries.

Don't worry if you can't find chestnut honey—any interesting honey that you enjoy will make a memorable flan. This is a good chance to try some of the wonderful "varietal" honeys that are becoming more available at upscale markets, farmers' markets, and through special mail-order sources (327). Lavender honey is a favorite in the south of France, while the ultradark, earthy, buckwheat honey is traditional in Brittany. Beekeepers here in America are producing some excellent varieties. Delicate, sweet, lightly herbal acacia honey and the deeply floral tupelo honey are just a couple you may want to taste and experiment with.

EQUIPMENT AND ADVANCE PREPARATION: Six 6-ounce custard cups (I use Pyrex) or ramekins • If you do not know the size of your custard cups, see note on page 164 to figure it out. • A roasting or baking pan large enough to hold all the cups without touching each other or the sides of the roasting pan

FOR THE CARAMEL
⅓ cup (2½ ounces) water

1 cup (7 ounces) sugar

1¼ cups (10 ounces) heavy cream

¾ cup (6 ounces) whole milk

¼ cup (3 ounces) chestnut honey

Zest of ½ orange, in strips

2 large eggs

2 large egg yolks

FOR SERVING

Softly whipped cream (54), unsweetened

Candied orange zest (236), optional

To caramelize the custard cups, place the water in a medium saucepan, add the sugar, and set the pan over medium heat. Stir constantly with a wooden spoon or swirl the pan frequently until the sugar has dissolved and the liquid is clear. Turn the heat to high and boil rapidly, swirling the pan occasionally (do not stir at this point) so the sugar cooks evenly, until it turns a deep golden brown. Remove the pan from the heat and immediately divide the caramel among the custard cups. Working quickly, swirl each cup to distribute the caramel evenly around the sides, to about an inch up from the bottom—be careful, the caramel is very hot (you may want to keep a small bowl of ice water nearby in case a bit of caramel escapes onto a finger during the swirling process). Set the cups in the roasting pan.

Preheat the oven to 325°F. Position an oven rack in the center of the oven.

To flavor the custard, place the heavy cream, milk, honey, and orange zest in a small saucepan over medium-low heat. Cook, stirring several times to dissolve the honey, just until the mixture begins to simmer. Remove the pan from the heat, cover with a lid, and allow the mixture to steep for 15 minutes.

To finish the custard, place the pan back over medium heat, remove the lid, and reheat the mixture just until it begins to simmer. In a medium bowl, whisk together the eggs and egg yolks. Slowly whisk the hot milk into the eggs. Pour the mixture through a fine-mesh strainer into a pitcher or large measuring cup with a spout. Discard the orange zest.

Divide the warm custard among the custard cups in the roasting pan. Place the pan in the oven, then pour enough hot tap water into the pan to come halfway up the sides of the cups. Cover the pan with foil and crimp it loosely around the edges (in about 4 places—do not make it airtight). Bake just until the centers of the custards are barely set, about 35 to 50 minutes.

Use a pair of tongs (or your hand protected with a kitchen towel) to immediately remove the cups from the pan and place them on a rack to cool, about 40 minutes. Refrigerate, covered with plastic wrap, for at least 6 hours, preferably overnight, before serving.

SERVING AND STORAGE NOTES: To unmold the custards, run a thin, sharp, flexible knife around the edges of each cup, pressing the knife into the cup rather than gouging the custard. Place a serving plate upside down on top of the cup, then holding the two together, flip them over so that the plate is right side up—the custard should slide out of the cup and onto the plate. If the custard is a bit hesitant, pick up the plate, hold the cup in place on the plate, and give the two a firm but gentle shake once or twice. Serve each custard with a small spoonful of unsweetened softly whipped cream and a sprinkling of candied orange zest strands, if desired. The custards are at their best the first day or two after baking—as they sit, the texture becomes more dense and less delicate.

GETTING AHEAD: The custards may be baked 1 or 2 days in advance. Store in the refrigerator, covered with plastic wrap. Unmold just before serving.

CLEANING TIP: Place the empty custard cups in a large pot and fill with water. Bring to a gentle boil and cook until the caramel remaining in the cups dissolves.

Black and White Mascarpone Parfait

serves 6

This dessert resides firmly in the "ooh and ahh" category of endings, both in flavor and appearance. Alternating layers of silky, rum-spiked white and chocolate mascarpone mousses are separated by layers of crunchy bitter chocolate cookie crumbs for a fun, sophisticated play on an old-fashioned ice cream parlor favorite.

EQUIPMENT AND ADVANCE PREPARATION: Six 8-ounce parfait glasses or champagne flutes • Bake about ½ roll of Bitter Chocolate Wafers (261). • If you wish to make your own mascarpone (42), you will need to begin at least 3 days before assembling the dessert. • 2 large pastry bags fitted with plain ½-inch tips. If you do not have 2 pastry bags, substitute 2 gallon-sized zip-top bags.

FOR THE MASCARPONE MOUSSES

1 pound mascarpone

½ cup plus 2 tablespoons (2½ ounces) sugar

2 to 3 tablespoons (1 to 1½ ounces) good-quality dark rum

1 tablespoon pure vanilla extract

1 cup (8 ounces) heavy cream

2 tablespoons unsweetened Dutch-process cocoa powder (262)

2 to 3 tablespoons (1 to 1½ ounces) warm water

About 1 cup (3½ ounces) coarsely crushed Bitter Chocolate Wafers (261)

FOR SERVING

Cigarette cookies, optional (available in the cookie aisle of the supermarket)

To make the rum mousse, place the mascarpone, sugar, rum, and vanilla in the bowl of an electric mixer fitted with the paddle attachment (this can also be done by hand in a medium bowl with a wooden spoon). Beat on medium-low speed for 30 to 60 seconds, or until they are well blended and the mixture is the consistency of thick pudding. With some brands of mascarpone, you may need to blend a bit longer to thicken the filling. If the filling becomes too thick or begins to appear grainy, stir in 1 or 2 tablespoons of heavy cream to smooth it out.

In a clean mixing bowl, using a clean whisk attachment, whip the cream on medium speed to firm peaks. Be careful not to overwhip the cream, or it will begin to separate and look curdled. If this happens, remove the bowl from the mixer and use a rubber spatula to gently stir in several tablespoons of cream, just until the whipped cream has smoothed out again. Use the rubber spatula to gently fold the whipped cream into the mascarpone. Taste and adjust the sugar and/or rum content to your liking.

To make the chocolate mousse, place the cocoa powder and 2 tablespoons warm water in a small bowl and stir with a small whisk or spoon until blended and smooth. It should be the consistency of a thin pudding, easily pouring from the spoon. This texture will make it easy to combine with the mousse—if it is too thick and paste-like, add more warm water, 1 teaspoon at a time, until the desired consistency is reached. Remove one-third of the rum mousse (about 10 ounces, or 1½ cups) and place it in a separate medium bowl. Using a rubber spatula, gently but thoroughly fold the cocoa mixture into this smaller portion of mousse. Again, if the filling becomes too thick or begins to appear grainy, gently stir in 1 or 2 tablespoons of heavy cream to smooth it out.

If you are using pastry bags, place a tip in each one, then twist the portion of the bag just above the tip and stuff it down into the tip (this seals off the tip and prevents any mousse from leaking out). Place each pastry or zip-top bag into a medium plastic storage container and fold any excess bag back over the top of the container. Spoon each mousse into one of the bags, then cover the top with a piece of plastic wrap or seal the zip-top bags and place them in the refrigerator. Keep chilled until serving time.

To crush the cookies, place them in a small plastic bag and gently crush them to coarse crumbs with a meat pounder, rolling pin, or the bottom edge of a heavy saucepan. The crumbs should be a bit chunky and crunchy—do not crush them to a fine powder. Place the crumbs in an airtight container until serving time.

To assemble the parfaits, line up the parfait glasses or champagne flutes in front of you. Use half the rum mousse to pipe a layer in the bottom of the glasses (if using zip-top bags, squeeze the mousse into one corner, then snip off and discard the very tip of the corner with a pair of scissors—you can always make the piping hole larger if needed, but it's best to start small). When piping, concentrate on directing the mousse against the sides of the glass—this will give a better visual delineation of the layers. Sprinkle this first layer of mousse in each glass with 1 tablespoon of the bitter Chocolate Wafer Crumbs, concentrating some of the crumbs up against the glass. Use the entire quantity of chocolate mousse to pipe the middle layer in the glasses. Sprinkle again with 1 tablespoon of cookie crumbs. Use the remaining half of the rum mousse to pipe the top layer in each glass. Finish with a light sprinkling of cookie crumbs.

SERVING AND STORAGE NOTES: Serve the parfaits immediately (or within 1 hour), while the cookie crumbs are still crunchy. I like to garnish this dessert by topping each parfait with a couple of long, thin "cigarette" cookies to mimic straws.

GETTING AHEAD: The mousses are best when prepared within 12 hours of being served (so the whipped cream retains its full volume) but, if necessary, can be prepared up to 1 day in advance.

The chocolate cookies can be baked and crushed 2 or 3 days in advance. Store in an airtight container.

The dessert must be assembled at the last moment so that the cookie crumbs retain their vital crunch. Assembly is a snap if you fill the pastry (or zip-top) bags ahead of time and have them ready to go in the refrigerator.

Tuscan Bread Pudding

When the olive trees in Tuscany are shivering in the fall wind and the air is perfumed with the first warming fires of the season, this is the ideal dessert. Tuscany is a region rich with wonderful foodstuffs, yet much of its cuisine is made up of simple, earthy, abundantly satisfying dishes like this one. Here, a rustic bread pudding is filled with fresh and dried fruits, then drizzled with delicate olive oil and baked to soft, custardy perfection, the fruit melting into the bread, the figs and olive oil providing a savory counterpoint to the sweet, soft interior. This recipe is an adaptation of one I learned from Lorenza de Medici of Badia a Coltibuono in Tuscany.

EQUIPMENT AND ADVANCE PREPARATION: One 9 x 2-inch round cake pan or a 9- to 9½-inch round gratin or deep pie dish, brushed with a light coating of butter • You will need to begin 24 hours in advance, as the bread cubes need to sit out overnight to dry slightly (do not try to "quick-dry" them in the oven—the bread will become too dry).

FOR THE CUSTARD

3 large eggs

2 large egg yolks

⅓ cup (2¼ ounces) sugar

1¼ cups (10 ounces) heavy cream

1 cup (8 ounces) whole milk

1 tablespoon pure vanilla extract

Zest of 1 lemon, very finely chopped (145)

1 small loaf challah or other rich bread, crusts trimmed, cut into ½-inch cubes and left out overnight to dry slightly (about 4 to 4½ cups of cubes)

FOR THE FRUIT

½ cup (2¾ ounces) tightly packed dried sour cherries

1½ cups (12 ounces) water

1 large (about 10 to 11 ounces) tart apple, such as Granny Smith

1 large (about 9 to 11 ounces) winter pear, such as Bosc or Anjou

12 (about 3 ounces) small, moist, dried Black Mission figs

2 tablespoons (1 ounce) extra virgin olive oil

3 tablespoons sliced natural almonds or whole pine nuts

FOR SERVING

Heavy cream

To make the custard, place the eggs and yolks in a medium bowl and whisk to blend. Whisk in the sugar. Add the cream and milk and whisk until well blended. Stir in the vanilla and chopped lemon zest. Place the bread cubes in a large mixing bowl. Pour the custard over the bread cubes and stir with a rubber spatula to thoroughly coat the bread cubes with the liquid. Place a dinner plate on top of the bread cubes and set a weight on top of the plate to keep the bread submerged in the custard (I use a large can of tomatoes). Let soak for 45 minutes, stirring once or twice during that time to make sure the bread absorbs the custard evenly.

To prepare the fruit, place the dried sour cherries in a small bowl. Bring the water to a boil in a small saucepan and immediately pour it over the cherries. Set aside to soak for 15 minutes. Peel and core the apple and pear and cut them into ½-inch cubes. Place them in a bowl. Pour the plumped dried cherries into a strainer and discard the water. Press the excess water from the fruit by gently squeezing handfuls of the cherries over the sink. Add the cherries to the apple and pear.

Preheat the oven to 350°F. Position an oven rack in the center of the oven.

To finish the pudding, remove the weight and plate from the soaked bread cubes and gently stir the fruit into the bread until it is evenly distributed. Pour the mixture into the prepared baking pan. Trim the hard stems from the dried figs and discard. Slice each fig in half lengthwise and nestle the halves, cut side up, in the top of the bread pudding. Drizzle the surface of the pudding with the olive oil and sprinkle with the sliced almonds or pine nuts. Bake for 60 to 70 minutes, or until the custard is set in the center (press the center gently with your finger and make sure that no liquid custard oozes out) and the top is golden brown.

SERVING AND STORAGE NOTES: Serve the bread pudding warm from the oven (if you're feeling very decadent, pour some heavy cream around each serving). It is at its best the same day it is baked. If the pudding has cooled, or has been refrigerated, reheat in a 325°F oven for about 15 to 20 minutes. If you will be serving the bread pudding the same day you bake it, just leave it at room temperature.

Coconut Rice Pudding Brûlée with Mango in Lime Caramel Sauce

serves 6

Coconut, though certainly not a "traditional" flavoring of the Mediterranean, has been enthusiastically embraced there and can be found in desserts throughout the region. Mangoes, another tropical import, are especially popular in North Africa and the Middle East. In this dessert a creamy coconut rice pudding hides a layer of sweet mangoes tossed with lime caramel sauce and is topped off with a burnt sugar crust. It's a dessert that guests remember, and continue to ask for, months later.

EQUIPMENT AND ADVANCE PREPARATION: Six 6-ounce custard cups (I use Pyrex) or ceramic ramekins • If you do not know the size of your custard cups, see note on page 164 to figure it out. • A double boiler (or a medium saucepan coupled with a medium stainless-steel mixing bowl that will fit about halfway into the saucepan when sitting on top of it) • A propane torch (see explanation, 168) to brûlée the puddings

FOR THE COCONUT RICE PUDDING

2 cans (13½ to 14 ounces each) coconut milk (192)

½ cup (3½ ounces) arborio rice

½ vanilla bean

½ cup (3½ ounces) sugar

⅓ cup (1 ounce) finely shredded unsweetened coconut (see Note)

⅔ cup (5¼ ounces) heavy cream

FOR THE LIME CARAMEL SAUCE

2 tablespoons plus 2½ tablespoons water

¼ cup (1¾ ounces) sugar

1½ tablespoons freshly squeezed lime juice

FOR ASSEMBLING

1 medium to large (8 to 10 ounces) ripe mango

FOR SERVING

¼ cup (1¾ ounces) sugar

NOTE: If the only coconut you can find is the large-shred variety, pulse it in the food processor until it is finely chopped.

To cook the rice pudding, fill the bottom of the double boiler with 3 inches of water and bring to a boil (the water should be at least 1 inch from the top of the double boiler). In a small saucepan, heat the coconut milk just until it begins to simmer (it may look curdled at this point—don't worry, it will smooth out when combined with the starch of the rice). Place the rice in the top of the double boiler. Use the tip of a sharp knife to split the vanilla bean lengthwise. Scrape out the tiny seeds and add them to the rice, along with the pod. Pour the hot coconut milk over the rice and set the mixture over the boiling water. Whisk well to evenly distribute the vanilla seeds. Cook for 1 hour, whisking every 5 to 10 minutes. Check the level of the boiling water and add water as necessary so it doesn't go dry.

After 1 hour, add the sugar to the rice mixture and continue cooking for another 15 to 30 minutes, or until the rice has absorbed most of the milk and is very tender—the mixture will be very thick. If the rice is not tender, add ¼ cup milk and continue cooking for another 15 minutes. Remove the pudding from the heat and stir in the coconut. Transfer the pudding to a clean container, place a piece of plastic wrap directly on the surface (so a skin doesn't form), and refrigerate until very cold, at least 2 hours.

To finish the rice pudding, remove and discard the vanilla bean pod. In the bowl of an electric mixer fitted with the whisk attachment, whip the cream on medium speed to firm peaks. Be careful not to overwhip the cream, or it will begin to separate and look curdled. If this happens, remove the bowl from the mixer and use a rubber spatula to gently stir in several tablespoons of cream, just until the whipped cream has smoothed out again. Use a rubber spatula to stir one-third of the whipped cream into the rice pudding to loosen it a bit, then gently fold in the remaining cream. Refrigerate until needed.

To make the lime caramel sauce, place 2 tablespoons of water in a small saucepan, then add the sugar and set the pan over medium heat. Stir constantly with a wooden spoon or swirl the pan frequently until the sugar has dissolved and the liquid is clear. Turn the heat to high and boil rapidly, swirling the pan occasionally (do not stir at this point) so the sugar cooks evenly, until it turns a deep amber color. Remove the pan from the heat and immediately add the remaining

2½ tablespoons water and the lime juice—be careful, the mixture will rise in the pan and sputter (you may want to wear on oven mitt on the hand holding the pan). Stir with the wooden spoon to blend. If the caramel has solidified, set the pan back over low heat and stir until it melts again. Cool. Store in a covered container in the refrigerator until needed.

To assemble the dessert, peel the mango using a vegetable peeler or paring knife, then slice off the plump "cheeks" located on either side of the large, fibrous pit. Slice off the smaller pieces of the fruit on the narrow sides of the pit. Chop the fruit into ¼-inch pieces. Place the fruit in a bowl and toss with 3 tablespoons of the cooled lime caramel sauce—you will not use all of the sauce (save the remainder to toss with fresh fruit for a quick compote, or stir it into iced mineral water for a refreshing drink). Divide the mango mixture among the custard cups or ramekins—the fruit should be in a single layer in the bottom of the dishes. Top with the coconut rice pudding, using a metal spatula or the flat side of a knife to level the top of the pudding with the edges of the custard cups or ramekins. Chill until serving time.

SERVING AND STORAGE NOTES: To serve, sprinkle the top of each pudding with 2 teaspoons sugar. Use a propane torch to caramelize the sugar (see page 168). Do not try to caramelize the sugar under the broiler, or the whipped cream will melt.

GETTING AHEAD: The rice pudding may be prepared 1 day in advance. Store in the refrigerator, covered with plastic wrap.

The lime caramel sauce may be prepared up to 5 days in advance.

The sugar topping may be caramelized up to 1 hour in advance.

Buying Coconut Milk

Coconut milk, contrary to popular belief, is not simply the liquid in the center of the coconut. Instead, it is made by infusing hot water with the shredded meat of the coconut (usually the liquid in the center is added too). Then every last drop of flavorful "milk" is squeezed from the meat. While it is certainly possible to make your own from fresh coconuts, most of us find it easier, and just as flavorful, to use canned coconut milk.

Pistachio Layer Cake with Nougat Cream, 30

Orange Flower and Pine Nut Armadillos with Apricot Sauce, 51

**Marbleized
Chocolate
Velvet Tart, 104**

**Siena Tart
with Almonds, Cherries,
Honey, and Spices, 107**

Galataboureko with Spiced Blood Orange Caramel Sauce, 229

Snake Pastry with Fig, Almond Paste, and Lemon, 233

BACK TO FRONT: **Brown Sugar and Almond Biscotti with Cinnamon and Orange, 286;**
Dried Sour Cherry and Bittersweet Chocolate Chip Biscotti, 272;
and Pistachio, Apricot, and Cardamom Biscotti, 276

Tangerine Sorbet, 317,
and Blood Orange Granita, 318

In general, canned coconut milk of very high quality is from Thailand and the Philippines. A particularly good brand I rely upon, Chaokoh, is from Thailand. I have recently noticed several "American" brands of coconut milk and can heartily recommend Thai Kitchen Pure Coconut Milk (see Mail-Order Sources, 327). There are some brands of coconut milk labeled "light," meaning some or most of the fat has been removed. Since fat is the vehicle for flavor throughout cooking (whether it is butter, olive oil, sesame oil, lard, or another fat), I recommend that you avoid these brands—especially in dessert making.

When you open a can of coconut milk, you may find that the fat has separated from the liquid portion of the milk—this is normal. If you like, stir the two in the can until blended, though most often I just pour the entire separated contents into my saucepan or mixing bowl. As the milk is heated, it may separate, but in most dessert recipes, the milk is then blended with ingredients that bind and smooth it (such as the arborio rice in Coconut Rice Pudding Brûlée, 190), so the separation is not a concern. Leftover coconut milk may be stored in a glass container in the refrigerator (do not leave it in the can) for 5 to 7 days.

Apricot Fool with Almond Cream

serves 6

A fool is an old-fashioned dessert both simple and sublime, consisting of fruit puree partially folded into whipped cream, so that ribbons of fruit run through the cream. The key to a good fool is using a fruit with plenty of acidity to offset the voluptuousness of the cream—in this case, the complex sharpness of apricots is paired with orange and amaretto. Amaretto is an especially fine accent in this recipe because it obtains its distinctive almond flavor from the pits of apricots.

EQUIPMENT AND ADVANCE PREPARATION: Six 12-ounce compote dishes or 8-ounce champagne glasses

FOR THE APRICOT PUREE

1½ pounds ripe apricots

¼ cup (2 ounces) freshly squeezed and strained orange juice

¾ cup (5¼ ounces) sugar

1 teaspoon Amaretto di Saronno

FOR THE WHIPPED CREAM

1½ cups (12 ounces) heavy cream

¼ cup (1¾ ounces) sugar

¼ teaspoon pure almond extract

FOR SERVING

Lacy Sesame Crisps (267), Toasted Almond and Dried Sour Cherry
Biscotti (274), or other crispy cookies

To make the apricot puree, halve and pit the apricots, then slice them very thinly. Place the sliced apricots, orange juice, and sugar in a medium nonaluminum saucepan over medium-low heat and cook until the mixture comes to a boil. Continue to cook at a low boil, stirring frequently with a wooden spoon to avoid scorching, until the mixture is very thick and almost jam-like in texture, about 50 to 60 minutes. The apricot slices should be very soft and melting into a roughly textured puree. Remove the pan from the heat, pour the apricots into a medium mixing bowl, and refrigerate until very cold, about 1 hour. When chilled, stir in the amaretto.

To finish the fool, place the cream, sugar, and almond extract in the bowl of an electric mixer fitted with the whisk attachment and whip on medium speed to firm peaks. Be careful not to overwhip the cream, or it will begin to separate and look curdled. If this happens, remove the bowl from the mixer and use a rubber spatula to gently stir in several tablespoons of cream, just until the whipped cream has smoothed out again. Use a rubber spatula to gently fold the cream into the apricot puree, but do not completely blend the two. There should be ribbons of apricot puree clearly visible in the cream. Divide the mixture among the compote dishes or champagne flutes and refrigerate, covered with plastic wrap, until serving time.

SERVING AND STORAGE NOTES: Serve the fools accompanied by crispy cookies such as Lacy Sesame Crisps or Toasted Almond and Dried Sour Cherry Biscotti.

GETTING AHEAD: The apricot puree may be made up to 2 days in advance. Store in an airtight container in the refrigerator.

The fool is best when prepared within 3 to 4 hours of serving so that the whipped cream retains its full volume but, if necessary, can be made up to 8 hours in advance.

Champagne Jelly
with Raspberries

serves 6

This recipe, an elegant after-dinner "drink," is perfect for the long, hot days of summer when we crave something light, chilled, and exhilarating. The alcohol in the champagne is not cooked off, so beware of its potency. Because the champagne is blended with sugar and lemon, do not use your best bottle here—a moderate to inexpensive bottle will serve the purpose well. This recipe comes from friend and food writer Brigit Binns.

EQUIPMENT AND ADVANCE PREPARATION: Six 8-ounce champagne flutes, wiped very clean (any dust or fingerprints on the inside of the glasses will show with this dessert)

> 3 tablespoons (1½ ounces) plus 1¼ cups (10 ounces) water
>
> 1 cup (7 ounces) sugar
>
> Zest of 1 lemon, in strips
>
> Juice of 1 lemon (about 3 tablespoons)
>
> 1 half-pint basket (about 6 ounces) fresh raspberries
>
> 2 packages (¼ ounce each) powdered unflavored gelatin
>
> 2 cups (16 ounces) champagne
>
> **FOR SERVING**
> Mint sprigs

To flavor the jelly, place the sugar, lemon zest, lemon juice, and 1¼ cups water in a small saucepan over medium-low heat. Cook, stirring several times to dissolve the sugar, just until the mixture begins to simmer. Remove the pan from the heat, cover with a lid, and allow the mixture to steep for 20 minutes. Pour the mixture through a fine-mesh strainer into a medium bowl and discard the lemon zest.

To make the raspberry puree, sort through the raspberries and discard any debris or moldy berries (do not wash fresh raspberries, as they will absorb water and disintegrate and are virtually impossible to dry, which leads to mushy berries with watered-down flavor), then divide the berries in half. Reserve one-half for garnish. Place the remaining berries (about 3 ounces, or ¾ cup loosely packed) in the bowl of a food processor or blender and process until smooth. Pour the puree into a fine-mesh strainer set over a medium bowl and use a rubber spatula to press the puree through the strainer, extracting as much juice as possible (you should have about 3 tablespoons, but a little less or more is fine). Discard the seeds and reserve the raspberry puree.

To finish the jelly, place the gelatin in a small bowl and stir in 3 tablespoons of water, just until there are no bits of dried gelatin remaining. Let sit for 5 minutes. Place an inch of water in a small skillet and heat just until it begins to simmer. Remove the pan from the heat and place the bowl with the gelatin into the water. In 1 or 2 minutes, the gelatin will warm and melt into a liquid. Add the melted gelatin to the lemon mixture. Cool the mixture quickly by placing the bowl in a larger bowl of ice water. Stir slowly and constantly with a rubber spatula to prevent the gelatin from hardening on the bottom of the bowl. When the liquid is cold and the gelatin begins to "tighten" (it will look like oil rather than water), remove the bowl from the ice bath and stir in the raspberry puree and the champagne. Immediately divide the mixture among the champagne flutes and drop a few whole raspberries into the top of each glass. Refrigerate, covered with plastic wrap, for at least 2 hours before serving.

SERVING AND STORAGE NOTES: To serve, garnish each glass with a mint sprig. I like to serve these the same day they are made, when the surface of the jelly is a bit loose. As gelatin sits, its hold becomes stronger, and the mixture will eventually take on a rubbery quality, so serve them within 1 or 2 days.

VARIATION

Tiny Bubbles: This dessert looks especially pretty with a string of berries floating up from the bottom of the glass like large red champagne bubbles. The buoyancy of the gelatin, however, keeps the berries from sinking into the liquid, so to accomplish this look, you will need to fill the glasses with an inch or so of champagne jelly, drop in a raspberry, then chill until set (the gelatin sets very quickly in the freezer). Then you add another layer of jelly and fruit and continue to the top. It's details like this that turn a good dessert into an all-out showstopper.

In preparation for this presentation, do not cool the mixture quickly in an ice bath as directed above—just leave it at room temperature and stir in the champagne (it will be much easier to pour the champagne into the glasses while it is still liquid). If the mixture begins to gel before you've finished making the layers, you can do one of two things: add the jelly to the glasses in its gloppy state (once it's chilled, no one will know), though it is hard to add it in even increments when chunky, or place the bowl of champagne jelly over a saucepan with 2 inches of water that has been brought to a boil, then removed from the heat. The residual heat will keep the mixture warm enough that the gelatin will not set.

Baklava and Filo Desserts

Filo or phyllo (the word means leaf in Greek) is a tissue-thin dough that is layered with butter to produce a crisp, flaky pastry—an ancestor to puff pastry. Filo has been used in the Mediterranean for hundreds of years, though no one knows its exact origin. It may have been an attempt to copy the versatile food wrapping of the Far East known as wonton skins. Or it may have been a refinement of the pasta-like dough still used to make an early form of baklava in some areas east of Turkey. Its beginnings remain a mystery, but we do know that filo was spread through Europe and North Africa by the conquering armies of the Byzantine, Islamic, and Ottoman empires. This light, flaky pastry can be found throughout the Mediterranean in dishes that range from sweet to savory and from appetizers to desserts.

Baklava is the filo dessert that Americans are most familiar with, though most may not realize that almost any nut-filled filo dessert in the Middle East is called baklava, and the range of shapes is surprisingly diverse. Filo can be found rolled up into big "cigarettes" that are then layered in a pan, or curled into a coil (sometimes several are connected end to end and coiled in a large pan to form a "cake"). A dowel may be rolled up in these cigarettes, then removed, and the ends of the cigarette gently squeezed toward each other to form a crinkled, more rustic-looking roll. Or filo may be stuffed and rolled like large Thai spring rolls, then nestled close together in a baking pan. These are just a few of the many, many shapes filo can take, and they are almost all referred to as baklava.

I have kept the shapes in this chapter to a few, emphasizing the style of baklava we are most accustomed to (layers of filo and filling in a square pan) while imbuing this versatile dough with some fun American flavor and texture combinations. And whereas most baklava recipes (and, in general, most recipes calling for filo) make enough to feed a small city, I have reduced the quantity to a much more manageable size—an 8-inch square baking pan. The baklavas here are tall (almost 2 inches!), sexy, glistening specimens, lush with color and exuberant in flavor.

I've included a classic-style almond and hazelnut baklava (Antibes Baklava) that is rich, light, and a revelation for those used to the sticky, gloppy commercial versions, as well as my take on Quince and Walnut Baklava, which features the lovely fragrance and beautiful rose color of this ancient fruit so popular in the Middle East. Baklava has always struck me as being more of a confection than a pastry, and I have veered in that free-spirited direction by including dried fruits and even chocolate in versions that range from Pistachio and Apricot Baklava with Orange Cardamom Syrup to Hazelnut and Chocolate Baklava to Sour Cherry and Almond Baklava. For a twist on the Greek favorite of semolina-filled filo called Galataboureko, try my recipe using the extracrispy shredded-wheat-like pastry called shredded filo (also known as *kunafeh* or *kataifi*) and a blood orange caramel sauce instead of the usual sugar syrup. A dramatic coiled snake pastry is filled with dried figs, almond paste, and lemon zest; sweet summer cherries are crowned with a cheesecake-like topping and baked in spiced shredded filo; and golden triangles, plump with a filling of dried apricots, bittersweet chocolate, and amaretto, are piled high on a platter for a fun, help-yourself ending to a party. This chapter will awaken you to filo's endless, and endlessly exciting, possibilities.

Notes on Equipment

Though I admit that hand-chopped nuts make the best baklavas, I know that very few people (me included) want to spend the required 20 minutes or so that this task requires. To that end, I encourage you to use a food processor to chop your nuts. Just watch to be sure they are finely chopped, not ground—the difference is only about 15 seconds or so in the machine. In fact, most of the recipes in this chapter call for finely chopped nuts, chocolate, and/or dried fruits, so a food processor with a good sharp blade is practically a necessity.

The syrups that moisten the baklavas in this chapter are cooked to 218°F, or the upper end of the thread stage. The consistency of syrup cooked to this stage is the best for baklava, so while I am reluctant to require a piece of kitchen equipment that most readers will not use very often, I do so here because a candy thermometer is the easiest and most reliable way to ensure your syrup is cooked to the correct temperature.

Candy thermometers can vary in accuracy, even when brand new. Always test your thermometer before you use it for the first time (or if you haven't used yours in a while) so you know you can trust the reading. It's a very simple test. Place the thermometer in a pot of cold water and then heat the water to a full rolling boil. It should register 212°F. If it reads above that, add the number of degrees above 212°F to the reading called for in a recipe; if it reads below 212°F, subtract the same number of degrees from the reading called for in a recipe. If the reading is more than 5 to 6 degrees off or if you see gaps in the mercury, replace the thermometer. Test the thermometer periodically, and always run this test if you happen to drop it.

When using the thermometer, warm it by placing it in a glass of hot water before inserting it into the heating syrup—this helps to prevent the thermometer from breaking. Always try to be eye level with the thermometer when you read the temperature. When you remove the thermometer from the syrup, place it back into the glass of hot water so that any syrup clinging to the thermometer will dissolve away.

Antibes Baklava with Almonds, Hazelnuts, Cinnamon, and Cloves

makes 18 pieces

I first tasted baklava at large school and church events, where the requirements for dessert were that it be cheap and plentiful—and baklava often fit the bill. The golden layered pastry was always enticing but failed to offer anything other than a sodden, ultrasweet mouthful, and it wasn't long before I vowed to avoid it forever. I kept this promise for many years, until one day in the south of France. Waiting for the Picasso Museum in Antibes to open, my friend and I shopped leisurely for lunch in the open-air market nearby. We each bought provisions, then sat on a small wall to share our purchases. When it came to dessert, she pulled out a piece of baklava, and I cringed as memories came flooding back. Just try it, she said, and with one taste my opinion was transformed. Now this was baklava! Crisp and light, with a crunch of almonds and hazelnuts, rich with spice and a hint of orange flower water, it was sweetened with just enough honey to make it interesting. That baklava became the model against which all future baklavas were judged, and this recipe is about as close as I can get to duplicating that wonderful pastry.

EQUIPMENT AND ADVANCE PREPARATION: One 8 x 8 x 2-inch baking pan • A soft-bristle brush • A candy thermometer • If you are using frozen filo, allow 24 hours for it to thaw in the refrigerator, then place the filo box on the counter to come to room temperature, about 1½ to 2 hours

FOR THE FILLING
1 cup (6½ ounces) whole natural almonds

1 cup (5¾ ounces) hazelnuts

3 tablespoons (1½ ounces) sugar

1 teaspoon ground cinnamon

¼ teaspoon ground cloves

1 pound filo, room temperature

6 tablespoons (3 ounces) unsalted butter, melted and lukewarm

FOR THE SYRUP

¾ cup (8 ¾ ounces) honey

1½ teaspoons orange flower water (260)

To prepare the filling, place the almonds and hazelnuts in the bowl of a food processor and process until the nuts are finely chopped (the largest should be the size of small dried lentils), about 15 to 20 seconds. Remove 3 tablespoons and reserve in a small bowl for garnish. To the remaining nuts, add the sugar, cinnamon, and cloves and pulse 3 or 4 times to blend. Transfer the mixture to a medium bowl.

To prepare the filo, remove it from its packaging and unfold it so that the stack lies flat on your work surface. Cut the stack in half crosswise, then trim each half to measure 8 by 8 inches. Stack them on top of each other, then cover with plastic wrap and a damp towel to prevent the filo from drying out. Discard the excess trimmings. Remove one sheet of filo and place it in the bottom of the pan to see that it fits snugly. It should touch the edges but not creep up the sides of the pan—trim the sheet of filo so that it fits correctly. Some square pans are smaller at the bottom than the top (where the measurements are taken), and if this is true of yours, use this first piece as a template to trim the remaining sheets of filo in the stack to the same size (they will be slightly smaller than the pan as you work toward the top, but this is fine).

To assemble the baklava, take out a sheet of filo and re-cover the rest (be sure to cover the remaining sheets each time you remove a new one). Place the filo in the bottom of the pan and brush it lightly with the melted butter. The sheerest coating of butter is all that is needed. Don't worry if the entire sheet is not evenly coated—too much butter will result in a heavy, greasy pastry. Repeat with 5 more sheets of filo. Sprinkle the top sheet of filo with ⅓ cup of the nut filling (to measure, just scoop the nuts from the bowl and level the top with your hand or the back of a knife—do not compact the nuts in the cup). Top with 3 more sheets of filo, buttering each one lightly. Sprinkle with ⅓ cup of the nut filling. Continue in this manner—3 sheets of buttered filo followed by ⅓ cup of nuts—until you have used up all the chopped nuts (you will have 7 layers of nuts).

When the last of the nuts have been added to the pan, top them with 6 sheets of buttered filo to match the original 6 sheets in the bottom of the pan. You should have just enough butter to coat the top piece of filo. If you have any excess butter, refrigerate it and reserve for another use. Roll and rewrap any remaining filo sheets twice in plastic wrap. Return to the refrigerator and use within 3 days. Place the pan of baklava in the freezer for 30 minutes—this makes it much easier to cut the pastry.

Preheat the oven to 350°F. Position an oven rack in the center of the oven.

To cut the chilled baklava, use a thin, sharp knife. I have a number of good knives, but the best one I've found for this purpose is a steak knife with tiny, sharp serrations. You may want to try a couple of different knives as you work to see which one is best. When cutting, use a gentle sawing motion and try not to compress the pastry by pressing down on it with one hand while cutting with the other. You shouldn't need to do this, as the chilling solidifies the butter and keeps the filo from bouncing about as you cut. Cut the pastry, all the way to the bottom of the pan, into thirds in one direction, then turn the pan 90 degrees and cut the pastry into thirds again. You should have 9 squares. Cut each square in half diagonally to form 18 triangles as shown.

Place the pan in the oven and bake for 25 minutes, then turn the oven down to 300°F and continue to bake for another 20 to 25 minutes, until the top is a lovely golden color. Remove from the oven and place on a rack to cool completely.

To make the syrup, place the honey in a small saucepan over medium heat. Insert the candy thermometer and cook until it registers 218°F. Remove the pan from the heat and set the candy thermometer aside. Stir the orange flower water into the hot honey. Pour the mixture evenly over the surface of the cooled baklava, making sure not to neglect the outer edges. Sprinkle the reserved 3 tablespoons of nuts over the top and let the baklava sit, uncovered, at room temperature. Allow the baklava plenty of time to absorb the honey before serving, at least 2 to 3 hours. Baklava is at its best 8 hours after it is made, when the syrup is evenly absorbed and the flavors have begun to meld.

SERVING AND STORAGE NOTES: Loosen the pieces of baklava by running your knife along the cut marks. Gently lift each piece out using the tip of your knife or a small spatula (the first piece is always the hardest to remove). Serve 1 or 2 triangles per person (if serving 2, set them at a 90-degree angle to each other for some drama on the plate). Store, loosely covered with plastic wrap or foil, at room temperature for up to 5 days.

GETTING AHEAD: The assembled and cut baklava can be covered tightly with plastic wrap and refrigerated overnight or frozen for up to 1 month (if freezing, wrap the entire pan twice with plastic wrap so the pastry will not dry out or pick up any odors). Refrigerated baklava will bake in the specified period of time, but allow a few extra minutes in the oven for baklava that has been frozen.

Do *not* grind the nuts in advance. As they sit, they compact, and you won't get as many layers of nuts as the recipe calls for (unless you have a scale and can divide the nuts into the layers needed by weight).

VARIATION

Walnut Baklava: Some feel walnuts make the best (and most classic) of all baklavas. Follow the recipe above, substituting 3 cups (10¾ ounces) walnuts for the almonds and hazelnuts. For a more typically Persian flavor, substitute 1½ teaspoons cardamom for the cinnamon and cloves.

The process for making fresh filo is time-consuming, but luckily, frozen filo is perfectly acceptable and available in almost every supermarket. If you live in a large, ethnically diverse city, you may find a shop that sells fresh filo, which is always the best choice, for the dough is supple and easy to use when freshly made. Fresh filo can also be purchased through the mail (see Mail-Order Sources, 327), and if you're the sort of person who plans ahead, I would highly recommend this alternative. Filo is exceptionally easy to work with, as long as you follow a few guidelines.

About Frozen Filo

- When buying frozen filo dough, always choose packages from the back of the freezer case, where the temperature is more constant.

- I always buy an extra box or two of frozen filo, just in case. Frozen filo may thaw during delivery to the supermarket, and even if it arrives frozen, it may thaw as it waits its turn to be placed in the freezer case. The trouble with thawed and refrozen filo is that the sheets tend to stick together, ripping and tearing unmercifully as you try to pry them apart. For this reason, I always buy extra frozen filo, so that if I get a bad box, I can finish the dessert with the filo in the second box.

- Thaw frozen filo overnight in the refrigerator so it has a chance to thaw gradually. When it is thawed at room temperature, moisture condenses on the filo, which can cause the sheets to stick together, causing the same problems described above. A long, slow thawing can reduce these problems dramatically.

- Once it has thawed in the refrigerator, place it on the counter and let it come to room temperature, about 1½ to 2 hours, before using the dough. Cold filo cracks more easily than soft, room-temperature dough.

About All Filo (Frozen or Fresh)

- When you're working with filo, keep in mind that it dries out quickly when exposed to the air and becomes very brittle. To prevent this from happening, always keep the filo sheets not in use covered with a piece of plastic wrap that is topped with a damp towel.

- Always use a soft, natural-bristle brush—a pastry brush or a new, soft-bristle paintbrush—to coat the filo sheets with the melted butter. Stiff bristles, particularly the hard, plastic variety, will tear the delicate dough.

- Many filo recipes call for butter that is clarified, a process that removes the milk solids (which go rancid quickly), resulting in pastry that has a long shelf life. It also results in a crisper pastry because milk solids tend to soften filo as it sits. This step is unnecessary if you're going to serve the baklava within a couple of days, which, of course, you will. I've made baklava with plain old melted butter as well as clarified butter, and the difference is negligible, not large enough to warrant the extra step of clarifying. Melt the butter slowly over low heat and remove it from the heat when it is melted but still creamy-looking.

- Use the melted butter sparingly. Each layer of filo needs only the barest touch of butter, so work quickly and with a light hand. A common mistake is to coat each sheet heavily, which results in a heavy, greasy pastry rather than a flaky, crispy one.

About Shredded Filo (*Kunafeh* or *Kataifi*)

This popular Middle Eastern pastry, which looks very similar to shredded wheat or fine vermicelli noodles, is not, as many believe, made from sheets of filo that have somehow been mechanically shredded. Rather, it is an entirely different pastry, made from a liquid batter rather than the dough used for making sheets of filo. The shredded filo batter is a mixture of flour and water, though sometimes milk is used as well. A very large griddle is heated, and the batter is poured into a *kunaffahiah,* which looks like a small metal canister into which dozens of tiny holes have been poked. The batter is then thrown from the *kunaffahiah* over the hot griddle in a circular pattern, and the small, thin strands that result are set almost instantly. Technically, they are not cooked, for the strands are still very white and pliable, but they are ready to be used in dessert preparation.

Shredded filo may be found in the frozen section of the supermarket with the other filo products and is more commonly found in markets catering to a Middle Eastern clientele (for a mail-order source, see page 327). There is really no substitute for this light and crispy dough.

Shredded filo is not nearly as fragile as the thin sheets of filo, and you do not have to worry about condensation ruining the pastry. To thaw frozen shredded filo, either place it on the counter and let it come to room temperature (about 2 to 3 hours) or let it thaw overnight in the refrigerator, then place on the counter for an hour to come to room temperature.

Pistachio and Apricot Baklava with Orange Cardamom Syrup

makes 18 pieces

This version is my favorite way to introduce baklava to nonbelievers. A golden-hued pastry with striking layers of bright green nuts and glistening orange fruit, it bursts with Middle Eastern dessert flavors. The moistening syrup combines fresh orange juice with honey and is scented with the seductive fragrance of cardamom. I like to use dried California apricots, which tend to be the tart Blenheim, or Royal, variety, but Turkish or Mediterranean apricots are good as well.

EQUIPMENT AND ADVANCE PREPARATION: One 8 x 8 x 2-inch baking pan • A soft-bristle brush • A candy thermometer • If you are using frozen filo, allow 24 hours for it to thaw in the refrigerator, then place the filo box on the counter to come to room temperature, about 1½ to 2 hours • If you find only pistachios in shells, buy double the weight given and shell them by hand.

FOR THE FILLING

6 ounces dried apricots, preferably California

1 cup (4¼ ounces) plus ½ cup (2½ ounces) raw unsalted shelled pistachios

¼ cup (1¾ ounces) plus 1 tablespoon sugar

1 pound filo, room temperature

6 tablespoons (3 ounces) unsalted butter, melted and lukewarm

FOR THE SYRUP

⅓ cup (2¾ ounces) freshly squeezed and strained orange juice

½ cup plus 2 tablespoons (4½ ounces) sugar

¾ teaspoon ground cardamom

¼ cup (3 ounces) honey

To prepare the filling, place the dried apricots, 1 cup pistachios, and ¼ cup sugar in the bowl of a food processor and process until the mixture is very finely chopped, about 20 to 30 seconds. Each component should still be discernible, though in very small pieces—not a puree. Transfer the mixture to a medium bowl. Place the remaining ½ cup pistachios and 1 tablespoon sugar in the bowl of the food processor and process until the nuts are very finely chopped (the largest should be the size of small dried lentils), about 10 to 15 seconds. Transfer the mixture to a small bowl.

To prepare the filo, remove it from its packaging and unfold it so that the stack lies flat on your work surface. Cut the stack in half crosswise, then trim each half to measure 8 by 8 inches. Stack them on top of each other, then cover with plastic wrap and a damp towel to prevent the filo from drying out. Discard the excess trimmings. Remove one sheet of filo and place it in the bottom of the pan to see that it fits snugly. It should touch the edges but not creep up the sides of the pan—trim the sheet of filo so that it fits correctly. Some square pans are smaller at the bottom than the top (where the measurements are taken), and if this is true of yours, use this first piece as a template to trim the remaining sheets of filo to the same size (they will be slightly smaller than the pan as you work toward the top, but this is fine).

To assemble the baklava, take out a sheet of filo and re-cover the rest (be sure to cover the remaining sheets each time you remove a new one). Place the filo in the bottom of the pan and brush it lightly with the melted butter. The sheerest coating of butter is all that is needed. Don't worry if the entire sheet is not evenly covered—too much butter will result in a heavy, greasy pastry. Repeat with 5 more sheets of filo. Sprinkle the top sheet of filo with 2 tablespoons of the chopped pistachios. Top with 3 more sheets of filo, buttering each one lightly. Sprinkle with another 2 tablespoons of chopped pistachios. Top with 3 more sheets of lightly buttered filo. Evenly spread about ½ cup of the apricot-nut filling over the top (to measure, just scoop the filling from the bowl and level the top with your hand or the back of a knife—do not compact the filling in the cup). You should be using about one quarter of the total apricot-nut filling at this point, and it may be slightly more than ½ cup, depending on the type of apricots and how finely the mixture was ground. Top with 3 more sheets of filo, buttering each one lightly. Sprinkle with another ½ cup of the apricot-nut filling. Repeat this procedure twice more, using all the remaining filling. Top with 3 sheets of lightly buttered filo, then sprinkle with 2 tablespoons of chopped pistachios. Repeat this once more. Reserve the remaining pistachios for garnish.

Finish the baklava by topping the pistachios with 6 sheets of lightly buttered filo to match the original 6 sheets in the bottom of the pan. You should have just enough butter to coat the top piece of filo. If you have any excess butter, refrigerate it and reserve for another use. Roll and rewrap any remaining filo sheets twice in plastic wrap. Return to the refrigerator and use within 3 days. Place the pan of baklava in the freezer for 30 minutes—this makes it much easier to cut the pastry.

Preheat the oven to 350°F. Position an oven rack in the center of the oven.

To cut the chilled baklava, use a thin, sharp knife. I have a number of good knives, but the best one I've found for this purpose is a steak knife with tiny, sharp serrations. You may want to try a couple of different knives as you work to see which one is best. When cutting, use a gentle sawing motion and try not to compress the pastry by pressing down on it with one hand while cutting with the other. You shouldn't need to do this, as the chilling solidifies the butter and keeps the filo from bouncing about as you cut. Cut the pastry, all the way to the bottom of the pan, into thirds in one direction, then turn the pan 90 degrees and cut the pastry into thirds again. You should have 9 squares. Cut each square in half diagonally to form 18 triangles (see illustration, 205).

Place the pan in the oven and bake for 25 minutes, then turn the oven down to 300°F and continue to bake for another 20 to 25 minutes, until the top is a lovely golden color. Remove from the oven and place on a rack to cool completely.

To make the syrup, place the orange juice, sugar, and cardamom in a small saucepan over medium heat. Insert the candy thermometer and cook until it registers 218°F. Remove the pan from the heat and set the candy thermometer aside. Stir in the honey, return the pan to the heat, and cook, just until the mixture returns to a boil. Immediately pour the syrup evenly over the surface of the cooled baklava in a thin, steady stream, making sure not to neglect the outer edges. Sprinkle the reserved pistachios over the top and let the baklava sit, uncovered, at room temperature. Allow the baklava plenty of time to absorb the syrup before serving, at least 2 to 3 hours. Baklava is at its best 8 hours after it is made, when the syrup is evenly absorbed and the flavors have begun to meld.

SERVING AND STORAGE NOTES: Loosen the pieces of baklava by running your knife along the cut marks. Gently lift each piece out using the tip of your knife or a small spatula (the first piece is always the hardest to remove). Serve 1 or 2 triangles per person (if serving 2, set them at a 90-degree angle to each other for some drama on the plate). Store, loosely covered with plastic wrap or foil, at room temperature for 3 to 5 days.

GETTING AHEAD: The assembled and cut baklava can be covered tightly with plastic wrap and refrigerated overnight or frozen for up to 1 month (if freezing, wrap the entire pan twice with plastic wrap so the pastry will not dry out or pick up any odors). Refrigerated baklava will bake in the specified period of time, but allow a few extra minutes in the oven for baklava that has been frozen.

Do *not* grind the nuts in advance. As they sit, they compact, and you won't get as many layers of nuts as the recipe calls for (unless you have a scale and can divide the nuts into the layers needed by weight).

VARIATION

Almond and Apricot Baklava with Orange Cardamom Syrup: Almonds and apricots make superb flavor partners in baklava, though the color of the almonds is not nearly as dramatic as that of pistachios. Follow the recipe above, substituting ¾ cup plus 2 tablespoons (4½ ounces) whole natural almonds to grind with the dried apricots, and ½ cup (2½ ounces) whole natural almonds to grind with the tablespoon of sugar.

Pistachios

Small, green, tender pistachios are well loved throughout the Mediterranean, from France to the Middle East, and are found in everything from dense, silky ice cream to nougat to classic baklava. In fact, many think the best baklava and, not coincidentally, the best pistachios come from the Turkish city of Gaziantep, near the Syrian border. It is thought the nut originated in this area, for the pistachio gardens here are centuries old. The pistachio was a local secret, though, until A.D. 820, when the Syrian consul to Italy took seedlings with him to his new post. From Italy the pistachio spread across the Mediterranean.

That said, unless you buy imported pistachios or travel to the Mediterranean source, your pistachios are most likely to be a California-grown variety from Iran called Kerman, named for the major city at the center of Iran's largest pistachio-producing region. Pistachios are a relatively new nut crop in California—the first harvest of any size was in 1978. The industry has expanded quickly since then and is now able to supply the entire country with its pistachios.

When buying pistachios for baking, be sure to buy raw unsalted nuts and always avoid those that have been dyed that awful artificial red. Shelled nuts are more practical for baking, and they are available in most stores that carry nuts in their baking section. If you can't find pistachios without shells, you will have to shell them yourself—a relatively quick and easy task. Be aware, however, that you will need to purchase about twice the weight of nuts called for in the recipe to make up for the weight that is lost when the shells are discarded.

Because of their high oil content, pistachios should be kept in the refrigerator or freezer until needed to prevent them from turning rancid. I always buy my nuts at the farmers' market, where I can be assured of purchasing pistachios from the current year's harvest. Admittedly, this is a lot easier to do in California than in other parts of the country. An alternate source is a store that has a high turnover—natural food stores are usually a good bet.

To toast pistachios: Preheat the oven to 350°F. Spread the pistachios on a baking sheet in a single layer and place in the oven. Cook for 6 to 8 minutes, or until the nuts are hot to the touch, smell nutty, and look lightly golden. Toasting should warm the oils and bring their flavor to the foreground, as well as lightly crisp the meat. Toasted pistachios should not be brown on the inside or the outside, as they become bitter at this point. Remove the nuts from the oven and transfer them to a plate for cooling (if they are left on the hot pan, the residual heat will continue to cook them). Cool the toasted nuts completely before using them in a recipe. Pistachios may be toasted several days in advance and stored at room temperature. Since their flavor is best when freshly toasted, do not toast pistachios you will be storing in the refrigerator or freezer.

Quince and Walnut Baklava

makes 18 pieces

Quinces and walnuts are a classic combination in the Middle East, in both desserts and savory dishes, and this baklava offers the beautiful rose-colored flesh and exquisite apple-pineapple-citrus flavor of quince in a single layer in the center, surrounded by layers of walnuts and flaky filo. The fruit's poaching liquid is reduced to a pastel-colored, highly aromatic syrup and poured over the baklava, giving the pastry has a pretty, pale pink cast.

EQUIPMENT AND ADVANCE PREPARATION: One 8 x 8 x 2-inch baking pan • A soft-bristle brush • A candy thermometer • If you are using frozen filo, allow 24 hours for it to thaw in the refrigerator, then place the filo box on the counter to come to room temperature, about 1½ to 2 hours.

FOR THE POACHING LIQUID AND QUINCE

1 medium (about 9 to 11 ounces) quince (217)

2 cups (16 ounces) water

¾ cup (5¼ ounces) sugar

Zest of ½ orange, in strips

Zest of ½ lemon, in strips

Two 3-inch sticks cinnamon

2 tablespoons freshly squeezed and strained lemon juice

FOR THE NUT FILLING

2½ cups (9 ounces) walnuts

2 teaspoons sugar

1 teaspoon ground cinnamon

1 pound filo, room temperature

6 tablespoons (3 ounces) unsalted butter, melted and lukewarm

To prepare the poaching liquid, wash the quince and pat dry. Peel, halve, and core the quince (218), reserving the peels and core. Cut each half into 4 slices, then set aside in a small bowl covered with plastic wrap. The quince will turn brown, but don't worry—the fruit will turn pink when cooked.

Place the peels and core in a small saucepan with the water, sugar, orange and lemon zests, cinnamon sticks, and lemon juice. Heat until the mixture begins to simmer, then cover the pan and cook for 30 minutes (the peels and core are very flavorful and will make a quince "stock" in which to poach the fruit). Strain out the peels, core, and zests and return the liquid and cinnamon sticks to the pan.

To poach the quince, add the 8 slices of quince to the liquid and return the mixture to a simmer, then cover the top of the liquid with a round of parchment or wax paper to keep the fruit submerged and continue to cook at the lowest possible simmer until the fruit is tender and a lovely pink to orange color, about 1½ to 2 hours, depending on the variety and ripeness of the fruit. Do not simply cover the pan with a lid and cook—the parchment paper allows you to monitor the fruit's progress and watch that the liquid does not boil rapidly. Even more important, it also lets moisture evaporate and concentrates the fruit flavor.

When the quince is tender, use a slotted spoon or a fork to gently pluck the fruit from the liquid. Blot the slices dry on paper towels and set them on a plate to cool. You should have about ½ cup of poaching liquid left (if you have a bit more, simply boil it until you have about ½ cup). Discard the cinnamon sticks. Cover and set the liquid aside in the pan until needed.

To prepare the nut filling, place the walnuts in the bowl of a food processor and process until the nuts are finely chopped (the largest should be the size of small dried lentils), about 10 to 15 seconds. Remove 2 tablespoons and reserve in a small bowl for garnish. To the remaining nuts, add the sugar and cinnamon and pulse 3 or 4 times to blend. Transfer the mixture to a medium bowl.

To prepare the filo, remove it from its packaging and unfold it so that the stack lies flat on your work surface. Cut the stack in half crosswise, then trim each half to measure 8 by 8 inches. Stack them on top of each other, then cover with plastic wrap and a damp towel to prevent the filo from drying out. Discard the excess trimmings. Remove one sheet of filo and place it in the bottom of the pan to see that it fits snugly. It should touch the edges but not creep up the sides of the pan—trim the sheet of filo so that it fits correctly. Some square pans are smaller at the bottom than the top (where the measurements are taken), and if this is true of yours, use this first piece as a template to trim the remaining sheets of filo to the same size (they will be slightly smaller than the pan as you work toward the top, but this is fine).

To assemble the baklava, take out a sheet of filo and re-cover the rest (be sure to cover the remaining sheets each time you remove a new one). Place the filo in the bottom of the pan and brush it lightly with the melted butter. The sheerest coating of butter is all that is needed. Don't worry if the entire sheet is not evenly coated—too much butter will result in a heavy, greasy pastry. Repeat with 5 more sheets of filo. Sprinkle the top sheet of filo with ¼ cup of the nut filling (to measure, just scoop the nuts from the bowl and level the top with your hand or the back of a knife—do not compact the nuts in the cup). Top with 3 more sheets of filo, buttering each one lightly. Sprinkle with ¼ cup of the nut filling. Repeat this procedure 2 more times, then top the fourth layer of nuts with 3 sheets of lightly buttered filo. Slice the cooled quince crosswise into ¼-inch-thick pieces (they will look like small pink triangles), then lay them on top of the filo in an even layer. They should just cover the pastry in a single layer.

Continue assembling the baklava by adding another 3 sheets of buttered filo topped with ¼ cup of nut filling. Repeat 3 more times. When the last of the nut filling has been added to the pan, top it with 6 sheets of buttered filo to match the original 6 sheets in the bottom of the pan. You should have just enough butter to coat the top piece of filo. If you have any excess butter, refrigerate it and reserve for another use. Roll and rewrap any remaining filo sheets twice in plastic wrap. Return to the refrigerator and use within 3 days. Place the pan of baklava in the freezer for 30 minutes—this makes it much easier to cut the pastry.

Preheat the oven to 350°F. Position an oven rack in the center of the oven.

To cut the chilled baklava, use a thin, sharp knife. I have a number of good knives, but the best one I've found for this purpose is a steak knife with tiny, sharp serrations. You may want to try a couple of different knives as you work to see which one is best. When cutting, use a gentle sawing motion and try not to compress the pastry by pressing down on it with one hand while cutting with the other. You shouldn't need to do this, as the chilling solidifies the butter and keeps the filo from bouncing about as you cut. Cut the pastry, all the way to the bottom of the pan, into thirds in one direction, then turn the pan 90 degrees and cut the pastry into thirds again. You should have 9 squares. Cut each square in half diagonally to form 18 triangles (see illustration, 205).

Place the pan in the oven and bake for 25 minutes, then turn the oven down to 300°F and continue to bake for another 20 to 25 minutes, until the top is a golden color. Remove from the oven and place on a rack to cool completely.

To make the syrup, place the reserved poaching liquid over medium heat. Insert the candy thermometer and cook until it registers 218°F. Remove the pan from the heat and set the candy thermometer aside. Pour the syrup evenly over the surface of the cooled baklava, making sure not to neglect the outer edges. Sprinkle the reserved 2 tablespoons of nuts over the top and let the baklava sit, uncovered, at room temperature. Allow the baklava plenty of time to absorb the syrup before serving, at least 2 to 3 hours.

SERVING AND STORAGE NOTES: Loosen the pieces of baklava by running your knife along the cut marks. Gently lift each piece out using the tip of your knife or a small spatula (the first piece is always the hardest to remove). Serve 1 or 2 triangles per person (if serving 2, set them at a 90-degree angle to each other for some drama on the plate). Store, loosely covered with plastic wrap or foil, at room temperature for up to 2 days. This version, with the freshly poached fruit, does not keep as well as the dried fruit and nut versions and should be eaten within a couple of days.

GETTING AHEAD: The quince may be poached 1 day ahead. Remove the quince slices from the poaching liquid, blot them dry on paper towels, and wrap them tightly in plastic wrap. Refrigerate. Store the poaching liquid separately in a small airtight container in the refrigerator.

The assembled and cut baklava can be covered tightly with plastic wrap and refrigerated overnight. Baking time will not change.

Quinces

Quinces are an ancient fruit, believed to have originated in Iran and the Caspian region, for wild quinces can still be found there. Interestingly, while we think of this fruit as being inedibly astringent in its raw state, there are cultivated trees in these regions that bear fruit that, though tart, is sweet enough to eat fresh. Quinces can be found throughout the Mediterranean and are used in savory as well as dessert preparations. Western Europeans like to turn quinces into candies or jellies, while North Africans and Middle Easterners also enjoy them sliced and cooked with meat stews or stuffed with a rice and meat filling and baked. They were at one time also popular in America, though they have fallen out of favor in the last fifty to seventy-five years, probably because they take such a long time to cook. Under the heading "everything old is new again," quinces are now becoming trendy and can be found in the "specialty" area of the produce section, usually at specialty prices. Your best bet for finding fresh quinces in season (late fall into winter) is stores that specialize in Middle Eastern foods. They can also sometimes be found at farmers' markets, for older orchards often have several quince trees tucked in among the apples.

Quinces are either round (like an apple) or oblong (resembling a pear) in shape. They have yellow skin that is tinged with green and covered with a downy fuzz. The fuzz can be rubbed off with a towel or rinsed away under running water. The flesh is a creamy white that turns brown when cut, just as an apple's does. For the purposes of this book, however, you needn't drop quince slices in lemon water or rub them with lemon juice, for the recipes here require the prolonged cooking that turns them a deep rose to red-orange color, obscuring any browning that may have occurred.

When buying quinces, choose fruit that is firm and free of blemishes, although very ripe, yellow quinces will always have a few brown spots. Handle the fruit gently, for though they are hard, they also bruise easily. If the quinces are green, ripen them by placing them, uncovered, on a plate in a cool place in your house. Their sweet perfume will scent the air as they reach their peak of ripeness. Once ripe, use within a few days or store in a paper bag in the refrigerator for up to one week.

When preparing quinces, use a sharp, heavy knife and a good vegetable peeler, because their flesh is very hard. I use a heavy knife to cut the fruit, a sharp peeler to remove the skin, and a sturdy melon baller to remove the tenacious core (you can also cut the core out with your knife).

Sour Cherry and Almond Baklava

makes 18 pieces

I love dried sour cherries from Michigan because they pack the same sort of intense sweet-sour punch as dried California apricots. I find myself tossing the little morsels into all sorts of desserts, from biscotti to tarts, so it was a short kitchen walk to basing a baklava on their chewy lusciousness. Baklava is a great vehicle for dried sour cherries, for their bright, acerbic flavor and gentle chewiness are the perfect counterpoint to flaky, buttery pastry and sweet, honeyed syrup. Here, layer upon layer of chopped almonds is built, then a layer of dried sour cherries blended with crushed amaretti cookies and apricot jam is hidden in the center of the pastry. Almonds, apricots, and cherries create a natural harmony of flavors, as all three are members of the same botanical family.

EQUIPMENT AND ADVANCE PREPARATION: One 8 x 8 x 2-inch baking pan • A soft-bristle brush • A candy thermometer • If you are using frozen filo, allow 24 hours for it to thaw in the refrigerator, then place the filo box on the counter to come to room temperature, about 1½ to 2 hours.

FOR THE NUT FILLING

1¼ cups (6½ ounces) whole natural almonds

2 tablespoons (1 ounce) sugar

1½ teaspoons ground cinnamon

FOR THE SOUR CHERRY FILLING

6 ounces dried sour cherries (327)

8 amaretti cookies

¼ cup (2 ounces) low-sugar apricot jam (Smucker's brand if available)

1 pound filo, room temperature

6 tablespoons (3 ounces) unsalted butter, melted and lukewarm

FOR THE SYRUP

⅓ cup (2¾ ounces) water

½ cup (3½ ounces) sugar

¼ cup (3 ounces) honey

2 tablespoons Amaretto di Saronno

FOR FINISHING

3 tablespoons (1½ ounces) chopped toasted almonds (254)

To prepare the nut filling, place the almonds in the bowl of a food processor and process until the nuts are finely chopped (the largest should be the size of small dried lentils), about 15 to 20 seconds. Add the sugar and cinnamon and pulse 3 or 4 times to blend. Transfer the mixture to a medium bowl.

To prepare the sour cherry filling, place the dried sour cherries and amaretti cookies in the bowl of the food processor and process until the mixture is very finely chopped—20 seconds to 1½ minutes, depending on the texture of the dried sour cherries you are using. Each component should still be discernible, though in very small pieces—not a puree. Add the apricot jam to the bowl and pulse until thoroughly combined. You will have a moist, coarse paste. Transfer the mixture to a small bowl.

To prepare the filo, remove it from its packaging and unfold it so that the stack lies flat on your work surface. Cut the stack in half crosswise, then trim each half to measure 8 by 8 inches. Stack them on top of each other, then cover with plastic wrap and a damp towel to prevent the filo from drying out. Discard the excess trimmings. Remove one sheet of filo and place it in the bottom of the pan to see that it fits snugly. It should touch the edges but not creep up the sides of the pan—trim the sheet of filo so that it fits correctly. Some square pans are smaller at the bottom than the top (where the measurements are taken), and if this is true of yours, use this first piece as a template to trim the remaining sheets of filo in the stack to the same size (they will be slightly smaller than the pan as you work toward the top, but this is fine).

To assemble the baklava, take out a sheet of filo and re-cover the rest (be sure to cover the remaining sheets each time you remove a new one). Place the filo in the bottom of the pan and brush it lightly with the melted butter. The sheerest coating of butter is all that is needed. Don't worry if the entire sheet is not evenly coated—too much butter will result in a heavy, greasy pastry. Repeat with 5 more sheets of filo. Sprinkle the top sheet of filo with a scant ⅓ cup of the nut filling (to measure, just scoop the nuts from the bowl; they should be about ¼ inch from the top of the cup—do not compact the nuts in the cup). Top with 3 more sheets of filo, buttering each one lightly. Sprinkle with another scant ⅓ cup of the nut filling. Repeat once more. Top with 3 sheets of lightly buttered filo, then use a small offset spatula or the back of a spoon to spread the entire sour cherry filling in an even layer on top. Add 3 sheets of buttered filo followed by a scant ⅓ cup of nut filling 3 more times. At this point, you should have used up all the nut filling.

When the last of the nut filling has been added to the pan, top it with 6 sheets of buttered filo to match the original 6 sheets in the bottom of the pan. You should have just enough butter to coat the top piece of filo. If you have any excess butter, refrigerate it and reserve for another use. Roll and rewrap any remaining filo sheets twice in plastic wrap. Return to the refrigerator and use within 3 days. Place the pan of baklava in the freezer for 30 minutes—this makes it much easier to cut the pastry.

Preheat the oven to 350°F. Position an oven rack in the center of the oven.

To cut the chilled baklava, use a thin, sharp knife. I have a number of good knives, but the best one I've found for this purpose is a steak knife with tiny, sharp serrations. You may want to try a couple of different knives as you work to see which one is best. When cutting, use a gentle sawing motion and try not to compress the pastry by pressing down on it with one hand while cutting with the other. You shouldn't need to do this, as the chilling solidifies the butter and keeps the filo from bouncing about as you cut. Cut the pastry, all the way to the bottom of the pan, into thirds in one direction, then turn the pan 90 degrees and cut the pastry into thirds again. You should have 9 squares. Cut each square in half diagonally to form 18 triangles (see illustration, 205).

Place the pan in the oven and bake for 25 minutes, then turn the oven down to 300°F and continue to bake for another 20 to 25 minutes, until the top is a lovely golden color. Remove from the oven and place on a rack to cool completely. Use the same thin, sharp knife to gently retrace the cutting lines in the pastry, all the way to the bottom of the pan. This will ensure that the sour cherry filling in the center does not prevent the syrup from reaching the lower half of the pastry.

To make the syrup, place the water and sugar in a small saucepan over medium heat. Insert the candy thermometer and cook until it registers 218°F. Remove the pan from the heat and set the candy thermometer aside. Stir the honey and amaretto into the syrup, then return the pan to the heat and bring to a boil. Pour the syrup evenly over the surface of the cooled baklava, making sure not to neglect the outer edges. Sprinkle the chopped toasted almonds over the top and let the baklava sit, uncovered, at room temperature. Allow the baklava plenty of time to absorb the syrup before serving, at least 2 to 3 hours. Baklava is at its best 8 hours after it is made, when the syrup is evenly absorbed and the flavors have begun to meld.

SERVING AND STORAGE NOTES: Loosen the pieces of baklava by running your knife along the cut marks. Gently lift each piece out using the tip of your knife or a small spatula (the first piece is always the hardest to remove). Serve 1 or 2 triangles per person (if serving 2, set them at a 90-degree angle to each other for some drama on the plate). Store, loosely covered with plastic wrap or foil, at room temperature for up to 5 days.

GETTING AHEAD: The assembled and cut baklava can be covered tightly with plastic wrap and refrigerated overnight or frozen for up to 1 month (if freezing, wrap the entire pan twice with plastic wrap so the pastry will not dry out or pick up any odors). Refrigerated baklava will bake in the specified period of time, but allow a few extra minutes in the oven for baklava that has been frozen.

Do *not* grind the nuts for the almond layers in advance. As they sit, they compact, and you won't get as many layers of nuts as the recipe calls for (unless you have a scale and can divide the nuts into the layers needed by weight).

Baklava Syrup: Hot versus Cold

Experienced baklava cooks will tell you that for the filo to absorb the syrup evenly, either the pastry has to be hot and the syrup cold, or the pastry cold and the syrup hot. The question I always wanted answered was, which is best? Pastry chefs tend to be a rather opinionated lot, and the answer I heard most frequently was to pour cold syrup over baklava hot from the oven. So this is the way I proceeded for many baklavas, but they just weren't quite as crispy as I wanted. Even after reducing the quantity of the syrup I was adding, I was still dissatisfied, so I decided to give the cold pastry/hot syrup a try. I was an immediate convert. Letting the pastry cool and settle in a dry state keeps the layers separate and crisp even after the addition of the syrup. When the pastry is hot, it absorbs the syrup more readily and softens more quickly, just as hot potatoes or vegetables absorb a vinaigrette more readily than cold ones. At last I discovered the secret to the crispy baklava I love, and I've been pouring hot syrup over cold pastry ever since.

Hazelnut and Chocolate Baklava

makes 18 pieces

Here, hazelnuts and bittersweet chocolate are chopped together and sprinkled layer after luscious layer between sheets of buttery-crisp filo to create a powerfully satisfying baklava. Their earthy pairing is enhanced with a touch of cinnamon and a syrup laced with espresso and Frangelico (hazelnut liqueur).

EQUIPMENT AND ADVANCE PREPARATION: One 8 x 8 x 2-inch baking pan • A soft-bristle brush • A candy thermometer • If you are using frozen filo, allow 24 hours for it to thaw in the refrigerator, then place the filo box on the counter to come to room temperature, about 1½ to 2 hours.

FOR THE FILLING

1½ cups (7¼ ounces) whole hazelnuts (remove the skins without toasting the nuts, as directed on page 228)

4 ounces bittersweet or semisweet chocolate, coarsely chopped

2 tablespoons (1 ounce) sugar

1 teaspoon ground cinnamon

1 pound filo, room temperature

6 tablespoons (3 ounces) unsalted butter, melted and lukewarm

FOR THE SYRUP

⅓ cup water

½ cup (3½ ounces) sugar

1 teaspoon instant espresso granules, preferably Medaglia d'Oro brand

¼ cup (3 ounces) honey

1 tablespoon Frangelico

To prepare the filling, place the skinned hazelnuts and chocolate in the bowl of a food processor and process until they are finely chopped (the largest should be the size of small dried lentils), about 10 to 15 seconds. Remove 2 tablespoons and reserve in a small bowl for garnish. To the remaining nuts, add the sugar and cinnamon and pulse 3 or 4 times to blend. Transfer the mixture to a medium bowl.

To prepare the filo, remove it from its packaging and unfold it so that the stack lies flat on your work surface. Cut the stack in half crosswise, then trim each half to measure 8 by 8 inches. Stack them on top of each other, then cover with plastic wrap and a damp towel to prevent the filo from drying out. Discard the excess trimmings. Remove one sheet of filo and place it in the bottom of the pan to see that it fits snugly. It should touch the edges but not creep up the sides of the pan—trim the sheet of filo so that it fits correctly. Some square pans are smaller at the bottom than the top (where the measurements are taken), and if this is true of yours, use this first piece as a template to trim the remaining sheets of filo in the stack to the same size (they will be slightly smaller than the pan as you work toward the top, but this is fine).

To assemble the baklava, take out a sheet of filo and re-cover the rest (be sure to cover the remaining sheets each time you remove a new one). Place the filo in the bottom of the pan and brush it lightly with the melted butter. The sheerest coating of butter is all that is needed. Don't worry if the entire sheet is not evenly coated—too much butter will result in a heavy, greasy pastry. Repeat with 5 more sheets of filo. Sprinkle the top sheet of filo with ⅓ cup of the hazelnut-chocolate filling (to measure, just scoop the filling from the bowl and level the top with your hand or the back of a knife—do not compact the filling in the cup). Top with 3 more sheets of filo, buttering each one lightly. Sprinkle with ⅓ cup of the nut-chocolate filling. Continue in this manner—3 sheets of buttered filo followed by ⅓ cup nut-chocolate filling—until you have used up all the filling (you will have 8 layers of filling).

When the last of the filling has been added to the pan, top it with 6 sheets of buttered filo to match the original 6 sheets in the bottom of the pan. You should have just enough butter to coat the top piece of filo. If you have any excess butter, refrigerate it and reserve for another use. Roll and rewrap any remaining filo sheets twice in plastic wrap. Return to the refrigerator and use within 3 days. Place the pan of baklava in the freezer for 30 minutes—this makes it much easier to cut the pastry.

Preheat the oven to 350°F. Position an oven rack in the center of the oven.

To cut the chilled baklava, use a thin, sharp knife. I have a number of good knives, but the best one I've found for this purpose is a steak knife with tiny, sharp serrations. You may want to try a couple of different knives as you work to see which one is best. When cutting, use a gentle sawing motion and try not to compress the pastry by pressing down on it with one hand while cutting with the other. You shouldn't need to do this, as the chilling solidifies the butter and keeps the filo from bouncing about as you cut. Cut the pastry, all the way to the bottom of the pan, into thirds in one direction, then turn the pan 90 degrees and cut the pastry into thirds again. You should have 9 squares. Cut each square in half diagonally to form 18 triangles (see illustration, 205).

Place the pan in the oven and bake for 25 minutes, then turn the oven down to 300°F and continue to bake for another 20 to 25 minutes, until the top is a golden color. Remove from the oven and place on a rack to cool completely.

To make the syrup, place the water, sugar, and espresso granules in a small saucepan over medium heat. Insert the candy thermometer and cook until it registers 218°F. Remove the pan from the heat and set the candy thermometer aside. Stir the honey and Frangelico into the syrup, then return the pan to the heat and bring to a boil. Pour the mixture evenly over the surface of the cooled baklava, making sure not to neglect the outer edges. Sprinkle the reserved 2 tablespoons of nuts and chocolate over the top and let the baklava sit, uncovered, at room temperature. Allow the baklava plenty of time to absorb the syrup before serving, at least 2 to 3 hours. Baklava is at its best 8 hours after it is made, when the syrup is evenly absorbed and the flavors have begun to meld.

SERVING AND STORAGE NOTES: Loosen the pieces of baklava by running your knife along the cut marks. Gently lift each piece out using the tip of your knife or a small spatula (the first piece is always the hardest to remove). Serve 1 or 2 triangles per person (if serving 2, set them at a 90-degree angle to each other for some drama on the plate). Store, loosely covered with plastic wrap or foil, at room temperature for up to 5 days.

GETTING AHEAD: The assembled and cut baklava can be covered tightly with plastic wrap and refrigerated overnight or frozen for up to 1 month (if freezing, wrap the entire pan twice with plastic wrap so the pastry will not dry out or pick up any odors). Refrigerated baklava will bake in the specified period of time, but allow a few extra minutes in the oven for baklava that has been frozen.

Do *not* grind the filling in advance. As it sits it will compact, and you won't get as many layers of filling as the recipe calls for (unless you have a scale and can divide the filling into the layers needed by weight).

Almond and Chocolate Baklava: This favorite candy bar combination takes on a more exotic form when layered with flaky pastry. Follow the recipe above, substituting 1½ cups (7¾ ounces) whole natural almonds for the hazelnuts. There is no need to remove the skins from the almonds, though you may use blanched almonds if you prefer them.

Walnut and Chocolate Baklava: Follow the recipe above, substituting 2 cups (7¼ ounces) walnuts for the hazelnuts. There is no need to remove the skins from the walnuts.

Hazelnuts

When I think of hazelnuts, I think of Oregon, and indeed this state grows enough hazelnuts to supply the entire country with this little round nut. The first tree, still standing, was planted there in 1858, but it wasn't until 1885 and the introduction of the Barcelona variety of hazelnut that production really took off. Of course, the hazelnut has a much longer history than that, having been cultivated in China for at least 4,500 years. It is the Mediterranean countries, however, that supply much of the world with hazelnuts. In fact, Turkey is the world's largest producer of hazelnuts.

Hazelnuts are sometimes referred to as filberts. The husks that grow around the nut are the main distinction between the two names, for the shelled nuts are almost all identical. In general, those trees that have husks that are longer than the shell are called filberts, while those whose husks allow the shells to be seen are called hazelnuts. It is believed the *hazel* comes from the Anglo-Saxon word *haesel*, meaning hood or bonnet.

When buying hazelnuts, always buy raw unsalted nuts. Hazelnuts have a high oil content and should be kept in the freezer until needed to prevent them from turning rancid. Try to buy your nuts from a store that has a high turnover to ensure you are purchasing nuts from the current year's harvest. Natural food stores that sell in bulk are usually a good bet.

To toast hazelnuts: Preheat the oven to 350°F. Spread the hazelnuts on a baking sheet in a single layer and place in the oven. Cook for 8 to 10 minutes, or until the skins have cracked. Remove from the oven and immediately transfer the nuts to a clean kitchen towel and wrap them tightly (the steam created will help to loosen the skins). After 5 minutes, rub the nuts furiously inside the towel to remove as much of their skin as possible. Don't worry about any skin remaining on the nuts—it will add color and flavor to your baking. Cool the toasted nuts completely before using them in a recipe. Hazelnuts may be toasted several days in advance and stored at room temperature. Since their flavor is best when freshly toasted, do not toast hazelnuts that you will be storing in the freezer.

To skin the hazelnuts without toasting them: This technique is adapted from *The Cake Bible* by Rose Levy Beranbaum. Amounts given are for 1½ cups (7¼ ounces) whole hazelnuts. Preheat the oven to 200°F. Bring 4½ cups (36 ounces) water to a rolling boil in a medium saucepan over high heat. Add ¼ cup (2¼ ounces) baking soda and then the hazelnuts. Cook at a boil for 3 minutes. Test a nut to see if the skin slips off easily—if not, cook a little longer. When the skins are loose, pour the nuts into a strainer in the sink and run cold water over them as you pop off their skins. As you work, transfer the cleaned nuts to a kitchen towel. Pat the nuts dry, then place them on a baking sheet in the oven for 12 to 18 minutes, or until dry and lightly crisped (do not let them brown). Cool completely before using in recipes.

Galataboureko with Spiced Blood Orange Caramel Sauce

serves 6 to 9

Galataboureko is a traditional Greek dessert featuring a semolina pudding baked between layers of filo and then moistened, baklava style, with a honey syrup. I always liked the idea of this dessert, but between the moisture in the pudding and the syrup, the texture seemed sodden to me. Needless to say, I've made a few changes. Instead of sheets of filo surrounding the pudding, I've substituted shredded filo, which has a texture similar to shredded wheat, bakes up light and crisp, and holds its texture against moisture much better than regular filo. Then, instead of pouring a syrup over the hot pastry, I let the pastry cool "dry" and pour a blood orange caramel sauce over each slice just before serving. The caramel sauce provides just enough moisture and sweetness to soften and accent the buttery shredded filo for a toothsome bite, while the color of the blood oranges is a striking contrast to the pastry's creamy white pudding filling.

EQUIPMENT AND ADVANCE PREPARATION: One 8 x 8 x 2-inch baking pan • 8 ounces of shredded filo, or ½ box (rewrap the remaining filo and return it to the refrigerator where it will keep for several weeks). • To thaw frozen shredded filo, place it on the counter and let it come to room temperature (2 to 3 hours) or thaw overnight in the refrigerator.

> 8 ounces (½ box) shredded filo (also called *kunafeh* or *kataifi*), room temperature
>
> 12 tablespoons (6 ounces) unsalted butter, melted
>
> **FOR THE SEMOLINA PUDDING**
> 2 ¾ cups (22 ounces) whole milk
>
> 6 tablespoons (3 ounces) sugar
>
> 1 teaspoon finely chopped lemon zest (145)
>
> Two 3-inch sticks cinnamon
>
> Pinch of salt
>
> ½ cup (3 ounces) fine semolina

3 large eggs

1½ teaspoons pure vanilla extract

FOR SERVING
Spiced blood orange caramel sauce (231)

Preheat the oven to 350°F. Position an oven rack in the center of the oven.

To prebake the filo, lightly brush the baking pan with a little of the melted butter. Place half of the shredded filo (4 ounces) in a medium bowl and use your hands to gently separate and fluff the strands, discarding any hard pieces or clumps of dough. Pour half of the melted butter over the filo and toss gently with your hands until it is evenly coated. Arrange the filo in an even layer in the bottom of the baking pan. Bake for 20 to 30 minutes, or until the pastry is lightly golden and crisp (do not let it brown). Remove from the oven and place on a rack to cool completely.

To make the semolina pudding, place the milk, sugar, lemon zest, cinnamon sticks, and salt in a small saucepan over medium heat and bring to a simmer. Whisk in the semolina in a steady stream and bring the mixture back to a boil. Cook, whisking constantly, for 3 to 4 minutes, or until the pudding is very thick and holds a shape on the surface when a bit is dropped from the whisk. Remove the pan from the heat and place a piece of plastic wrap directly on the surface of the pudding to keep a skin from forming. Let the pudding cool for 30 minutes, then remove and discard the cinnamon sticks. Whisk in the eggs and vanilla until thoroughly blended. Pour the pudding over the cooled filo in the baking pan.

To finish the galataboureko, place the remaining half (4 ounces) of shredded filo in the medium bowl and again gently separate the strands with your hands, discarding any hard clumps. Pour the rest of the melted butter over the filo and toss gently with your hands until it is evenly coated. Place small handfuls of filo over the surface of the pudding, spreading it gently to form an even layer. Place the pan in the oven and bake for 45 to 50 minutes, or until the pudding is set when the pan is gently shaken and the filo is a lovely golden color. Remove from the oven and place on a rack to cool.

SERVING AND STORAGE NOTES: This dessert is very good warm or at room temperature. To serve warm, cool on the rack for about 30 minutes (the pastry can also be reheated in a 325°F oven for about 15 minutes). Otherwise, cool completely. Use a thin, sharp knife to cut the pastry into thirds, then turn the pan 90 degrees and cut into thirds again to form 9 pieces. For hearty eaters or for a breakfast portion (delicious!), cut it into 6 pieces. Slide a small spatula into the pan to lift out each piece (the first one is always the hardest—and messiest—to remove). Place on a plate and spoon a tablespoon or two of the spiced blood orange caramel sauce over each piece. Store at room temperature for 1 day, or cover with plastic wrap and refrigerate for up to 3 days. Reheat the galataboureko in a 325°F oven for 15 to 20 minutes before serving if it has been refrigerated.

Spiced Blood Orange Caramel Sauce

makes about 1¼ cups

I like to make caramel sauces with fruit juice or fruit puree in place of the cream. Their flavor is pure and clean, and rather than coating your mouth with the richness of cream, these fruit sauces heighten and enhance whatever they're paired with. I especially enjoy them with fruit desserts, such as Mascarpone-Stuffed Dates (134) and flaky, buttery pastry desserts, such as Galataboureko (229). This blood orange sauce is one of my favorites. Its beautiful hue of deep red tinged with brown is striking, and when it hits your tongue, there is an explosion of flavors as vibrant as the color—sweetness tempered with the slight bitterness of caramel; full, round orange tones heightened with a bit of orange liqueur; and a wonderful, warming complexity of spices.

¼ cup (2 ounces) water

½ cup (3½ ounces) sugar

½ cup (4 ounces) freshly squeezed and strained blood orange juice, room temperature (if blood oranges are unavailable, substitute navel oranges)

⅛ teaspoon ground cinnamon

⅛ teaspoon ground cloves

2 tablespoons orange liqueur, such as Grand Marnier or Cointreau

Place the water in a small saucepan, add the sugar, and set the pan over medium heat. Stir constantly with a wooden spoon or swirl the pan frequently until the sugar has dissolved and the liquid is clear. Turn the heat to high and boil rapidly, swirling the pan occasionally (do not stir at this point) so that the sugar cooks evenly, until it turns a golden brown. Remove the pan from the heat and immediately add the orange juice, spices, and liqueur—be careful, the mixture will rise dramatically in the pan and sputter (you may want to wear an oven mitt on the hand holding the pan). Stir with the wooden spoon to blend. If the caramel has solidified, set the pan back over low heat and stir until it melts again. Cool. Transfer to an airtight container and refrigerate until needed.

GETTING AHEAD: The caramel sauce may be made up to 5 days in advance. Keep refrigerated in an airtight container.

Snake Pastry with Fig, Almond Paste, and Lemon

serves 8 to 10

Looking for all the world like a golden brown snake coiled up for a nap, this dessert is an adaptation of a Berber dessert from North Africa, where it is called m'hencha, *or the serpent. The flavors here are a luxuriant cross between a sophisticated Fig Newton and the richest, chewiest almond macaroon, with an accent of lemon and anise. Relatively easy to make, it is a beautiful and unusual ending to a Mediterranean meal. I prefer to use dried Black Mission figs, which are usually moist and pliable—very important here—as well as flavorful. Whatever variety you choose, avoid dried fruit that is very hard or brittle, because there is no addition of liquid in this recipe to plump it up.*

EQUIPMENT AND ADVANCE PREPARATION: One 9 x 2-inch round cake pan. Brush the sides and bottom of the pan with a generous coating of melted butter. • A soft-bristle brush • A serving platter that is perfectly flat (or nearly so). A curving platter might distort the shape of the pastry as it sits and will make slicing the snake more difficult. • If you are using frozen filo, allow 24 hours for it to thaw in the refrigerator, then place the filo box on the counter to come to room temperature, about 1½ to 2 hours.

FOR THE FILLING

8 ounces moist dried figs, preferably Black Mission

7 ounces almond paste, cut into ½-inch pieces

¼ teaspoon anise seed

Zest of 1 lemon, very finely chopped (145)

3 tablespoons (1½ ounces) sugar

2 tablespoons (1½ ounces) honey

10 sheets filo (the sheets should be 17 inches long if possible), room temperature

2 large egg yolks

6 tablespoons (3 ounces) unsalted butter, melted and lukewarm

Powdered sugar, optional

Candied lemon zest (236)

Preheat the oven to 375°F. Position an oven rack in the center of the oven.

To prepare the filling, trim the hard stems from the figs and discard. Place the figs, almond paste, anise seed, lemon zest, sugar, and honey in the bowl of a food processor and process until the mixture is very finely chopped, about 15 to 20 seconds. Each component should be discernible, though in very small pieces—do not grind to a homogeneous paste. Remove the mixture from the processor bowl and divide it into 5 equal portions (about 3½ ounces, or a little less than ½ cup, each) on a plate.

To prepare the filo, remove it from its packaging and unfold it so that the stack lies flat on your work surface. Remove 10 sheets. Stack them on top of each other on your work surface, then cover with plastic wrap and a damp towel to prevent the filo from drying out. Roll and rewrap any remaining filo sheets twice in plastic wrap. Return to the refrigerator and use within 3 days.

To assemble the snake pastry, place the egg yolks in a small bowl and stir just to blend. Take out a sheet of filo and re-cover the rest (be sure to cover the remaining sheets each time you remove a new one). Place the sheet on your work surface, with one of the long sides toward you. Brush the surface lightly with melted butter. Place another sheet of filo on top and brush lightly with melted butter. Take one of the portions of fig mixture and make a long, even mound with it on the filo, about 1 inch from the edge nearest you, that extends all the way to the two short edges of the dough.  Fold the bottom of the filo over the filling, then proceed to roll it up, jelly-roll fashion, as shown, to within 1 inch of the opposite long edge. Do not try to roll it very tightly, or the filo will crack as you try to bend it—give it a little push and let it roll up naturally. Use your finger or a small brush to apply a small amount of egg yolk along the top edge, then continue to roll the dough on top of it so the seam side is down. Arrange the roll, seam side down, along the outer edge of the buttered cake pan as shown on the following page. Brush the inside of the roll with a light coating of egg yolk.

Prepare 4 more rolls as directed above and place each one in the cake pan, extending the coil by attaching the new roll to the end of the last roll with a dab of egg yolk. Brush the inside of each roll with egg yolk so that as the rolls coil around and touch each other, they will adhere to the roll on each side of them—this is very important when slicing the pastry for serving. Brush the final roll with egg everywhere except the bottom before you put it in the pan, as the last roll fits snugly and there will not be room to add the egg afterward. The last roll should curl tightly around itself, filling the center of the pan. If your filo sheets are short (the sheets for this recipe should be 17 inches in length) and the 5 rolls do not fill the cake pan, quickly adjust the coil (while the egg yolk is still damp) so that the center is filled—if the outer edges do not touch the cake pan, that's okay. Brush the top of the pastry evenly with the remaining egg yolk.

Place the pan in the oven and bake for 25 to 30 minutes, or until golden. Remove from the oven and place on a rack to cool completely.

To unmold, run a thin, sharp knife around the edges of the pan, loosening any filo that may have stuck. As you do this, gently press the knife into the side of the pan to avoid gouging the pastry. Gently set a plate upside down on top of the cake pan and, holding the pan and plate together, flip the two over. The pastry should slide out onto the plate. (If the pastry sticks to the bottom of the pan, place the pan in a hot oven or over a burner for a few seconds, just long enough to warm and loosen the butter and egg, then try turning it out again.) Place your serving platter upside down on top of the pastry, then flip the two over so that the pastry is right side up.

SERVING AND STORAGE NOTES: Dust the top of the snake very lightly with powdered sugar if you like, allowing the golden filo to show through. Use a thin, sharp knife to cut wedges of the pastry, transferring each to a plate using a pie wedge or cake server (the coil is delicately bound with the egg yolk and could break apart if not supported). Top each slice with a few pieces of candied lemon zest and sprinkle a few pieces around each plate as well. Store at room temperature, lightly covered with plastic wrap or foil, for up to 4 days. This pastry is at its best about 8 hours after it has been baked, as the flavors begin to meld.

Snake Pastry with Apricots, Almond Paste, and Orange: The bright flavor of dried apricots is a perfect pairing with the sweet, slightly bitter essence of almond paste. Try to find tart California dried apricots for this recipe. If your only option is Mediterranean or Turkish apricots, reduce the sugar in the recipe to 1 tablespoon. Otherwise, follow the recipe above, substituting 8 ounces dried apricots for the figs and the finely chopped zest of 1 orange for the lemon. Omit the anise seed altogether. Garnish with candied orange zest (below).

Candied Lemon or Orange Zest

Translucent little strips of lemon or orange zest are a sweet addition to cakes, tarts, or baked goods of all kinds, as well as a lovely garnish. Much easier—and faster—to make than candied peel (which uses the whole rind, rather than just the colored part), these sweet little bites of citrus hold well in the refrigerator for at least 1 month. You can double or triple the recipe as needed.

> 1½ cups (12 ounces) water
>
> 1½ cups (10½ ounces) sugar
>
> ¼ cup (3 ounces) corn syrup
>
> 1 tablespoon freshly squeezed lemon juice
>
> Zest of 4 large lemons or oranges, in strips (see Note)

NOTE: If your zester is not sharp enough to remove the zest of a fruit in long strips, then use a vegetable peeler, but be sure to scrape off any of the bitter white pith clinging to the back of the zest with a small, sharp knife or the edge of a spoon. A vegetable peeler will result in wide strips of zest, so use a knife to slice them into thin strips (julienne) before poaching.

Place the water, sugar, corn syrup, and lemon juice in a small saucepan over medium heat. Cook, stirring occasionally, until the sugar has dissolved and the liquid is clear. Then add the zest and bring the mixture to a very low boil, with bubbles barely breaking the surface. Cover and cook for 30 to 40 minutes, or until the zest is translucent and tender. Remove from the heat and pour the zest and syrup into a storage container. Cool to room temperature, then cover and refrigerate. The candied zest will keep for at least 1 month.

To use the candied zest, remove the needed amount from the storage container. Rinse the zest under cold running water to remove excess syrup and pat dry. Use as directed. When using as garnish, leave the zest in long strips, which look beautiful on a serving plate.

Konafa with Tangerine Lime Syrup

serves 6 to 8

Konafa is an Arabic dessert consisting of two layers of shredded filo sandwiching ricotta cheese and coated with a sugar syrup as it comes from the oven (other versions contain a layer of nuts or a cooked cream filling in the center). This dish is also known as kadaif in Greece and Turkey. Some versions of konafa call for a tiny bit of orange flower water to be added to the ricotta, but I felt it needed a bigger punch of flavor for my American table. As I was working on the recipe, there happened to be a bowl of tangerines on a table nearby, and I suddenly realized that the concentrated sweet-and-sour essence of this fruit combined with a twist of lime might be the perfect contrast to the ricotta filling. Give this recipe a try, and I think you'll agree that the combination of crunchy, buttery pastry, warm, creamy ricotta, and sweet-sour tangerine syrup is hard to resist. I serve this true to the original style—hot out of the oven and topped with cold syrup, which creates a slight sizzling sound and a heady aroma.

EQUIPMENT AND ADVANCE PREPARATION: One 8 x 3-inch round cake pan. Brush the sides and bottom of the pan with a generous coating of melted butter. • A candy thermometer • A serving plate that is lower in the center than the sides so that the syrup poured over the cake will not run off the edges of the platter • 8 ounces of shredded filo, or ½ box (rewrap the remaining filo and return it to the refrigerator, where it will keep for several weeks) • To thaw frozen shredded filo, place it on the counter and let it come to room temperature (2 to 3 hours) or thaw overnight in the refrigerator. • If you find only pistachios in shells, buy double the weight given below and shell them by hand.

FOR THE SYRUP

1⅓ cups (about 10¼ ounces) freshly squeezed and strained tangerine juice (see Note)

1½ cups (10½ ounces) sugar

¼ cup (2 ounces) freshly squeezed and strained lime juice

8 ounces (½ box) shredded filo (also called *kunafeh* or *kataifi*), room temperature

12 tablespoons (6 ounces) unsalted butter, melted

One 15-ounce container whole-milk ricotta

FOR SERVING

3 tablespoons (about ¾ ounce) raw unsalted shelled pistachios, toasted (213) and coarsely chopped

NOTE: If you purchase freshly squeezed tangerine juice at the supermarket, make sure you buy enough to measure 1⅓ cups *after* you have strained off all the pulp. Two 8-ounce containers should be sufficient.

To make the syrup, place the tangerine juice in a small saucepan over medium heat and bring to a boil. Lower the heat and simmer the juice until it has reduced by half—you should have ⅔ cup concentrated tangerine juice. Add the sugar and lime juice to the tangerine juice and turn the heat to medium. Insert the candy thermometer and cook until it registers 218°F. Remove the pan from the heat and set the candy thermometer aside. Pour the syrup into a medium bowl and cool to room temperature. Cover and refrigerate until needed.

Preheat the oven to 350°F. Position an oven rack in the center of the oven.

To prebake the filo, place half of the shredded filo (4 ounces) in a medium bowl and use your hands to gently separate and fluff the strands, discarding any hard pieces or clumps of dough. Pour half of the melted butter (3 ounces, or 6 tablespoons) over the filo and toss gently with your hands until it is evenly coated. Arrange the filo in an even layer in the bottom of the buttered baking pan. Bake for 25 to 35 minutes, or until the pastry is golden and crisp (do not let it brown). Remove from the oven and place on a rack to cool completely.

To finish the konafa, spoon the ricotta in an even layer over the cooled filo, leaving a ¾-inch border around the edges. Place the remaining half (4 ounces) of shredded filo in the medium bowl and again gently separate the strands with your hands, discarding any hard clumps. Pour the rest of the melted butter over the filo and toss gently with your hands until it is evenly coated. Place small handfuls of filo over the surface of the ricotta, spreading it gently to form an even layer. Place the pan in the oven and bake for 40 to 50 minutes, or until the filo is golden.

SERVING AND STORAGE NOTES: Serve this dessert hot from the oven. To unmold, remove the pan from the oven and run a thin, sharp knife around the edges of the pan to loosen any filo that may have stuck. Place a plate on top of the pan, then flip it over and remove the cake pan. Place your serving dish on the bottom of the konafa, then turn it right side up. Sprinkle the chopped toasted pistachios over the surface. Bring the hot konafa to the table and pour 1 cup of the tangerine lime syrup evenly over the surface of the cake. Serve the remaining syrup in a pitcher so guests can add extra syrup if they like. Slice or spoon the pastry onto each guest's plate.

Fresh Cherries and Sweet Cheese in Shredded Filo

serves 6

In this very American adaptation of baklava, sweet summer cherries topped with a layer of luscious cheesecake-like filling are encased in a crisp, buttery shell of cinnamon-scented shredded filo.

EQUIPMENT AND ADVANCE PREPARATION: One 8 x 8 x 2-inch baking pan • 6 ounces of shredded filo, or slightly less than half of a 1-pound box (rewrap the remaining filo and return it to the refrigerator, where it will keep for several weeks) • To thaw frozen shredded filo, place it on the counter and let it come to room temperature (2 to 3 hours) or thaw overnight in the refrigerator.

FOR THE FILO

6 ounces shredded filo (also called *kunafeh* or *kataifi*), room temperature

12 tablespoons (6 ounces) unsalted butter, melted and lukewarm

1 tablespoon sugar

FOR THE FILLING

10 ounces fresh sweet cherries, preferably Bing

1 teaspoon plus ¼ cup (1¾ ounces) sugar

4 ounces cream cheese, room temperature

4 ounces sour cream

1 large egg

1 large egg yolk

1½ teaspoons Amaretto di Saronno

1 teaspoon finely chopped orange zest (145)

FOR FINISHING THE PASTRY

2 tablespoons plus 1 teaspoon sugar

½ teaspoon ground cinnamon

⅛ teaspoon ground cardamom

FOR SERVING

Powdered sugar

Fresh stem cherries

Preheat the oven to 350°F. Position an oven rack in the center of the oven.

To prebake the filo, place 2 ounces of the shredded filo in a medium bowl. Gently separate and fluff the strands of filo with your hands, discarding any hard pieces or clumps of dough. Pour 4 tablespoons (2 ounces) of the melted butter over the dough, sprinkle with the tablespoon of sugar, and toss gently with your hands until it is evenly coated. Arrange the filo in an even layer in the bottom of the baking pan. Bake for 15 to 18 minutes, or just until crisp and lightly golden (do not let it brown). Remove from the oven and place on a rack to cool completely.

To make the filling, rinse the cherries in cold water and pat them dry. Pit the cherries, then cut each one in half. Place in a small bowl and toss with 1 teaspoon of sugar. Set aside. Place ¼ cup sugar and the cream cheese in the bowl of an electric mixer fitted with the paddle attachment (a handheld mixer is fine; just allow a little extra time to reach each stage specified in the recipe). Beat on medium speed until the mixture is smooth and creamy, about 2 to 3 minutes. Scrape down the bowl with a rubber spatula and add the sour cream. Beat on medium for another minute, then scrape down the bowl again. Add the egg and yolk and beat until well blended. Add the amaretto and orange zest and beat well, 15 to 20 seconds. Place the cherries in an even layer in the cake pan, covering the bottom layer of filo. Pour the cheese filling evenly over the cherries.

To finish the pastry, in a small bowl, stir together 2 tablespoons sugar, the cinnamon, and cardamom. Place the remaining 4 ounces of filo in the medium bowl and again gently separate the strands with your hands, discarding any hard clumps. Pour the rest of the melted butter (4 ounces) over the filo, then add the sugar and spice mixture. Toss gently with your hands until the filo is evenly coated. Place small handfuls of filo over the surface of the cheese filling, spreading it gently to form an even layer. Sprinkle the top with the remaining 1 teaspoon sugar. Place the pan in the oven and bake for 40 to 45 minutes, or until the filling is set (the center of the filling will feel firm if you press lightly on the filo covering it) and the filo is golden. Remove from the oven and place on a rack to cool.

SERVING AND STORAGE SUGGESTIONS: Serve this pastry warm, about 20 to 30 minutes after removing it from the oven (if completely cool, it should be reheated in a 325°F oven for about 15 minutes). Lightly dust the top of the pastry with powdered sugar. Use a thin, sharp knife to cut the pastry into thirds, then turn the pan 90 degrees and cut in half to form 6 pieces. Slide a small spatula into the pan to lift out each piece (the first one is always the hardest—and messiest—to remove). Place each slice on a plate and garnish with a few fresh cherries, stems attached (they are much prettier this way). Store the pastry at room temperature for 1 day. For longer storage, cover with plastic wrap and refrigerate for up to 2 days (after this point the cherries make the bottom soggy, but it still tastes good). Reheat the pastry in a 325°F oven for 15 to 20 minutes before serving if it has been refrigerated.

GETTING AHEAD: The bottom layer of filo can be prebaked up to 8 hours in advance.

VARIATION

Cinnamon Apple and Sweet Cheese in Shredded Filo: Follow the recipe above, substituting 1 large (10 to 12 ounces), tart baking apple (such as Granny Smith), peeled, cored, and cut into ½-inch cubes, for the cherries. Toss in a bowl as directed with an additional teaspoon of sugar (2 teaspoons total), ¼ teaspoon ground cinnamon, and 1 teaspoon freshly squeezed lemon juice.

Tiropetes with Chocolate and Apricot Filling

makes 20 tiropetes

Golden brown, crispy little triangles are filled with the bright, mouth-awakening flavor of sweet-tart apricots combined with deeply bittersweet chocolate pieces. There is a layering effect of flavor and texture here, for the soft filling is just barely sweet—the real sweetening is in the crystallized sugar sprinkled between the flaky layers of filo. The finished triangles glitter from an additional sprinkling of sugar before they go in the oven. Crystallized sugar is crunchy, sparkling sugar that does not melt when baked (it is often used to top cookies in bakeries) and is available from cake-decorating stores or general cake and baking suppliers (327), as well as some supermarkets (especially around the holidays).

EQUIPMENT AND ADVANCE PREPARATION: Two 18 x 13 x 1-inch baking sheets with sides, each sheet lined with parchment paper • A soft-bristle brush • If you are using frozen filo, allow 24 hours for it to thaw in the refrigerator, then place the filo box on the counter to come to room temperature, about 1½ to 2 hours.

> 8 ounces dried apricots, preferably California
>
> 3 tablespoons (1½ ounces) water
>
> 3 tablespoons (1½ ounces) sugar
>
> 2 tablespoons (1 ounce) Amaretto di Saronno
>
> ½ cup (2½ ounces) whole natural almonds
>
> 3 ounces (½ cup) miniature bittersweet chocolate chips (274) or finely chopped chocolate, pieces no larger than ⅜ to ½ inch
>
> 10 sheets filo dough, room temperature
>
> 8 tablespoons (4 ounces) unsalted butter, melted and lukewarm
>
> 10 tablespoons (5 ounces) crystallized sugar plus additional for sprinkling the top of the tiropetes
>
> 1 large egg yolk

To make the filling, place the apricots in the bowl of a food processor and process until they are very finely chopped, about 15 to 20 seconds. Transfer them to a medium bowl. Place the water, sugar, and amaretto in a small saucepan over medium-low heat and stir constantly until the sugar has dissolved and the liquid is clear. Bring the mixture just to a boil, then pour it over the chopped apricots, stirring to distribute the liquid evenly. Set aside, stirring every minute or so, until the liquid is absorbed and the mixture is cool.

Place the almonds in the bowl of the food processor and process until they are finely chopped, about 10 to 15 seconds. Stir the almonds and the chocolate into the cooled apricot mixture.

Preheat the oven to 375°F. Position an oven rack in the center of the oven.

To prepare the filo, remove it from its packaging and unfold it so that the stack lies flat on your work surface. Remove 10 sheets. Stack them on top of each other on your work surface, then cover with plastic wrap and a damp towel to prevent the filo from drying out. Roll and rewrap the remaining filo twice in plastic wrap. Return to the refrigerator and use within 3 days.

To assemble the tiropetes, take out a sheet of filo and re-cover the rest (be sure to cover the remaining sheets each time you remove a new one). Place the sheet on your work surface with one of the short sides toward you. Brush the filo with melted butter. Sprinkle the dough evenly with 2 tablespoons of crystallized sugar. Place another sheet of filo on top and brush it lightly with melted butter. Use a sharp knife to cut the dough lengthwise into 4 pieces—you should have 4 long strips of filo.

Place a level tablespoon of the apricot-chocolate filling near the end of one of the strips, toward the left side. Take the right corner and fold it over the filling to make a triangle. Continue folding the strip, just as you would a flag (keeping the triangular shape), until you reach the opposite end as shown. If there is a bit of dough left at the end, simply trim it off. Place the triangle on one of the prepared baking sheets, with the final fold of dough downward. Brush the top with butter to keep it from drying out. Repeat with the remaining 3 strips.

Repeat the process until all of the filling has been used. You will have 20 triangles.

Bake the tiropetes one pan at a time. Before baking, brush the top of the triangles lightly with the egg yolk and sprinkle each one with about ¼ teaspoon of crystallized sugar. Place the pan in the oven and bake for 15 to 20 minutes, or until the pastry is a golden color. Remove from the oven and place on a rack to cool.

SERVING AND STORAGE NOTES: These pastries may be served warm or at room temperature. I like to serve them at a party piled on a platter, allowing guests to serve themselves. They're also good served warm in a bowl with a scoop of vanilla ice cream. Store, uncovered, at room temperature for 1 day. These are at their best the same day they are baked but can be held in an airtight container for up to 3 days.

GETTING AHEAD: The assembled tiropetes can be covered tightly with plastic wrap and refrigerated overnight or frozen for 1 month. (Freeze them on the baking sheets and, when frozen, transfer the triangles to a freezer bag and store as desired.) To bake the frozen pastries, do not let them thaw. Bake them directly from the freezer, allowing an extra minute or two in the oven.

Cookies

Though I love desserts of all kinds, it's cookies I turn to most often when I'm entertaining casually at home. Adults and kids alike love them, they're quick and easy to make, and they're especially great for last-minute guests, since most can be made ahead to some point, then frozen and baked to order in a matter of minutes. Most of all, nothing beats the heart-warming aroma of fresh-from-the-oven cookies. Add a scoop of great ice cream, either homemade or store bought, and you have a supremely satisfying dessert that will delight everyone.

In the Mediterranean, many cookies have a historical, often religious meaning and an association with a particular holiday, feast, or saint's day. Though each one of us may experience some of this tradition according to our cultural background or favorite family traditions, mostly we Americans just like to eat a really good cookie. And whether you like it crunchy or chewy, chocolatey or lemony, rich and decadent or light and elegant, there's a cookie here for you.

If you like crunch, there's plenty of that in an assortment of biscotti that will keep you dipping, from the Moorish-influenced Spanish Olive Oil and Spice Biscotti to Pistachio, Apricot, and Cardamom Biscotti. Brown Sugar and Almond Biscotti with Cinnamon and Orange are ever so slightly chewy in the center, and all-American Double-Chocolate Toffee Biscotti are reminiscent of a deep, dark, luscious brownie. If it's something soft you crave, try the irresistibly dense and chewy Almond and Hazelnut Chip Macaroons or the tender, cake-like Lemon and Rose Madeleines, which are perfect with a cup of tea or coffee. Nonna's Rugelach are the flakiest, most tender version of this cinnamony walnut-filled pastry you'll ever try, while Lacy Sesame Crisps are thin, exotic wafers that can be served as such or turned quickly into elegant cigarette cookies or edible bowls for holding ice cream, sorbet, or mousse. Company's coming? Turn the page.

Almond and Hazelnut Chip Macaroons

makes sixteen 3-inch cookies or fifty to sixty 1-inch cookies

These thick, chewy, roughly textured cookies are a far cry from the refined, diminutive macaroons often found in bakeries, but one bite will convert you forever. All nut macaroons are basically equal parts of ground almonds and sugar with a little egg white stirred in to bind the mixture. This recipe follows the classic equation, then goes a step further by reducing the sugar (for a more pronounced almond flavor) and adding a bit of apricot jam (for an extra layer of flavor and a chewier texture) and a zing of lemon zest, plus a crunch of texture from coarsely chopped hazelnuts. I particularly like the contrast in flavors of an almond cookie with little chunks of hazelnuts, but they're awfully good with chopped almonds or pine nuts as well (see the variations at the end of the recipe). In fact, these would be fine macaroons even if you left out the nut "chips" altogether. This recipe is an adaptation of a recipe I learned from the gifted chef and teacher Madeleine Kamman.

EQUIPMENT AND ADVANCE PREPARATION: 2 baking sheets with sides, lined with parchment paper

> 2 cups (11 ounces) whole natural almonds, toasted (254)
>
> 1¼ cups (8¾ ounces) sugar
>
> 2 to 3 large egg whites
>
> 2 tablespoons (1¼ ounces) apricot jam
>
> 1 teaspoon finely minced lemon zest (145)
>
> ⅔ cup (3 ounces) whole hazelnuts, toasted and skinned (227), chopped to about the size of currants or chocolate chips

Preheat the oven to 325°F. Position 2 oven racks in the top and center thirds of the oven. (If you are baking only one pan at a time, bake it in the center of the oven.)

To make the batter, place the almonds and sugar in the bowl of a food processor and process until the nuts are very finely ground, about 30 to 40 seconds. Add

2 egg whites, the jam, and lemon zest and pulse until thoroughly blended. Stop and touch the dough at this point—it should be thick and tacky when pressed with a fingertip. If the mixture seems a little dry, add the remaining egg white, a small amount at a time. The dough should not be loose or very sticky, so add the extra white slowly. To do this, place the remaining egg white in a small bowl and whisk it just until frothy. Then add the white to the dough teaspoon by teaspoon, pulsing after each addition, until the correct consistency is reached—at most you will use a quarter to half of the remaining egg white.

To form the macaroons, remove the mixture from the processor and knead in the chopped hazelnuts by hand. As you work, keep a small bowl of cold water nearby and lightly wet your hands occasionally, shaking off any excess water, to keep the dough from sticking to them. Divide the dough into 16 pieces. The easiest way to do this is to divide the dough in half, pat each half into a 5-inch round, then cut each round into 8 wedges. Roll each wedge between your dampened palms to shape it into a ball.

Place 8 balls of dough on each baking sheet. Use your damp fingers or the palm of your hand to gently press each ball into a 3-inch round. Bake for 18 to 22 minutes, reversing the baking sheets from front to back and from top to bottom racks halfway through the baking time. The cookies should be golden brown on top and look dry and set. Remove from the oven and place the pans on a rack to cool.

NOTE: The cookies in this recipe are large, about 3 inches in diameter. That size is used in making Lemon and Almond Macaroon Ice Cream Sandwiches (311), and it feels satisfyingly substantial in a snacker's hand. However, this dough can be used to make bite-sized cookies as well. Reduce the baking time by 3 to 5 minutes for 1-inch cookies.

SERVING AND STORAGE NOTES: When the macaroons are completely cool, gently peel them off the parchment paper, then transfer them to an airtight container, layering them between sheets of parchment or wax paper. These are at their best the first day or two after baking but will hold well for up to a week in an airtight container.

GETTING AHEAD: The macaroons freeze very well. Place the baked cookies flat on a baking sheet in the freezer until hard, then wrap tightly in plastic wrap, layered between sheets of parchment or wax paper, place in a freezer bag, and freeze for up to 1 month. Thaw in the refrigerator overnight, still wrapped in plastic. Let the cookies come to room temperature before serving.

VARIATIONS

Double-Almond Macaroons: Substitute ⅔ cup (3 ounces) whole natural almonds, toasted (254) and coarsely chopped for the chopped hazelnuts in the original recipe.

Almond and Pine Nut Macaroons: Place ⅓ cup (1½ ounces) whole pine nuts on a baking sheet and bake in a 350°F oven for 5 to 7 minutes, or until lightly toasted. Remove from the oven and immediately transfer the nuts to a plate to cool completely (if left on the pan, they could overcook from the residual heat). Substitute these toasted pine nuts (do not chop) for the chopped hazelnuts in the original recipe.

Almonds

Almonds are one of a trio of flavors that, for me, define the Mediterranean. A veritable map of the region can be drawn by following the spread of almond, olive, and citrus trees through this beautifully rugged area. Although the almond was well known in the Mediterranean for at least several centuries B.C., it was during the occupation of the Arabs (about A.D. 700 to 1500), with their love of marzipan, that the region became known for its use of almonds in desserts.

Almonds arrived in California with the Spanish missionaries, who planted them in their mission gardens, beginning in San Diego at the Mission San Diego de Alcala in 1769. The Central Valley in particular is an important growing region because of its warm, dry location. This interior valley, sheltered from frosts or heavy rains during the critical blooming period, is the perfect location—so perfect, in fact, that almonds are currently the most important nut grown there. Among all the fruit and nut crops in California, almonds are second only to grapes in both acreage and commercial importance.

Happily, this importance directly affects another vital, though unheralded aspect of the agricultural industry—beekeeping. Because the commercial almond varieties must be cross-pollinated, almond growers rent beehives during the blooming period to ensure a fruitful crop. A drive through the valley in early spring is a breathtaking sight, with seemingly endless rows of trees practically exploding with delicate white blossoms. And set out at regular intervals among the trees are small, simple white boxes—the mobile homes of hard-working honeybees.

Botanically, the almond is a member of the Rosaceae, or rose, family. More specifically, it is found under the *Prunus,* or plum, genus. This places the almond in direct relation to plums, peaches, nectarines, and apricots, which perhaps explains its special affinity for flavoring desserts made with these fruits. In its early growing stages, the almond is covered with a velvety green down, just like the peach. Where they differ is in maturity, when the outer covering of the almond becomes dry and hard and the covering of the peach becomes soft, sweet, and juicy.

Green almonds, considered a delicacy in much of the Mediterranean, are simply very young almonds. The meat of the nut has passed through the milky stage but has not yet reached the hard, mature stage we are familiar with. The meat itself is not green—it is the soft, fuzzy green shell that gives this product its name. The meat is sweeter, milder, and somehow more evocative of the essence of almond than the fully mature nut. Green almonds can be found in the early spring at farmers' markets in California and at some stores catering to a Middle Eastern clientele. To serve, split the nuts in half (the shell is soft, so is easily accomplished by hand or with a small knife) and present the nut meat fresh, still nestled in its pod, "on the half shell."

Once mature, almonds are harvested by mechanical tree shakers—a kind of tractor with eerie long arms protruding from the front, à la Edward Scissorhands. The arms grab hold of the tree and vibrate the trunk until the nuts drop to the ground. The nuts are collected, dried, and processed according to use. I almost always use natural almonds (with the brown skin on the nut), because I feel the skin adds both beauty and flavor to baked goods. Blanched almonds have had their skins removed and are a creamy white color (you can blanch natural almonds, if you wish, by dropping them into boiling water for a minute or two—the nuts will slip easily from the skins). Sliced almonds are thin ovals of nut and are available either blanched or natural. Slivered almonds, cut to resemble little matchsticks, are always cut from blanched almonds. Almond meal and almond flour are very finely ground nuts (finer than is possible in a food processor) and are available from professional supply companies.

Because they have a high oil content, almonds should be purchased in the spring and kept in the refrigerator or freezer until needed to prevent them from turning rancid. I always buy my nuts at the farmers' market, where I can be assured of purchasing almonds from the current year's harvest. Otherwise, buy them from a store that has a high turnover—a natural food store that sells in bulk is usually a good bet.

To toast almonds: Preheat the oven to 350°F. Spread the whole almonds on a baking sheet in a single layer and place in the oven. Cook for 7 to 9 minutes (5 to 6 minutes for sliced or slivered almonds), or until the nuts are hot to the touch and smell nutty. Toasting should warm the oils and bring their flavor to the foreground, as well as lightly crisp the meat. Toasted nuts should not be brown on the inside, as they become bitter at this point. Remove the nuts from the oven and transfer them to a plate for cooling (if left on the hot pan, they will continue to cook from the residual heat). Cool completely before using toasted nuts in a recipe. Almonds may be toasted several days in advance and stored at room temperature. Since their flavor is best when freshly toasted, do not toast almonds you will be storing in the refrigerator or freezer.

Nonna's Rugelach

makes 36 cookies

My grandmother has been making these tender, flaky, cinnamon-sugar and walnut-filled crescents for as long as I can remember. They are the lightest, crispiest version I've ever tried because of the addition of sour cream to the dough rather than the usual, heavier cream cheese. She always cuts them in wedges and rolls them up croissant style, so that's the way I shape them as well.

Rugelach is a cookie that has long been associated with eastern European cultures but is now increasingly found in the Mediterranean because of the migration of Ashkenazic Jews to Israel, who have brought their cookie traditions with them. The dough is like a flaky tart or pie dough and should be handled similarly—that is, use very cold butter, work quickly so the butter doesn't warm, and do not overwork the dough.

EQUIPMENT AND ADVANCE PREPARATION: 2 baking sheets with sides, lined with parchment paper, plus 2 extra baking sheets to slip under the first (this is known as "double-panning") to ensure the bottom of the cookies do not burn during baking. If you do not have enough baking sheets, simply bake one pan of cookies at a time.

FOR THE DOUGH

2 cups (10 ounces) unbleached all-purpose flour

½ teaspoon salt

2 sticks (8 ounces) very cold unsalted butter, cut into 1-inch pieces

1 egg yolk

¾ cup (6 ounces) sour cream

FOR THE FILLING

¾ cup (5¼ ounces) sugar

1 teaspoon ground cinnamon

¾ cup (3¼ ounces) walnuts, toasted (follow the directions for toasting almonds, 254) and finely chopped

To make the dough, place the flour and salt in the bowl of a food processor. Pulse to blend. Add the cold butter pieces and process until the mixture resembles peas and cornmeal in texture, about 10 to 15 pulses. (This step can also be done in the bowl of a standing mixer using the paddle attachment or by hand in a medium bowl using a pastry blender, 2 knives, or your fingertips—for further instructions, see the directions for making Flaky Tart Dough on page 110). In a separate small bowl, whisk together the egg yolk and sour cream. Add this to the food processor and pulse until the mixture looks like coarse breadcrumbs or crumble topping (it should not form a cohesive dough at this point), about 15 to 20 pulses. Turn the mixture out onto a work surface and knead gently several times, just until the dough comes together. Divide the dough into 3 equal pieces (each piece should weigh about 8¼ ounces), then shape each piece into a 5-inch disc and wrap in plastic wrap. Chill for 2 hours or overnight.

To make the filling, in a medium bowl, stir together the sugar and cinnamon until well blended. Remove 3 tablespoons of this mixture and set aside. Add the walnuts to the remaining cinnamon sugar.

To shape the cookies, roll a disc of dough into an 11-inch round on a lightly floured work surface—the dough should be about ⅛ inch thick. Sprinkle one-third of the walnut filling evenly over the dough. Cut the round into 12 wedges— this makes small, bite-sized cookies (for larger rugelach, cut the round into eighths). Roll each wedge into a crescent shape by starting at the wide end and rolling it tightly toward the point as shown. Tuck the point under each cookie, then place it on one of the baking sheets—an inch between cookies is fine because these don't spread during baking. Repeat this process with each disc of dough until all the cookies have been shaped and are on the pans (18 cookies per pan). Place the pans in the refrigerator for 30 minutes to chill the dough thoroughly.

Preheat the oven to 350°F. Position 2 oven racks in the top and center thirds of the oven. (If you are baking only one pan at a time, bake it in the center of the oven).

Sprinkle the cookies with the reserved cinnamon sugar and slip the extra baking sheets under the filled pans. Bake for 30 to 35 minutes, or until nicely browned on the bottom and lightly golden on top, reversing the baking sheets from front to back and from top to bottom racks halfway through the baking time. Remove from the oven and place on a rack to cool completely.

SERVING AND STORAGE NOTES: These cookies are best served the same day they are baked. They may be stored in an airtight container between sheets of parchment or wax paper for 3 to 4 days, but they will lose their crispness.

GETTING AHEAD: The dough can be made, shaped into a disc and frozen for up to 3 months. Wrap in plastic wrap and store in a freezer bag—thaw overnight in the refrigerator before continuing with the recipe.

Once the cookies are shaped, they can be frozen on the baking sheets until hard, then transferred to a plastic freezer bag for storage for up to 1 month. Thaw the cookies on baking sheets in the refrigerator for an hour before baking.

Lemon and Rose Madeleines

makes 24 cookies

Madeleines are the little scalloped, cake-like cookies made famous by Marcel Proust in his Remembrance of Things Past, *in which a bite and the ensuing reflection on this childhood cookie led the man to write an entire series of books. I won't guarantee the same results, but I do find these light, tender morsels undeniably alluring. There is a trend afoot to make madeleines dense, buttery, and generally more like pound cake in texture. While cute, these are simply butter cakes baked in a madeleine pan. Classic madeleines fit into the sponge cake category, which means they are airy and slightly dry, which makes them the perfect partner for nibbling with a cup of tea or coffee. In this delightful variation on the classic, the soft cookies are flavored not only with lemon juice and lemon zest but with the lovely scent of rose water, which adds a gentle note of exoticism.*

EQUIPMENT AND ADVANCE PREPARATION: 2 madeleine pans, each pan containing 12 molds for 3-inch shell-shaped cookies (if you have only 1 pan, see baking instructions below) • Brush the pans generously with melted butter (or use pan spray), then dust with flour, tapping out the excess. • A sheet of parchment or wax paper

> **6 tablespoons (3 ounces) unsalted butter**
>
> **2 teaspoons very finely chopped lemon zest (145), about 1 large lemon**
>
> **1 cup (3½ ounces) cake flour, sifted, then spooned lightly into the cup for measuring**
>
> **½ teaspoon baking powder**
>
> **Pinch of salt**
>
> **2 large eggs, room temperature**
>
> **⅓ cup plus 1 tablespoon (2¾ ounces) sugar**
>
> **1 tablespoon freshly squeezed lemon juice**
>
> **2 teaspoons rose water (260)**
>
> **FOR SERVING**
> **Powdered sugar**

Preheat the oven to 375°F. Position an oven rack in the center of the oven.

To make the cookie batter, place the butter in a small saucepan and melt it over low heat—do not allow it to boil. Remove the pan from the heat and add the lemon zest. Set aside until the butter has cooled (it should be lukewarm or cool to the touch but still liquid).

Place the cake flour, baking powder, and salt in a medium bowl, whisk to blend, and set aside. Place the eggs and sugar in the bowl of an electric mixer fitted with the whisk attachment (a handheld mixer is fine; just allow a little extra time to reach each stage in the recipe). Whip on high speed until the mixture is very thick, light in color, and ribbons when it falls from the whisk to the surface of the mixture, about 3 to 4 minutes. Add the lemon juice and rose water and blend thoroughly, about 5 to 10 seconds. Sift half of the flour mixture over the eggs and use a rubber spatula to gently fold it in, then sift the remaining flour over the batter and repeat. Quickly but gently fold in the cooled butter until a homogeneous batter is formed.

To bake the cookies, immediately spoon the batter into the madeleine pans (about 1 level tablespoon per mold). Bake for 8 to 11 minutes, or until the center of the cookies springs back when lightly pressed with a fingertip and the edges are golden brown. (If you have only 1 pan, bake the first dozen, wash the pan—this will cool it as well—then butter and flour the pan again. Gently stir the batter to reblend it, as the butter may have separated. The second batch will be slightly heavier in texture than the first.)

Place a sheet of parchment or wax paper on the counter. Remove the pans from the oven and rap them sharply on the countertop, letting the cookies fall onto the paper. Transfer the madeleines to a cooling rack, shell side upward.

SERVING AND STORAGE NOTES: Just before serving, dust the cookies lightly with powdered sugar. These cookies are best served the same day they are baked. They may be stored in an airtight container between sheets of parchment or wax paper for 1 day.

VARIATION

Orange Madeleines with Orange Flower Water: These cookies remind me of spring in my old neighborhood in Los Angeles, when the fragrance of hundreds of orange trees in blossom perfumed the warm air. Follow the recipe above, substituting the very finely chopped zest of 1 orange for the lemon zest, 1 tablespoon freshly squeezed orange juice for the lemon juice, and 2 teaspoons orange flower water for the rose water.

Rose Water and Orange Flower Water

Fragrant waters are found in everything from salads to candy in the Mediterranean, though they are used most often in pastries. And while we associate rose and orange flower water most closely with the foods of North Africa and the Middle East, they enhance desserts in France, Italy, Spain, and Greece as well.

Both rose water and orange flower water are distilled using the same process employed to make fine liqueurs or eaux-de-vie, resulting in flavors that are the very essence of their namesake. Rose water is made from the most fragrant of roses, often the damask rose, while orange flower water is made from the blossoms of the bergamot (or bitter) orange tree. These waters are very concentrated and must be used sparingly. Add them to a recipe literally drop by drop, for too much of a good thing can quickly become overpowering. An eyedropper or baby medicine dispenser is a valuable tool when working with these flavorings.

Rose water and orange flower water are sold in markets catering to a Middle Eastern clientele, as well as stores specializing in imported western European foods (from Italian or Greek delis to pricy food boutiques) and even some upscale supermarkets (see Mail-Order Sources, 327). If possible, purchase fragrant waters imported from France, which seem to be of a higher quality than others. After opening, store the fragrant waters at room temperature—they will keep for at least a year.

Bitter Chocolate Wafers

These thin, crisp, intensely chocolate cookies with a pleasantly bitter edge are a great homemade alternative to chocolate wafers from the supermarket. They are the dessert equivalent of the little black dress, for though their pure chocolate flavor is enticing on its own (just ask my husband, who eschews most sweets but could eat these by the dozen), their real talent lies in enhancing all manner of dessert partners. In the Black and White Mascarpone Parfait (185), they add the perfect contrast of texture and flavor to the soft and silky rum-flavored mousse. They also make great bite-sized ice cream sandwiches (coffee ice cream is my favorite) and have an array of uses when crushed into crumbs: made into a cookie crust, layered with mousse, pressed into the sides of cakes, sprinkled on top of cream pies or ice cream, and so on. Everyone should have a couple of rolls in their freezer for easy last-minute desserts.

EQUIPMENT AND ADVANCE PREPARATION: 1 baking sheet with sides, lined with parchment paper

> 1½ sticks (6 ounces) unsalted butter, softened
>
> ¾ cup plus 1 tablespoon (5¾ ounces) sugar
>
> 1 large egg
>
> 2 teaspoons pure vanilla extract
>
> 1½ cups (7½ ounces) unbleached all-purpose flour
>
> ¾ cup unsweetened Dutch-process cocoa powder (262), sifted, then spooned lightly into the cup for measuring
>
> 1 teaspoon baking powder
>
> ¼ teaspoon salt

To make the dough, place the butter and sugar in the bowl of an electric mixer fitted with the paddle attachment (a handheld mixer is fine; just allow a little extra time to reach each stage in the recipe). Beat on medium speed until the mixture is light in color, about 2 to 3 minutes. Use a rubber spatula to scrape down the sides of the bowl. Add the egg and vanilla and blend well, about 1 minute. In a separate bowl, whisk together the flour, cocoa powder, baking powder, and salt. Add the dry ingredients to the butter mixture and combine on low speed, just until the dough is thoroughly blended, about 20 seconds.

To shape the dough, on a lightly floured surface, divide the dough in half and roll each half into a log 8 inches long and 1½ inches in diameter. Brush any excess flour off the logs, then wrap them in plastic wrap, twisting the ends of the plastic in opposite directions to form an even roll. Refrigerate on a flat surface for 1 hour before baking. (You will probably use only one roll at a time—freeze the extra roll as directed in Getting Ahead.)

Preheat the oven to 350°F. Position an oven rack in the center of the oven.

To bake the cookies, use a thin, sharp knife to slice the chilled roll into ¼-inch-thick discs and place the cookies on the parchment-lined pan. Bake for 15 to 18 minutes, or until the wafers can be easily lifted from the pan with your fingertips. They will crisp upon cooling. Remove from the oven and place the pan on a rack to cool completely.

SERVING AND STORAGE NOTES: These cookies are at their best the same day they are baked. Store extra cookies in an airtight container for 3 to 4 days.

GETTING AHEAD: The cookie dough may be frozen for up to 3 months. After shaping the dough into a log, wrap it tightly in plastic wrap and place the log on a baking sheet in the freezer. Once the log is frozen, remove the pan and store the cookie dough as desired. Thaw overnight in the refrigerator. If you're in a hurry, thaw on the counter for 15 to 20 minutes, just until soft enough to slice.

Choosing Cocoa Powder

Buying cocoa powder for baking can be confusing. Should you buy natural (also called nonalkalized) cocoa or Dutch-process cocoa? What's the difference? Why not just substitute hot chocolate mix?

Cocoa is unsweetened chocolate with most (up to 75 percent) of the cocoa butter removed. The very bitter chocolate mixture that remains is then pulverized into cocoa powder. All cocoa powder is unsweetened, so it may seem redundant for cookbooks to call for "unsweetened cocoa powder" in a recipe, but this is done to avoid confusion between the real stuff and the hot chocolate mix. Hot chocolate mix does indeed contain cocoa powder, but it also contains sugar and other ingredients, making it an impossible substitute for cocoa powder in baking.

There are two styles of cocoa powder to choose from—natural and Dutch process. The difference in these two types of cocoa is one step in the manufacturing process. Natural, or nonalkalized, cocoa is the type Americans are most familiar with (Hershey's is the most popular brand). It is light brown in color and very bitter, with a deep chocolate flavor. Dutch process is European-style cocoa, which means that during processing, the powder is treated with an alkali to reduce the natural acidity. This makes the cocoa less bitter, more soluble, and also mellows the flavor. Dutch-process cocoa is much darker in color than natural cocoa and the best-quality ones often take on a reddish hue. For some reason, many supermarkets stock Dutch-process cocoa powder in the hot chocolate section and natural cocoa powder in the baking aisle. No wonder people are confused.

How do you know which style to use? Alice Medrich, one of our country's foremost experts on all things chocolate, notes that many recipes can be made with either cocoa, according to your personal preference. She suggests the following guidelines: Choose natural cocoa for recipes that use a lot of sugar, have many ingredients, or are cooked for a period of time (such as brownies or hot fudge sauce); choose Dutch-process cocoa when the recipe has a minimal amount of sugar, few ingredients, and a shorter cooking time. When making recipes with leavening, such as cakes, use the cocoa specified, because the type and quantity of leavening is directly associated with the type of cocoa (nonalkalized cocoa needs baking soda, while Dutch-process cocoa works better with baking powder). I suggest that if you are following a recipe and you trust the taste and judgment of the author, rely upon his or her expertise to guide you to the best cocoa for that recipe.

Note: Because the percentage of cocoa butter contained in cocoa powder is not standardized, differing brands can vary widely in weight. So although I have included weights throughout this book for those who prefer the consistency and ease of using a scale for baking, it is not possible to include consistently accurate weights for cocoa powder. If you like to use a scale, I've found that the easiest way to solve this problem is to weigh your favorite cocoa in the traditional cup increments, record these weights, and refer to them whenever you bake with that cocoa.

Orange Cornmeal Rosettes with Apricot Jam

makes 26 to 28 cookies

Some cookies are special by virtue of their appearance, while others more homely in countenance are chosen for their extraordinary flavor. Here is a thinking man's cookie—enticing with its curvy ridges cradling a center of shiny jam—but with flavor to match. This cookie starts slow with a crumbly butteriness textured with cornmeal, then melts into a bright play of orange against the spicy ginger-like accent of cardamom and finishes with the soft, soothing sweetness of apricot jam. Excellent with sorbets and granitas or alongside a cup of tea, shaped butter cookies like these are popular around the world and can be found in great variety throughout the Mediterranean wherever friends gather for coffee and conversation.

This is a piped cookie and requires a very stiff dough to hold its beautiful shape in the heat of the oven. You will need to exert a good deal of pressure during the piping process—here's where your workouts will really pay off.

EQUIPMENT AND ADVANCE PREPARATION: 2 baking sheets with sides, lined with parchment paper. If you don't have 2 pans, just bake one at a time, reserving the remaining cookies on a piece of parchment paper on a tray or platter in the refrigerator. • A large pastry bag fitted with a ½-inch star tip • A small plain tip for the pastry bag (optional)

14 tablespoons (7 ounces) unsalted butter, softened

⅔ cup (4½ ounces) sugar

2 large egg yolks

2 tablespoons freshly squeezed orange juice

2 tablespoons finely chopped orange zest (145), about 2 large oranges

1½ cups (7½ ounces) unbleached all-purpose flour

⅔ cup (2½ ounces) fine cornmeal, spooned lightly into the cup for measuring

1 teaspoon ground cardamom

Pinch of salt

²/₃ cup (about 7 ounces) low-sugar apricot jam (Smucker's brand if
available)

To make the dough, place the butter and sugar in the bowl of an electric
mixer fitted with the paddle attachment (a handheld mixer is fine; just allow a little extra time to reach each stage in the recipe). Beat on medium speed until the
mixture is light in color, about 2 to 3 minutes. Use a rubber spatula to scrape
down the sides of the bowl. Add the egg yolks one by one, allowing the first to
incorporate fully before adding the next. Add the orange juice and zest and beat
another 15 to 30 seconds. Scrape down the sides of the bowl again.

In a separate bowl, whisk together the flour, cornmeal, cardamom, and
salt. Add the dry ingredients to the butter mixture and combine on low speed just
until the dough is thoroughly blended, about 20 to 30 seconds. Remove the bowl
from the mixer and stir the dough with the rubber spatula to be sure it is evenly
blended. (Do not walk away at this point, thinking you will come back later, even
in 10 minutes, to pipe the cookies. As the dough sits, it becomes very hard, making it impossible to pipe. If this happens, see the variation below.)

To pipe the dough, immediately spoon the dough into the
pastry bag fitted with the star tip. Pressing very hard, pipe
rosettes on the parchment-covered pans, spacing them
about an inch apart as shown. The rosettes should be
about ½ inch thick at the thickest point and about 1¾
inches in diameter. Continue piping until you have
used all the dough. Chill in the refrigerator for 20 minutes. Wash and dry the pastry bag if you wish to pipe the
jam in the center of the cookies.

Preheat the oven to 350°F. Position 2 oven racks in the top and center thirds of the oven (if you are only baking one pan at a time, place the rack in
the center of the oven).

Bake the rosettes for 15 to 20 minutes, until they are golden brown
around the edges. Remove from the oven and place the pan on a cooling rack.
While the cookies are still very hot, use your thumb or the rounded end of a
kitchen utensil to make a depression in the center of each rosette (do not push so
hard that you break through to the sheet pan or crack the cookie).

To add the filling, cook the apricot jam in a small saucepan over medium-low heat until very hot and liquid. Pour the jam through a strainer to remove any large lumps of fruit. Place the small plain tip in the pastry bag (this step can also be done using a zip-top bag with a tiny hole snipped in one corner or you can spoon the jam onto the cookies) and pour the warm jam into the bag. Pipe or spoon a little jam into each depression in the cookies as shown, filling them with an amount that looks appetizing to you. Adding the hot jam to the warm cookies gives the jam filling a professional smooth and shiny appearance. Allow the cookies to finish cooling completely.

SERVING AND STORAGE NOTES: These cookies are at their best the same day they are baked. Store extra cookies at room temperature in an airtight container between sheets of parchment or wax paper for up to 5 days.

GETTING AHEAD: Pipe the rosettes and place them on the baking sheets in the freezer until hard, about 1 hour. Transfer the rosettes to a freezer bag and store as desired. They will keep frozen for up to 2 months. Bake them straight from the freezer, allowing an extra minute or two in the oven.

VARIATION

Orange Cornmeal Wafers: Prepare the dough as directed. Shape into logs, chill, and bake as directed for Bitter Chocolate Wafers (261).

Lacy Sesame Crisps

makes about thirty-six 3-inch cookies or fourteen 5-inch cookies for making molded shapes

These rustic, wafer-thin cookies—a beautiful combination of caramel, orange, and sesame—have a shattering crispness that is barely tempered by a slight chewiness. An abundance of sesame seeds forms the lovely lace-like pattern over their roughly textured surface. Not too sweet, these wafers have barely enough sugar to put them into the cookie (rather than cracker) category of baked goods. Their earthy flavor is enhanced by a small amount of tahini, a paste of ground sesame seeds similar to peanut butter, which is available in natural and natural food stores and many supermarkets. The recipe comes from dear friend and inspired pastry chef Michele Fagerroos.

Once baked, these versatile cookies can be shaped and used in several different ways. Left au natural, they are appealing round wafers that can accompany all kinds of desserts, especially ice creams, sorbets, and mousses, or they can be used to sandwich whipped cream or mousse to form "new age" Napoleons. While still warm from the oven, the cookies can be rolled into elegant cigarettes, gently molded over upturned custard cups to form edible bowls for ice cream or mousse, rolled around cannoli forms for a fun variation on this Sicilian classic, draped over a rolling pin to form a gently curving tile shape, or rolled around a coronet mold to form a classic cream horn shape.

EQUIPMENT AND ADVANCE PREPARATION: 2 baking sheets with sides, as level as possible, lined with parchment paper

> **4 tablespoons (2 ounces) unsalted butter, cut into 4 pieces**
>
> **¼ cup (3 ounces) honey (one with a pourable consistency is best)**
>
> **¼ cup (2 ounces) tightly packed dark brown sugar**
>
> **1½ teaspoons finely chopped orange zest (145), about ½ large orange**
>
> **½ cup (2¾ ounces) toasted sesame seeds (101)**
>
> **1 tablespoon (½ ounce) tahini**
>
> **1 tablespoon unbleached all-purpose flour**
>
> **⅛ teaspoon baking powder**

Preheat the oven to 375°F. Position an oven rack in the center of the oven.

To make the cookie batter, place the butter in a small saucepan over low heat. When it is melted, add the honey and brown sugar and stir gently with a rubber spatula or flat-edged wooden spoon until the sugar is melted and the mixture is blended. Remove the pan from the heat. Stir in the orange zest, sesame seeds, and tahini. Add the flour and baking powder and blend thoroughly—the batter will be very thick.

To bake the cookies, place 6 level teaspoons of the cookie batter on one of the parchment-lined pans and gently pat each one with the edge of the teaspoon to make sure it is evenly thick—the rounds should be about 1½ inches in diameter. Keep in mind that the cookies will spread during the baking process to a little over 3 inches in diameter, so be sure to leave enough space both between the rounds and the edges of the pan. Bake for 6 to 7 minutes, or until caramel brown in color. The cookies will seem very soft but will crisp upon cooling. Remove from the oven and place the pan on a rack to cool. Place the next batch of cookies on the second pan and bake. The baking sheets may be reused while still warm. When cool, the cookies will easily release from the parchment paper.

SERVING AND STORAGE NOTES: These cookies quickly absorb moisture from the air, making them soft and stale tasting, so as soon as they are cool, transfer them to an airtight storage container until needed. They are at their crispest the same day they are made but, if stored airtight, will hold well for up to 5 days. Molded shapes (see variations below) should be stored similarly, though the bowl and tile shapes may lose their third dimension even if airtight, especially if the weather is very hot or humid, so should be used the same day they are baked. Do not fill the shapes with ice cream, sorbet, or mousse until just before serving.

VARIATIONS

If you want to make one of the molded shapes below, you will need to make larger cookies. Use a level tablespoon of batter for each cookie and bake 4 on a baking sheet at one time. The cookies will spread to a diameter of about 5 inches. After baking, slide the parchment, cookies still attached, off the baking sheet onto a work surface. Allow the cookies to cool for 45 to 60 seconds, or until still warm but cool enough to be lifted (carefully) off the paper with your fingertips. Work quickly to shape them as directed below. If the cookies cool, warm them briefly by placing them back on the pan and returning them to the oven for 30 to 60 seconds, until pliable.

To make cigarettes: Turn the cookies over so the smooth side is up. Roll the cookies tightly around a small dowel or pencil as shown, then slide the dowel out and set the cookies aside to cool.

To make bowls or tiles: Place the cookies, smooth side down, over an upside-down custard cup as shown (for bowls) or a rolling pin (for tiles) and gently use your fingers to press the warm cookie snugly against the mold. Let cool, then gently remove from the mold.

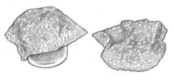

To make cannoli or cream horns: Turn the cookies over so the smooth side is up. Place the mold at the edge of a cookie, then roll it toward the opposite edge, curling the warm cookie tightly around the mold as shown. Let it cool for a few seconds, then slide the mold out and set the cookie aside to finish cooling.

A few filling suggestions:
Crème Fraîche Ice Cream (302)
Pistachio Ice Cream (294)
Pomegranate Ice Cream (312)
Tangerine (317) or Blood Orange Sorbet (318)
Quince Sorbet with Lemon (323)
Nougat cream (30)
Honey cream (53) topped with a handful of chopped toasted almonds
Pomegranate buttercream (68)
Apricot Fool with Almond Cream (194)

Biscotti

It's hard to believe that just fifteen years ago, biscotti were almost unknown in America outside Italian households. Since then, this traditional dunking cookie has taken the country by storm and become a new favorite. The coffeehouse explosion hasn't hurt their popularity either, for they are the perfect partner to a frothy cappuccino or latte. In fact, sometimes I think people are so accustomed to buying biscotti that they don't realize just how easy they are to make and—like almost everything else—how much better they are when made in your own kitchen. Because they are purposely dried to a hard crispness, they can be stored for weeks in an airtight container, ready to join the party at a moment's notice.

Biscotti are extremely versatile and endlessly variable, making them a good candidate for enjoyment any time of day. Italians often eat them for breakfast (a practice I can highly recommend) and dip them in their hearty red wine as well as their sweet *vin santo,* but they aren't the only culture to enjoy this type of dry dipping cookie. The Finns enjoy *rusks,* the Germans have *zwieback,* and the Jews munch on *mandelbrot,* to mention a few. In this country we enjoy biscotti dipped in coffee and hot chocolate, as a snack, a simple dessert, or alongside a glass of dessert wine. Their crisp texture also makes them a perfect accompaniment to ice creams and sorbets or light fruit desserts.

Biscotti get their name from being baked (*cotti*) twice (*bis*) in the oven. First the dough is baked in the shape of a log, then it is sliced crosswise and the individual cookies are placed back in the oven to dry out and lightly toast. The hardness of the biscotti depends on the recipe's formula (those containing butter are softer than those made without it), as well as how long and at what temperature you allow them to dry in the oven. Cookies toasted at 350°F for 10 to 15 minutes will be softer than those toasted in a 275°F oven for 30 to 35 minutes.

Keep in mind that the nuts, dried fruits, and flavorings in all the following recipes can be adapted to your personal taste. In fact, biscotti can be a great outlet for kitchen creativity. Don't like raisins? Use some chopped dried figs instead. Out of hazelnuts? Substitute almonds or pistachios. You can even leave the nuts or fruits out without harming the basic recipes. Just a bit of advice—when adapting a recipe to your taste, it's always a good idea to make it first as it is written so you can experience the taste and texture of the original before making changes. When you come up with ideas for variations, write the notes directly on the recipe so you don't forget them.

A few tips for success when making biscotti:

- Always lightly toast and cool the nuts before making the dough. The difference in flavor is immense.

- Make sure the cookie logs have baked completely before removing them from the oven. If they are underdone, they will have an unattractive raw dough line through the center of the cookie that will not disappear with toasting.

- Use a sharp serrated knife and slice the logs into cookies using as few motions as possible. In general, the cookie logs should be lukewarm before slicing (too hot and the slices squash; too cold and they may crack), but this can vary depending upon the type of dough, so it is best to follow each recipe's directions on cooling and slicing.

- When they are finished toasting, allow the biscotti to cool completely before transferring them to an airtight container.

- If the biscotti soften during storage, they can be recrisped before serving by placing them on a baking sheet in a 300°F oven to dry for about 10 to 15 minutes. Cool completely before serving.

Dried Sour Cherry and Bittersweet Chocolate Chip Biscotti

makes 45 to 50 biscotti

The absence of butter in this recipe results in a hard, crunchy style of biscotti known as cantucci in Italy—ideal for dipping into coffee, hot chocolate, or milk and especially popular in Prato, near Florence. I like the deep bittersweet flavor of top-quality chocolate in these biscotti, so I chop up some of my favorite brand, then whirl it in the food processor to make tiny little chips, which give a fun leopard-print look to the cookies.

EQUIPMENT AND ADVANCE PREPARATION: 2 baking sheets with sides, lined with parchment paper

- **4 large eggs**
- **1 cup (7 ounces) sugar**
- **1 tablespoon finely minced orange zest (145), about 1 large orange**
- **2 tablespoons (1 ounce) Amaretto di Saronno**
- **3 cups (15 ounces) unbleached all-purpose flour**
- **1 teaspoon baking powder**
- **¼ teaspoon salt**
- **1 cup (4 ounces) dried sour cherries**
- **½ cup (3 ounces) miniature bittersweet chocolate chips (274; if using store-bought mini chips, increase amount to ¾ cup)**

Preheat the oven to 350°F. Position an oven rack in the center of the oven.

To make the dough, place the eggs and sugar in the bowl of an electric mixer fitted with the whisk attachment (a handheld mixer is fine; just allow a little extra time to reach each stage in the recipe) and beat on high until the mixture is very thick, light in color, and ribbons when it falls from the whisk to the surface of the batter, about 3 to 4 minutes. Add the orange zest and amaretto and blend well. In a separate bowl, whisk together the flour, baking powder, and salt. Switch to the paddle attachment and add the flour mixture (if you are using a handheld mixer, stir it in by hand with a wooden spoon). Blend on low speed just until the dough comes together, about 10 to 15 seconds. Add the dried sour cherries and chocolate chips and blend thoroughly, another 10 to 15 seconds.

To shape the dough, working on a lightly floured surface, divide the dough in half and shape into 2 logs 15 inches long. (If this size is too long for your baking sheet, break enough dough off each log to make them fit comfortably, then shape the extra dough into a short third log—it should be the same thickness as the larger logs so they all bake in the same amount of time.)

Brush any excess flour from the surface. If you don't want to bake both rolls at once, freeze the extra log as directed in Getting Ahead. Place the logs on a parchment-lined baking sheet about 3 inches apart. Flatten each log until it is 2 inches wide. Place the second baking sheet under the first (to keep the bottom of the logs from browning too quickly). Bake for 30 to 35 minutes, or until the logs are firm to the touch and lightly golden brown. Transfer the pans to a rack to *cool completely* (if you cut these biscotti while the dough is warm, the still-soft chocolate chips will smear).

Turn the oven down to 275°F. Position 2 oven racks in the top and center thirds of the oven.

To toast the biscotti, remove the cookie logs from the baking sheet and slice on a slight diagonal into cookies ⅜ inch thick as shown. Place the cookies, cut side down, on the parchment-covered baking sheets (you will need both pans to hold all the cookies) and return to the oven to toast for 30 to 40 minutes, or until dry and lightly tinged with color, reversing the baking sheets from front to back and from top to bottom  halfway through the baking time. Remove from the oven and place the pans on a rack to cool completely.

SERVING AND STORAGE NOTES: Store the biscotti in an airtight container, where they will keep for at least 2 to 3 weeks. If the biscotti soften, recrisp them in a 300°F oven for about 15 minutes.

GETTING AHEAD: The cookie dough may be frozen for up to 3 months. After shaping the dough into a log, wrap it tightly in plastic wrap and place the log on a baking sheet in the freezer. Once the log is frozen, remove the pan and store the cookie dough as desired. To bake, remove the plastic wrap, set on a parchment-lined baking sheet, and thaw at room temperature for 1 hour before placing in the oven.

VARIATIONS

Hazelnut, Orange, and Chocolate Chip Biscotti: Follow the recipe above, substituting 2 tablespoons Frangelico for the Amaretto di Saronno and 1 cup (5 ounces) toasted, peeled, and coarsely chopped hazelnuts (227) for the dried sour cherries.

Toasted Almond and Dried Sour Cherry Biscotti: Follow the recipe above, substituting ¾ cup (3¾ ounces) toasted (254) and coarsely chopped whole natural almonds for the chocolate chips.

Miniature Chocolate Chips

1 pound of chocolate yields approximately 13 ounces (about 2⅓ cups) miniature chocolate chips and 3 ounces (about ½ cup) chocolate dust

Miniature chocolate chips are a snap to make and are perfect for adding to cakes, cookies, ice creams, or whatever you want to give a burst of deep chocolate flavor. They are made by simply chopping top-quality chocolate in a food processor until it is reduced to small chips. These chips are a whole different animal than store-bought chocolate chips, which contain shortening or oil and flavorings and are formulated to remain soft after baking. I use these home-made mini chips when I want their sophisticated flavor evenly dispersed through a dessert, so each bite carries a dozen nuggets of rich chocolate flavor.

To make the chips, use a high-quality bittersweet or semisweet bar chocolate, such as Lindt or Tobler, or bulk chocolate like Callebaut, Scharffen Berger, or Valrhona. Use a large, sharp chef's knife to chop the chocolate into pieces no larger than ½ to ¾ inch. Place the chopped chocolate in the bowl of a food processor fitted with the metal blade. Process until the chocolate is chopped into very small pieces, about 10 to 15 seconds. Some chips will be very tiny and others will be slightly larger—this is fine. For the purposes in this book, the largest should be no bigger than about ⅜ inch. Place the chocolate in a medium-fine strainer over a bowl. Shake the strainer to sift out the chocolate "dust" that formed in the processor. Save the dust and use it to coat truffles, sprinkle over cappuccino, and decorate cakes or other desserts, or use it in recipes that call for melted chocolate, melting it as you would any other type of chocolate. Place the chips in an airtight container and store at room temperature for up to a year. Store the chocolate dust in the same manner.

Pistachio, Apricot, and Cardamom Biscotti

makes 35 to 40 biscotti

The butter in this recipe results in a cookie that is richer in flavor, softer in texture, and a bit crumblier when broken than the biscotti in the preceding recipe. The deep coral of the apricots and the green flecks of pistachio create an enticing mosaic on the surface of each cookie and are warmly complemented by the orange zest and cardamom revealed in the first bite. Though the cookie is Italian, the flavor combination points to North Africa and the Middle East, making this, I suppose, a very Californian biscotti. For a much more traditional version of this biscotti, try the Pistachio, Sultana, and Anise variation at the end of the recipe.

EQUIPMENT AND ADVANCE PREPARATION: 2 baking sheets with sides, lined with parchment paper • If you find only pistachios in shells, buy double the weight given below and shell them by hand.

3/4 cup (about 5 ounces) tightly packed dried apricots, preferably California

1 stick (4 ounces) unsalted butter, softened

1/2 cup (3 1/2 ounces) sugar

2 tablespoons (1 1/2 ounces) honey

2 tablespoons finely minced orange zest (145), about 2 large oranges

3 large eggs

3 cups (15 ounces) unbleached all-purpose flour

2 teaspoons ground cardamom

1 teaspoon baking powder

1/4 teaspoon salt

3/4 cup (3 1/4 ounces) raw unsalted shelled pistachios

Preheat the oven to 350°F. Position an oven rack in the center of the oven.

To prepare the apricots, use a pair of kitchen scissors or a sharp chef's knife to snip the apricots in half, then cut each half into 3 or 4 pieces, resulting in nuggets no larger than 3/8 to 1/2 inch. Set aside.

To make the dough, place the butter, sugar, and honey in the bowl of an electric mixer fitted with the paddle attachment (a handheld mixer is fine; just allow a little extra time to reach each stage in the recipe). Beat on medium speed until the butter is light in color, about 2 to 3 minutes. Add the orange zest and blend well, another 15 to 20 seconds. Use a rubber spatula to scrape down the sides of the bowl. Add the eggs one at a time, beating well after each addition (about 15 to 20 seconds) and scraping down the sides of the bowl between each egg. In a separate bowl, whisk together the flour, cardamom, baking powder, and salt. Add the flour mixture to the butter and blend on low speed just until the dough comes together, about 10 to 15 seconds (if you are using a handheld mixer, stir it in by hand with a wooden spoon). Add the pistachios and apricots and blend thoroughly, another 10 to 15 seconds.

To shape the dough, working on a lightly floured surface, divide the dough in half and shape into 2 logs 13 inches long. (If this size is too long for your baking sheet, break enough dough off each log to make them fit comfortably, then shape the extra dough into a short third log—it should be the same thickness as the larger logs so they all bake in the same amount of time.)

Brush any excess flour from the surface. If you don't want to bake both rolls at once, freeze the extra log as directed in Getting Ahead. Place the logs on a parchment-lined baking sheet about 4 inches apart. Flatten each log until it is 2 inches wide. Place the second sheet under the first (to keep the bottom of the logs from browning too quickly). Bake for 30 to 35 minutes, or until the logs are firm to the touch and lightly golden brown. Transfer the pans to a rack and cool until lukewarm.

Turn the oven down to 275°F. Position 2 oven racks in the top and center thirds of the oven.

To toast the biscotti, remove the cookie logs from the parchment and slice on a slight diagonal into cookies ⅜ inch thick (see illustration, 273). Place the cookies, cut side down, on the parchment-lined baking sheets (you will need both pans to hold all the cookies) and return to the oven to toast for 30 to 40 minutes, or until dry and lightly tinged with color, reversing the baking sheets from front to back and from top to bottom halfway through the baking time. Remove from the oven and place the pans on racks to cool completely.

SERVING AND STORAGE NOTES: Store the biscotti in an airtight container, where they will keep for at least 2 to 3 weeks. Because of the butter, this type of biscotti tends to soften more quickly than others. If they become too soft, recrisp them in a 300°F oven for 10 to 15 minutes.

GETTING AHEAD: The cookie dough may be frozen for up to 3 months. After shaping the dough into a log, wrap it tightly in plastic wrap and place the log on a baking sheet in the freezer. Once the log is frozen, remove the pan and store the cookie dough as desired. To bake, remove the plastic wrap, set on a parchment-lined baking sheet, and thaw at room temperature for 1 hour before placing in the oven.

VARIATION

Pistachio, Sultana, and Anise Biscotti: Omit the orange zest and add ½ teaspoon pure anise extract instead. Omit the cardamom and add 1 tablespoon anise seeds instead. Omit the apricots and include ½ cup (about 3 ounces) tightly packed sultana (golden) raisins in their place.

Cardamom

This lovely spice, with its orange-lemon-lime scent and underlying hints of flowers, mint, and ginger, belongs to the ginger family. The rhizome-like root, which requires a tropical environment with 100 to 160 inches of rainfall a year, is indigenous to south India and Sri Lanka, though it is also now exported from Guatemala, Malaysia, and Cambodia. Cardamom's diminutive seed pods are harvested when they are almost ripe yet still green and firm. Because this harvesting takes place five or six times a year and is all done by hand, cardamom is one of the three costliest spices in the world, coming in third behind saffron and vanilla beans.

Though Americans have not yet grown to love cardamom, it is the most popular spice in the Arab countries, an indispensable ingredient in Indian cooking, and ubiquitous in Scandinavian baking. Cardamom is available in two forms—ground and whole pods containing the seeds. If you buy pods, look for the natural green pods and avoid those that have been bleached white, for their quality is inferior. To use, break open the pod and extract the tiny seeds. The seeds may be used whole (for infusing) or ground—because the seeds are so small, it is easiest to pulverize them with a mortar and pestle.

Spanish Olive Oil and Spice Biscotti

makes about 40 biscotti

This unusual biscotti recipe is made with olive oil instead of butter and is flavored with a Moorish blend of honey, sesame, orange, anise, and cinnamon. The olive oil creates a tender, tightly grained dough with a lightly herbal background flavor. The result is a cookie that, when broken, has a smooth, clean snap. This recipe comes from good friend and gifted chef Heidi Insalata Krahling, owner of Insalata's in San Anselmo, California. Heidi uses Spanish olive oil for these cookies, but any good, fruity extra-virgin olive oil will work well.

EQUIPMENT AND ADVANCE PREPARATION: Two baking sheets with sides, lined with parchment paper

- 2 tablespoons ($^3/_4$ ounce) sesame seeds, toasted (101), or 1$^1/_2$ tablespoons tahini
- 4 large eggs
- 1 cup (8 ounces) sugar
- 2 tablespoons (1$^1/_2$ ounces) honey
- $^1/_2$ cup (4 ounces) fruity extra-virgin olive oil
- 2 tablespoons finely minced orange zest (145), about 2 large oranges
- 3$^3/_4$ cups (18$^3/_4$ ounces) unbleached all-purpose flour
- 1 tablespoon plus 1 teaspoon baking powder
- $^1/_2$ teaspoon salt
- 2 teaspoons ground anise seeds
- 2 teaspoons ground cinnamon
- 1$^1/_2$ cups (7$^3/_4$ ounces) whole natural almonds, toasted (254) and coarsely chopped

Preheat the oven to 350°F. Position an oven rack in the center of the oven.

Place the toasted sesame seeds in a spice grinder (I use a coffee grinder) or a mortar and pestle, and grind them to a fine powder. Set aside.

To make the dough, place the eggs, sugar, and honey in the bowl of an electric mixer fitted with the whisk attachment (a handheld mixer is fine; just allow a little extra time to reach each stage in the recipe) and beat on high until the mixture is very thick, light in color, and ribbons when it falls from the whisk to the surface of the batter, about 3 to 4 minutes. With the mixer running, pour in the olive oil in a slow, steady stream, allowing the oil and eggs to emulsify into a smooth mixture—if you add the oil all at once, the mixture will look broken or curdled (this step is very similar to making mayonnaise or salad dressing). Add the orange zest and blend well. If you are using tahini instead of ground sesame seeds, add it here.

In a separate bowl, whisk together the ground sesame seeds, flour, baking powder, salt, anise, and cinnamon. Switch to the paddle attachment and add the flour mixture (if you are using a handheld mixer, stir it in by hand with a wooden spoon). Blend on low speed just until the dough comes together, about 10 to 15 seconds. Add the almonds and blend thoroughly, another 10 to 15 seconds.

To shape the dough, working on a lightly floured surface, divide the dough in half and shape into 2 logs 15 inches long. (If this size is too long for your baking sheet, break enough dough off each log to make them fit comfortably, then shape the extra dough into a short third log—it should be the same thickness as the larger logs so they all bake in the same amount of time.)

Brush any excess flour from the surface. If you don't want to bake both rolls at once, freeze the extra log as directed in Getting Ahead. Place the logs on a parchment-lined baking sheet about 3 inches apart. Flatten each log until it is 2 inches wide. Place a second baking sheet under the first (to keep the bottom of the logs from browning too quickly). Bake for 30 to 35 minutes, or until the logs are firm to the touch and lightly golden brown. Remove from the oven and place the pans on a rack to cool until lukewarm.

Turn the oven down to 275°F. Position 2 oven racks in the top and center thirds of the oven.

To toast the biscotti, remove the cookie logs from the pan and slice on a slight diagonal into cookies ½ inch thick (see illustration, 273). Place the cookies, cut side down, on the parchment-lined baking sheets (you will need both pans to hold all the cookies) and return to the oven to toast for 35 to 40 minutes, turning the cookies over twice during this toasting period and reversing the sheet pans from front to back and from top to bottom halfway through the baking time. The cookies should be dry and lightly tinged with color. Remove from the oven and place the pans on racks to cool completely.

SERVING AND STORAGE NOTES: Store the biscotti in an airtight container, where they will keep for at least 2 to 3 weeks. If the biscotti soften, recrisp them in a 300°F oven for 10 to 15 minutes.

GETTING AHEAD: The cookie dough may be frozen for up to 3 months. After shaping the dough into a log, wrap it tightly in plastic wrap and place the log on a baking sheet in the freezer. Once the log is frozen, remove the pan and store the cookie dough as desired. To bake, remove the plastic wrap, set on a parchment-lined baking sheet, and thaw at room temperature for 1 hour before placing in the oven.

Olive Oil and Desserts

Because much of the mountainous, dry landscape of the Mediterranean is not conducive to supporting herds of cows, olive oil has been the cooking fat of choice in the region for hundreds of years. It is not unusual, then, to find it in traditional dessert recipes. Of course, these days butter is readily available and is usually preferred in pastries for the special qualities it contributes. Still, cakes, cookies, tarts, and crêpes can all be made with this ever-abundant and flavorful oil.

There are many classic dessert recipes that contain olive oil and derive from a time when butter was either unknown or prohibitively expensive. *Castagnaccio,* a wonderful chestnut flour cake made with olive oil and rosemary, comes from the Tuscany region of Italy, and *pissota,* an olive oil cake flavored with lemon zest and rum, is made in the area around Verona. *Malomacarona* are very popular Greek cookies made with olive oil and semolina and dipped in a honey syrup, *qirshalli* are a kind of Lebanese biscotti made with olive oil and flavored with anise, and *thriba* are walnut cookies from Morocco that are made with olive oil and dusted with cinnamon. *Patoudia* are little pastries from Crete made with an olive oil dough and stuffed with a nut, honey, and sesame seed filling, and cannoli are Sicilian pastries made from a dough softened with olive oil, then fried and filled with a ricotta cream. And there are almost countless numbers of fried sweet doughs all around the Mediterranean that are first enriched and softened with olive oil, then deep-fried in it and showered with sugar, from the *churros* and *buñuelos* of Spain to the *deples* of Greece (coated with honey, nuts, and cinnamon), *zalabia* of Egypt (with a coating of rose and orange flower syrup), and *cenci* ("rags") of Italy that are dusted with powdered sugar.

Nowadays, modern cooks often experiment with new ways of using this ancient oil in their desserts, as Heidi has in Spanish Olive Oil and Spice Biscotti. Its presence in a sweet creates a tender crumb and a slightly elusive herbal or peppery flavor, depending on the type of olive oil you use. If you would like to experiment with olive oil in baking, use a good, fruity, extra virgin oil that you enjoy eating, and keep in mind that, in general, you will need to use only three-fourths as much olive oil as you would butter.

Double-Chocolate
Toffee Biscotti

makes about 50 biscotti

"Like a really great brownie, only crisp!" was my sister Toni's reaction when she first tasted these intensely chocolate, toffee-packed, completely over-the-top biscotti. I have a real weakness for chocolate-covered toffee, so it was inevitable that the convenient little toffee chips now available in the baking aisle would eventually find their way into my chocolate biscotti, which were already laden with miniature chocolate chips. The cookies are so full of chocolate and toffee that they are almost moist . . . almost. Don't worry—they're still crispy enough to be biscotti.

EQUIPMENT AND ADVANCE PREPARATION: 2 baking sheets with sides, lined with parchment paper

> 1 stick (4 ounces) unsalted butter, room temperature
>
> 1¼ cups (8¾ ounces) sugar
>
> 1 tablespoon pure vanilla extract
>
> 3 large eggs, room temperature
>
> 3 cups (15 ounces) unbleached all-purpose flour
>
> ½ cup unsweetened Dutch-process cocoa powder (262), sifted, then
>   spooned lightly into the cup for measuring
>
> ½ teaspoon baking powder
>
> ¼ teaspoon salt
>
> One 10-ounce package toffee chips (I use Skor brand)
>
> 1½ cups (about 10 ounces) miniature chocolate chips (274)

Preheat the oven to 350°F. Position an oven rack in the center of the oven.

To make the dough, place the butter and sugar in the bowl of an electric mixer fitted with the paddle attachment (a handheld mixer is fine; just allow a little extra time to reach each stage in the recipe). Beat on medium speed until the butter is light in color, about 2 to 3 minutes. Add the vanilla and blend well, another 15 to 20 seconds. Use a rubber spatula to scrape down the sides of the bowl. Add the eggs one at a time, beating well after each addition (about 15 to 20 seconds) and scraping down the sides of the bowl between each egg. In a separate bowl, whisk together the flour, cocoa powder, baking powder, and salt. Add the flour mixture to the butter and blend on low speed just until the dough comes together, about 10 to 15 seconds (if you are using a handheld mixer, stir it in by hand with a wooden spoon). Add the toffee chips and chocolate chips and blend thoroughly, another 10 to 15 seconds. Turn the dough out onto a lightly floured surface and knead gently several times, just to ensure the toffee and chocolate chips are evenly distributed.

To shape the dough, working on a lightly floured surface, divide the dough in half and shape into 2 logs 15 inches long. (If this size is too long for your baking sheet, break enough dough off each log to make them fit comfortably, then shape the extra dough into a short third log—it should be the same thickness as the larger logs so they all bake in the same amount of time.)

Brush any excess flour from the surface. If you don't want to bake both rolls at once, freeze the extra log as directed in Getting Ahead. Place the logs on a parchment-covered baking sheet about 4 inches apart. Flatten each log until it is 2 inches wide. Place a second sheet pan under the first (to keep the bottom of the logs from browning too quickly). Bake for 35 minutes. The ends of the logs will feel firm, but the rest of the dough will seem too soft to be cooked—don't worry, it will firm upon cooling. Remove from the oven and place the pans on a rack to *cool completely*—do not try to cut these while they are still warm, because the dough is very tender and breaks easily.

Turn the oven down to 300°F. Position 2 oven racks in the top and center thirds of the oven.

To toast the biscotti, gently remove the cookie logs from the parchment and slice them straight across into cookies ½ inch thick. Carefully transfer the cookies, cut side down, to the parchment-lined baking sheets (you will need both pans to hold all the cookies) and return to the oven to toast for 20 to 25 minutes, until they feel firm and dry to the touch, reversing the baking sheets from front to back and from top to bottom halfway through the baking time. Remove from the oven and place the pans on racks to cool completely.

SERVING AND STORAGE NOTES: Store the biscotti in an airtight container, where they will keep for at least 2 to 3 weeks. Because of the moisture in the toffee chips, these tend to soften quickly. If they become too soft, recrisp them in a 300°F oven for 10 to 15 minutes.

GETTING AHEAD: The cookie dough may be frozen for up to 3 months. After shaping the dough into a log, wrap it tightly in plastic wrap and place the log on a baking sheet in the freezer. Once the log is frozen, remove the pan and store the cookie dough as desired. To bake, remove the plastic wrap, set on a parchment-lined baking sheet, and thaw at room temperature for 1 hour before placing in the oven.

Brown Sugar and Almond Biscotti with Cinnamon and Orange

makes about 20 to 25 biscotti

I call these chunky red-brown cookies my Christmas biscotti because the fragrance of the brown sugar and cinnamon permeates the house like all those delicious spiced molasses holiday treats I love—and because I give an awful lot of them as gifts each December. This recipe is a bit sweeter than average, but that's the key to the cookie's unique texture—the extra level of moistness the sugar adds means that just under the crisp surface there's an irresistibly chewy center.

EQUIPMENT AND ADVANCE PREPARATION: 2 baking sheets with sides, one lined with parchment paper

> 2 cups (10 ounces) unbleached all-purpose flour
>
> 1 cup (3 ounces) blanched sliced almonds (see Note)
>
> 1 teaspoon ground cinnamon
>
> ¼ teaspoon baking powder
>
> 5 tablespoons (2½ ounces) unsalted butter, room temperature
>
> 1¾ cups (14 ounces) tightly packed light brown sugar
>
> 2 large eggs
>
> 1 tablespoon finely minced orange zest (145), about 1 large orange
>
> ¾ cup (4 ounces) whole natural almonds, toasted (254)

NOTE: If the only sliced almonds you can find have their skins (they look like beige little ovals circled with a brown marking pen), go ahead and use them. There will be attractive light flecks of brown throughout the cookies.

Preheat the oven to 350°F. Position an oven rack in the center of the oven.

To make the dough, place the flour, sliced almonds, cinnamon, and baking powder in the bowl of a food processor and process until the nuts are very finely ground, about 60 to 90 seconds. Set aside. Place the butter and brown sugar in the bowl of an electric mixer fitted with the paddle attachment (a handheld mixer is fine; just allow a little extra time to reach each stage in the recipe) and beat on medium speed for 2 to 3 minutes. The mixture will be very thick and clumpy rather than smooth and creamy—this is normal. Add the eggs one at a time, beating well after each addition (about 15 to 20 seconds) and scraping down the sides of the bowl after each egg. Add the orange zest and blend well, another 10 to 15 seconds. Add the flour mixture and blend on low speed just until the dough comes together, about 10 to 15 seconds (if you are using a handheld mixer, stir in by hand with a wooden spoon). Add the toasted whole almonds and blend thoroughly, another 10 to 15 seconds.

To shape the dough, working on a lightly floured surface, divide the dough in half and shape into 2 logs 14 inches long. This dough is crumbly, so form the logs by squeezing the dough into shape. (If this size is too long for your baking sheet, break enough dough off each log to make them fit comfortably, then shape the extra dough into a short third log—it should be the same thickness as the larger logs so they all bake in the same amount of time.)

Brush any excess flour from the surface. If you don't want to bake both rolls at once, freeze the extra log as described in Getting Ahead. Place the logs on a parchment-lined baking sheet about 4 inches apart. Flatten each log until it is 2 inches wide. Place the second baking sheet under the first (to keep the bottom of the logs from browning too quickly). Bake for 35 minutes. The ends of the logs will feel firm, but the rest of the dough will seem too soft to be cooked—don't worry, it will firm upon cooling. Remove from the oven and place the pan on a rack to *cool completely*—do not try to cut these while they are still warm, because the dough is very tender and breaks easily.

Turn the oven down to 300°F.

To toast the biscotti, gently remove the cookie logs from the parchment and slice them straight across into cookies ¾ inch thick (yes, these are thick biscotti, but it's necessary for the crisp-chewy texture). Place the cookies, cut side down, on the parchment-lined pan (you no longer need the second sheet underneath) and return to the oven to toast for 7 to 8 minutes. Remove the pan from the oven, turn each cookie over, and return them to the oven to toast for an additional 7 to 8 minutes. Remove from the oven and place the pan on a rack to cool completely.

SERVING AND STORAGE NOTES: Store the biscotti in an airtight container, where they will keep for at least 2 to 3 weeks. Remember, these cookies are supposed to be chewy in the center, so do not attempt to recrisp them.

GETTING AHEAD: The cookie dough may be frozen for up to 3 months. After shaping the dough into a log, wrap it tightly in plastic wrap and place the log on a baking sheet in the freezer. Once the log is frozen, remove the pan and store the cookie dough as desired. To bake, remove the plastic wrap, set on a parchment-lined baking sheet, and thaw at room temperature for 1 hour before placing in the oven.

Pear and Walnut Whole Wheat Biscotti

makes 45 to 50 biscotti

Whole wheat flour adds an unusual, hearty dimension to these biscotti and is an earthy complement to the pears and walnuts within. There's no butter here, so remember that this makes a naturally hard cookie (good for dipping). If you want them a bit softer for snacking, toast them for only 10 to 15 minutes total.

EQUIPMENT AND ADVANCE PREPARATION: 2 baking sheets with sides, lined with parchment paper

> 6 ounces dried pears
>
> 3 tablespoons (1½ ounces) Poire William (pear brandy)
>
> 3 large eggs
>
> 1 cup (7 ounces) sugar
>
> 1¾ cups (8¾ ounces) unbleached all-purpose flour
>
> 1½ cups (6¼ ounces) whole wheat flour
>
> ¾ teaspoon baking powder
>
> ½ teaspoon ground nutmeg
>
> ¼ teaspoon baking soda
>
> ¼ teaspoon salt
>
> 1 cup (3½ ounces) whole walnuts, toasted (follow directions for toasting whole almonds, 254) and coarsely chopped

To prepare the fruit, use a pair of scissors to snip the dried pears into ⅜-inch to ½-inch pieces, discarding any hard matter in the core areas. Place the pears in a small bowl. Add the Poire William and stir to blend. Set the bowl aside for 15 minutes, stirring several times to help the pears absorb the liquid evenly.

Preheat the oven to 350°F. Position an oven rack in the center of the oven.

To make the dough, place the eggs and sugar in the bowl of an electric mixer fitted with the whisk attachment (a handheld mixer is fine; just allow a little extra time to reach each stage in the recipe) and beat on high until the mixture is very thick, light in color, and ribbons when it falls from the whisk to the surface of the batter, about 3 to 4 minutes. In a separate bowl, whisk together the all-purpose flour, whole wheat flour, baking powder, nutmeg, baking soda, and salt. Switch to the paddle attachment and add the flour mixture (if you are using a handheld mixer, stir it in by hand with a wooden spoon). Blend on low speed just until the dough comes together, about 10 to 15 seconds. Add the dried pears, any remaining soaking liquid, and the chopped walnuts and blend thoroughly, another 15 to 20 seconds.

To shape the dough, working on a lightly floured surface, divide the dough in half and shape into 2 logs about 15 inches long. (If this size is too long for your baking sheet, break enough dough off each log to make them fit comfortably, then shape the extra dough into a short third log—it should be the same thickness as the larger logs so they all bake in the same amount of time.)

Brush any excess flour from the surface. If you don't want to bake both rolls at once, freeze the extra log as directed in Getting Ahead. Place the logs on a parchment-lined baking sheet about 4 inches apart. Flatten each log until it is 2 inches wide. Place the second baking sheet under the first (to keep the bottom of the logs from browning too quickly). Bake for 30 to 35 minutes, or until the logs are firm to the touch in the center and lightly golden brown. Transfer the pans to a rack and cool until the logs are lukewarm.

Turn the oven down to 300°F. Position 2 oven racks in the top and center thirds of the oven.

To toast the biscotti, gently remove the warm cookie logs from the baking sheet and slice them on a slight diagonal into cookies ½ inch thick (see illustration, 273). Place the cookies, cut side down, on the parchment-covered baking sheets (you will need both pans to hold all the cookies) and return to the oven to toast for 20 minutes, or until dry and lightly tinged with color, reversing the baking sheets from front to back and from top to bottom halfway through the baking time. Remove the pans from the oven and place on a rack to cool completely.

SERVING AND STORAGE NOTES: Store the biscotti in an airtight container, where they will keep for at least 2 to 3 weeks. If the biscotti soften, recrisp them in a 300°F oven for 10 to 15 minutes.

GETTING AHEAD: The cookie dough may be frozen for up to 3 months. After shaping the dough into a log, wrap it tightly in plastic wrap and place the log on a baking sheet in the freezer. Once the log is frozen, remove the pan and store the cookie dough as desired. To bake, remove the plastic wrap, set on a parchment-lined baking sheet, and thaw at room temperature for 1 hour before placing in the oven.

Ice Creams
and Sorbets

Ice creams, fruit ices, and sorbets are well loved throughout the Mediterranean, but nowhere as much as right here in the United States, where we have adopted them as some of our national foods. Though easily bought, ice cream and sorbet are far better when homemade for several reasons. First, *you* choose the flavor *and* the ingredients, which means you can pick the ripest, most flavorful fruit and freshest nuts (or coffee beans or vanilla beans or whatever), and transform them into dessert the same day. The result is an intensity of flavor that commercial brands just can't match. Second, since you get to enjoy your frozen desserts "fresh," you don't have to add the stabilizers and emulsifiers that commercial producers include for prolonged shelf life. Best of all, guests go wild for frozen desserts, which illicit the sort of "You did that for *me?*" response that is usually reserved for much more time-consuming desserts.

If the last time you made ice cream was with an old-fashioned hand-crank machine, you'll be thrilled with modern freezing equipment. A variety of efficient ice cream machines is available in all price ranges (295). If you can't muster an ice cream machine, there's always granita. Made with the same mixture as sorbet (fruit juice or puree sweetened with sugar syrup), granita is not machine frozen but is placed in a pan in the freezer and whisked occasionally over the course of several hours to form an icy, refreshing dessert of sparkling fruit crystals with a slightly slushy texture.

This chapter includes some of the best endings possible for Mediterranean-inspired meals, for the simplicity and vibrancy of ices capture the true essence of the region's culinary spirit. If it's ice cream that you crave, you'll find rich and creamy spectacles—from a Pistachio Ice Cream saturated with the warm and deep flavor of freshly roasted pistachios to a pucker-up-and-smile Double-Lemon Ice Cream to an incredible Lavender and Almond Praline Ice Cream that is richly evocative of Provence. And if you have a weakness for ice cream sandwiches, as I do, you'll love the marriage of childhood fun with grown-up flavors in Lemon and Almond Macaroon Ice Cream Sandwiches, in which the creamy tartness of Double-Lemon Ice Cream is paired with soft and chewy almond macaroons. For pure fruit refreshment, try the dramatically hued Blood Orange Sorbet, the exquisitely perfumed Lemon Verbena Sorbet, or the silky and exotic Quince Sorbet with Lemon. This week, skip the ice cream aisle in the supermarket and find a whole new world of dynamic flavors by creating your own exciting frozen desserts at home.

Pistachio Ice Cream

makes about 1 quart

If you've tasted only store-bought pistachio ice cream, you're in for a real treat. This ice cream tastes like the very essence of pistachios, thanks to the infusion of nuts and the accent of Amaretto di Saronno. Rather than adding a discernible almond flavor, the liqueur actually enhances the taste of toasted pistachios. Chocolate and pistachios are a classic match, so if you feel like going the extra mile, stir about ¼ to ⅓ cup of home-made miniature chocolate chips (274) into the ice cream after you transfer it to the storage container. For cookies and ice cream, pair with Bitter Chocolate Wafers (261).

Pistachios do not lend their color to ice cream, which is, instead, a delicate creamy beige. If you feel pistachio ice cream simply must be green, a drop or two of green food coloring will do the trick. Add the coloring to the cooled custard before you place it in the machine.

EQUIPMENT AND ADVANCE PREPARATION: An ice cream machine • If you have a frozen canister–style machine, be sure to allow 24 hours for the canister to freeze. • If you find only pistachios in shells, buy double the weight given below and shell them by hand.

> 2 cups (16 ounces) heavy cream
>
> 2 cups (16 ounces) half-and-half
>
> ¾ cup (5¼ ounces) sugar
>
> 1½ cups (6½ ounces) raw unsalted shelled pistachios, toasted (213) and coarsely chopped
>
> 4 large egg yolks
>
> 2 tablespoons Amaretto di Saronno

To flavor the custard, place the cream, half-and-half, sugar, and toasted nuts in a medium saucepan. Cook over medium-low heat to just below boiling, stirring several times with a wooden spoon to dissolve the sugar. Turn off the heat, cover the pan with a lid, and allow the mixture to steep for 30 to 40 minutes.

To finish the custard, place the pan back over medium-low heat and reheat the mixture to just below boiling. In a small bowl, lightly whisk the egg yolks, just to blend. Whisking constantly, slowly add about 1 cup of the hot cream to the yolks. Pour the yolk mixture back into the saucepan and cook, stirring constantly with the wooden spoon, until the custard thickens and coats the back of the spoon (about 170°F on an instant-read thermometer). Do not let the mixture boil, or the eggs will curdle. Immediately pour the custard through a fine-mesh strainer into a large bowl, pressing firmly against the nuts with a rubber spatula to remove as much liquid as possible. Discard the nuts. Stir the custard gently for a minute or two, just to cool it slightly. Stir in the amaretto. Cover and refrigerate until the custard is very cold.

Freeze in your ice cream machine according to the manufacturer's directions. Immediately transfer the ice cream to a storage container, cover, and place in the freezer.

SERVING AND STORAGE NOTES: If possible, let the ice cream "ripen" slightly in the freezer, about 2 to 3 hours. Homemade ice cream may get very hard after 1 or 2 days in the freezer. If this happens, let it soften in the refrigerator for 15 to 30 minutes before serving.

GETTING AHEAD: The custard may be prepared up to 4 days in advance. Keep refrigerated in an airtight container.

VARIATIONS

Hazelnut Ice Cream: Substitute 1½ cups (7¼ ounces) toasted (227) and skinned hazelnuts, coarsely chopped, for the pistachios in the recipe, and Frangelico (hazelnut liqueur) for the Amaretto di Saronno.

Almond Ice Cream: Substitute 1½ cups (7¼ ounces) toasted (254) whole natural almonds, coarsely chopped, for the pistachios in the recipe.

Warm Bittersweet Chocolate Sauce

makes about 2 cups

This chocolate sauce is the perfect partner to the nut ice creams presented here. I particularly like this recipe because it is made with milk and crème fraîche instead of all cream, so it is lighter than usual. The crème fraîche adds a nutty richness to the deep, round flavor of chocolate, creating an exceptionally silky sauce. Use this sparingly for a punch of liquid flavor—avoid "pools" of choco-

late sauce, which can easily overwhelm almost anything. The exception, of course, is an ice cream sundae, where a cascade of chocolate is practically a requirement.

8 ounces bittersweet or semisweet chocolate, finely chopped

1 cup (8 ounces) whole milk

½ cup (4 ounces) crème fraîche (303)

1 to 2 tablespoons (½ to 1 ounce) brandy, to taste

Place the chopped chocolate in a medium bowl. Place the milk and crème fraîche in a small saucepan over medium-low heat and warm to just below the boiling point. Immediately pour the mixture over the chocolate and let it sit for 2 minutes. Whisk gently to blend and smooth the sauce, then stir in the brandy. Serve warm.

This sauce can be made ahead and refrigerated in an airtight container until needed. To reheat, bring 2 inches of water to a simmer in a medium saucepan. Transfer the sauce to a medium bowl and place it on top of the saucepan. Stir frequently with a wooden spoon or rubber spatula while the sauce is warming. Use immediately, or turn off the heat and allow the sauce to stay warm over the steaming water. Do not overcook the sauce or allow it to boil, or it may separate.

If it's true that we all scream for ice cream, then it's also true that we are steadfastly cheering for one of two definitive styles of the stuff. "Philadelphia-style" ice cream is the classic American version consisting of heavy cream mixed with a bit of sugar and fruit or flavorings. While it can be very good, I prefer to do all my yelling for "French-style" ice cream, which is based on a cooked custard composed of heavy cream, milk, egg yolks, sugar, and flavorings. To me, custard ice cream has a deeper, richer flavor, and because egg yolks act as natural emulsifiers and stabilizers, they create a smoother, less icy texture, even after storage.

ABOUT THE INGREDIENTS

Cream

We Americans like our ice cream rich, dense, and full of flavor, and heavy cream is essential for each of these elements. In cooking as well as baking, fat is the prime medium that distributes flavor throughout a dish. In ice cream, the milkfat in the heavy cream both carries and enhances the flavorings you have chosen. It also inhibits whipping during the churning process, which means less air is incorporated, resulting in a denser ice cream. There are so few ingredients in these luscious homemade versions that the quality of ingredients really shines through, and this is especially true of the cream.

If at all possible, avoid the ultrapasteurized cream sold in supermarkets. "Ultra" means the cream has been pasteurized at a much higher temperature than needed so it can sit on the shelf longer, but the result is an odd, cooked-milk flavor. Much better is pasteurized heavy cream, often available in "gourmet" markets or in natural and natural food stores. Even better is manufacturing cream. This cream has a higher milkfat content—up to 40 percent or more, compared to the 30 percent to 36 percent of heavy cream. It is the cream used by fine restaurants and pastry shops to make their ice creams and desserts. Manufacturing cream is available in stores that cater to those businesses—restaurant supply stores, large membership stores, and "open to the public" supply stores.

Note on using manufacturing cream The ice cream recipes in this book were developed using heavy whipping cream. If you will be using manufacturing cream, replace the half-and-half in each recipe with whole milk—otherwise, the ice cream may be unpleasantly heavy and rich.

Sugar

Sugar is, of course, used as a sweetener, but it also plays an important part in the texture of ice cream. The right amount of sugar slightly reduces the freezing point of the custard, which means that the mixture takes longer to freeze, the dasher has more time to churn the ice cream smooth, and the end product has a pleasant softness to it, even when hardened in the freezer. Too much sugar, in addition to ruining the flavor, can take the freezing point so low as to result in a slushy texture, even after hardening. You can adjust the sugar slightly in these recipes, but remember that the custard should always taste a bit sweeter than you want it because freezing reduces our perception of sweetness. Too little sugar can result in a flat-tasting dessert.

Alcohol

Alcohol is a wonderful addition to ice cream for several reasons. First, it provides another layer of flavor, underscoring or complementing the predominant one. Second, it has a sharpness of flavor that cuts through the cream for a nice balance of flavor. Third, it can improve texture. This occurs because alcohol does not freeze, and when used in moderate quantities, it has a softening effect on the ice cream. Adding too much alcohol will keep the mixture from freezing, resulting in a milkshake texture. In general, do not use more than about 3 to 4 tablespoons of liquor for every 3 cups of cream and/or milk in a recipe.

ABOUT ICE CREAM MACHINES

Ice cream machines have come a long way since the 1846 invention of the classic hand-crank freezer. Though this old-fashioned machine still makes great ice cream, there are more efficient, electric models available. These machines use less manpower but still need ice and salt to freeze the mixture inside the canister. Though they can be messy and noisy, electric machines have a large capacity (usually 2 quarts) and allow you to make as many successive batches of ice cream or sorbet as you want per day (as long as you have enough ice and salt).

Frozen-canister ice cream makers were introduced in the 1980s and made churning easy and fun . . . and inexpensive. The thick metal canister has a coolant in its walls and needs to be stored in the freezer overnight before use. The canister's capacity is 2 to 4 cups, depending on the model. Many of these machines call for hand-churning (don't panic—it's easy), but there are now some canister machines with electric stirring mechanisms available. The one drawback (and this is for fanatics) is that because the canister needs to be frozen overnight between uses, you can make only one batch of ice cream per day.

Note: If you have a hand-churn frozen-canister model, ignore the manufacturer's directions for turning the dasher only every few minutes and stir slowly and constantly from the moment you add the ice cream mixture until it is frozen. My experience has been that by the time you wait a few minutes, the mixture against the wall has frozen hard and may prevent the dasher from turning (or you may break the plastic handle in the process of trying).

The Rolls-Royce of ice cream makers is the electric machine with a built-in cooling unit. It sits on the countertop and is about the size of a large toaster oven. It is simple to use, clean, and efficient and turns out fabulously smooth ice cream. Just turn it on, add the custard, and soon thereafter—almost effortless dessert. These machines usually hold 4 to 6 cups and can make batch after batch after batch. As you may have guessed, there's a price tag for this ease of use, but for those who love homemade ice cream and sorbet and make it regularly, it's a worthwhile investment.

SERVING SUGGESTIONS

My childhood love of mixed ice creams, such as Neapolitan (chocolate, strawberry, and vanilla) and hopscotch (vanilla ice cream and orange sorbet), has not diminished—it's the quality and flavor of the ingredients that has improved. Marbleizing two complementary ice creams (or an ice cream and a sorbet) creates a dramatic dessert with a flavor that is much more than the sum of its parts. Marbleizing is as simple as layering the ice creams in a storage container (each layer should be about ⅜ to ½ inch thick). When serving time comes, the mixture "self-marbleizes" as you pull the scoop through the layers. The layering is easiest to do when the ice creams are soft—preferably, straight from the machine. If that's not possible, just let the two flavors soften in the refrigerator for 15 to 30 minutes, until soft enough to spread. When I'm in a hurry, I put each flavor separately in the bowl of an electric mixer fitted with the paddle attachment and beat the ice cream on medium speed until it has softened (this takes just a few seconds).

For a presentation that is a bit more formal and dramatic, place a terrine mold, small cake pan, or other decorative mold in the freezer for 30 minutes. Line it with plastic wrap, then layer the ice creams in the pan as directed above. Cover the top with plastic wrap and return to the freezer until the ice cream has hardened, at least 2 hours. When you are ready to serve dessert, turn the ice cream out of the mold, peel off the plastic wrap, and cut into slices. Serve with warm bittersweet chocolate sauce (295) or caramel sauce (66) and garnish with fresh fruit of the season.

Here are a few pairing ideas for marbleizing the recipes in this book. Not all of these combinations are dramatic color contrasts, but the flavor combinations are dynamite. If you want visual drama in addition to flavor, then you will need to enhance the color of the ice creams marked with an asterisk (*) by adding a tiny bit of food coloring to the cooled custard before you place it in the machine. Be cautious here—add the coloring drop by drop and stir thoroughly before adding each drop to keep the colors "natural" and avoid the neon look of so many commerical ice creams. Use yellow food coloring for lemon, red or purple for pomegranate, and green for pistachio.

- Lavender and Almond Praline Ice Cream (305) and Blackberry Sorbet (320)

- Pomegranate Ice Cream (312) and Pomegranate Granita with Rose Water prepared as a sorbet (325)

- Crème Fraîche Ice Cream (302) and Raspberry or Blackberry Sorbet (320)

- Pomegranate Ice Cream★ (312) and Pistachio★ (294) or Almond (295) Ice Cream

- Double-Lemon Ice Cream★ (308) and Crème Fraîche Ice Cream (302)

- Double-Lemon Ice Cream★ (308) and Lemon Verbena Sorbet (321)

- Double-Lemon Ice Cream (308) and Tangerine (317) or Blood Orange Sorbet (318)

Gelato Affogato

serves 6

There's nothing like the contrast of eating cold, sweet ice cream while sipping hot, bitter espresso. The Italians have raised this combination to dessert status with gelato affogato. Literally "smothered ice cream," this dessert is a small dish of ice cream with a shot of hot espresso (or sometimes liqueur) poured over the top. The ice cream softens and blends with the coffee, and the play of warm against cold is irresistible. I particularly like it made with one of the nut ice creams (listed below), though Crème Fraîche Ice Cream is a good choice as well. In fact, this dessert is easily thrown together for last-minute entertaining if you have a pint of good store-bought coffee or vanilla ice cream in the freezer. No espresso machine? Use a flavorful, good-quality coffee and make it strong. As you can see below, I like to add a few extras to turn Gelato Affogato into a petite ice cream sundae.

1 recipe Pistachio (294), Almond (295), Hazelnut (295), or Crème Fraîche (302) Ice Cream

2 cups (16 ounces) hot espresso or strong coffee

6 tablespoons (3 ounces) Amaretto di Saronno, Frangelico, or other liqueur

1 recipe softly whipped cream (54)

Miniature chocolate curls (106)

For each serving, place 1 or 2 scoops of ice cream in a small dish. Pour over the ice cream 1 shot (about ⅓ cup) of espresso or strong coffee blended with 1 tablespoon liqueur (Amaretto di Saronno and Frangelico are my particular favorites and blend beautifully with the ice cream suggestions above). Top with a generous spoonful of softly whipped cream and 1 teaspoon miniature chocolate curls or shavings. Serve immediately, while the coffee is still warm.

Crème Fraîche
Ice Cream

makes about 1 quart

This is the perfect ice cream when you want something simple, out of the ordinary, and utterly sensational. Here, the cultured acidity of crème fraîche lends a lightly sour, wonderfully nutty flavor to ice cream, somewhere between cream cheese and sour cream. I like it best paired with fresh farmstand fruit, such as strawberries, sliced peaches, or cherries, that has been tossed with a sprinkling of sugar and a dash of Amaretto di Saronno.

EQUIPMENT AND ADVANCE PREPARATION: An ice cream machine • If you have a frozen canister–style machine, be sure to allow 24 hours for the canister to freeze. • If you are making crème fraîche (303), you will need to start 2 days before you want to make the ice cream.

> 3 cups (24 ounces) crème fraîche
>
> 4 large egg yolks
>
> ¾ cup plus 1 tablespoon (5²/₃ ounces) sugar
>
> 1 teaspoon pure vanilla extract

To make the custard, place the crème fraîche in a medium saucepan. Warm over medium-low heat to just below the boiling point. In a medium bowl, whisk together the egg yolks and sugar—the mixture will be stiff at first but will eventually smooth out. Whisking constantly, slowly add about 1 cup of the hot crème fraîche to the yolks. Pour the yolk mixture back into the saucepan and cook, stirring constantly with a wooden spoon, until the custard thickens and coats the back of a spoon (about 170°F on an instant-read thermometer). Do not let the mixture boil, or the eggs will curdle. Immediately pour the custard through a fine-mesh strainer into a large bowl. Stir the custard gently for a minute or two, just to cool it slightly. Stir in the vanilla extract. Cover and refrigerate until the custard is very cold.

Freeze in your ice cream machine according to the manufacturer's directions. Immediately transfer the ice cream to a storage container, cover, and place in the freezer.

SERVING AND STORAGE NOTES: If possible, serve within 1 hour of churning in the ice cream machine. Because of the high milkfat content of crème fraîche, it has a tendency to freeze into a hard block that is nearly impossible to scoop unless you soften it in the refrigerator for 15 to 30 minutes before serving.

GETTING AHEAD: The custard may be prepared up to 4 days in advance (just remember that the crème fraîche will continue to culture as it sits). Keep refrigerated in an airtight container.

VARIATION

Vanilla Bean Crème Fraîche Ice Cream: This variation on classic vanilla bean ice cream combines the floral quality of a whole vanilla bean with the slightly sour note of crème fraîche. Use the tip of a sharp knife to split 1 whole vanilla bean lengthwise. Scrape out the seeds and add them to the saucepan with the crème fraîche, along with the pod. Heat as directed above to just below the boiling point, then turn off the heat, cover the pan with a lid, and allow the mixture to steep for 20 to 30 minutes. Place the pan back over medium-low heat and reheat the mixture to just below boiling, then continue with the recipe above. After straining the custard, retrieve the vanilla pod from the strainer and add it to the cooling custard—remove it just before pouring the custard into the ice cream machine.

Crème Fraîche

makes 1 cup

Crème fraîche is a cultured sour cream with a nutty flavor that is very popular in France. It is often compared to sour cream, but sour cream has a harsher and more acidic edge to it than more mellow crème fraîche. Do not substitute sour cream for crème fraîche when making recipes in this book. Crème fraîche is available in cheese shops and in the dairy section of many supermarkets. It is very easy to make at home, and this recipe can be doubled, tripled, or more to make as much as you need (if you are making Crème Fraîche Ice Cream, 302, you will need to triple the recipe).

Crème fraîche is best when made with cream that is not ultrapasteurized, for in addition to adding an odd, cooked-milk flavor, this "ultra" cream becomes much more acidic during the culturing process. Regular pasteurized heavy cream is usually available in "gourmet" markets, as well as natural and natural food stores. If you can find manufacturing cream (see Note on page 294), it is perfect for making crème fraîche.

__Note:__ Homemade crème fraîche thickens as it sits but will remain a liquid. If you want to serve crème fraîche as an accompaniment to dessert instead of whipped cream, whip it to soft peaks, just as you would heavy cream.

1 cup (8 ounces) heavy cream

2 tablespoons (1 ounce) buttermilk

Place the heavy cream in a small saucepan over medium-low heat and warm just until lukewarm (about 95° to 100°F). Remove the pan from the heat and stir in the buttermilk. Pour the mixture into a jar, cover the opening with plastic, and let it sit at room temperature for 24 to 48 hours. The mixture will become thick and flavorful. Taste it every so often and refrigerate it once you like the flavor. I like it a bit thicker and more cultured, so I usually let it sit out for at least 36 to 48 hours. Keep in mind that the weather can affect the rate at which the cream sours—faster in the summer, slower in the winter. Once you like the flavor, refrigerate until needed. Crème fraîche will keep for at least a week, continuing to culture as time passes. If it looks a little watery or separated, just stir it until the mixture becomes homogeneous again.

Lavender and Almond Praline Ice Cream

makes about 1 quart

This recipe is richly evocative of Provence, where fields of lavender and graceful almond trees are an integral part of the landscape. I first tasted lavender ice cream in a tiny restaurant with just five tables (did it even have a name?) in the south of France. One bite and I knew I had to re-create the flavor, if not the exquisite setting, when I arrived back home. In this version I've added ground almond praline for a dramatic contrast in texture and also because the earthy flavors of caramel and toasted almonds perfectly complement the musky perfume of lavender. If you never thought you'd eat anything lavender flavored, give this ice cream a try. It will make you an herbal convert.

EQUIPMENT AND ADVANCE PREPARATION: 1 recipe almond praline (306). Grind enough praline to fill a ½-cup measure and save the remaining praline for another use. • An ice cream machine • If you have a frozen canister–style machine, allow 24 hours for the canister to freeze.

FOR THE CUSTARD

2 cups (16 ounces) heavy cream

1 cup (8 ounces) half-and-half

⅔ cup (4¾ ounces) sugar

2 tablespoons dried lavender flowers (see Note)

4 large egg yolks

FOR FINISHING

⅓ to ½ cup ground almond praline (306), to taste

NOTE: When cooking with lavender, always use flowers that have been grown for culinary purposes. Those available in flower shops and craft stores have been treated with chemicals that can be dangerous if ingested (see Mail-Order Sources, 327).

To flavor the custard, place the cream, half-and-half, and sugar in a medium saucepan. Warm over medium-low heat to just below the boiling point, stirring several times with a wooden spoon to dissolve the sugar. Turn off the heat, add the lavender flowers, cover the pan, and allow the mixture to steep for 5 minutes.

Pour the mixture through a fine-mesh strainer into a medium bowl, pressing firmly against the flowers with a rubber spatula to remove as much liquid as possible. Discard the flowers. Return the flavored cream to the saucepan.

To finish the custard, place the pan back over medium-low heat and reheat the mixture to just below the boiling point. In a small bowl, lightly whisk the egg yolks, just to blend. Whisking constantly, slowly add about 1 cup of the hot cream to the yolks. Pour the yolk mixture back into the saucepan and cook, stirring constantly with the wooden spoon, until the custard thickens and coats the back of the spoon (about 170°F on an instant-read thermometer). Do not let the mixture boil, or the eggs will curdle. Immediately pour the custard through a fine-mesh strainer into a large bowl. Stir the custard gently for a minute or two, just to cool it slightly. Cover and refrigerate until the custard is very cold.

Freeze in your ice cream machine according to the manufacturer's directions. Immediately transfer the ice cream to a storage container, then stir in the praline, to your taste. Cover and place in the freezer.

SERVING AND STORAGE NOTES: If possible, let the ice cream "ripen" slightly in the freezer, about 2 to 3 hours. Homemade ice cream may get very hard after 1 or 2 days in the freezer. If this happens, let it soften in the refrigerator for 15 to 30 minutes before serving.

GETTING AHEAD: The custard may be prepared up to 4 days in advance. Keep refrigerated in an airtight container.

Praline

makes 3 cups (14 ounces) finely ground praline

Praline, a caramelized sugar and toasted nut combination, is a staple flavoring in the French pastry kitchen. It is made with equal weights of sugar and nuts, and almost any nut (or combination of nuts) may be used—almonds and hazelnuts are a classic combination. In the fall I like to make praline with pecans or walnuts because they complement pumpkin, apples, and pears so well, and in the spring and summer I turn to almonds or hazelnuts, which blend with the berries and stone fruits of those seasons.

Once the praline is made, it can be used in several forms—broken into large pieces like candy, chopped coarsely, ground finely, or even processed to a paste, depending on your taste and the intended use. I almost always use it finely ground for flavoring fillings and mousses, as well as for decorating the sides of cakes or garnishing plates.

EQUIPMENT AND ADVANCE PREPARATION: A baking sheet with sides • Brush the pan with a thin, even coat of melted butter or flavorless vegetable oil.

> ¼ cup (2 ounces) water
>
> 1 cup (7 ounces) sugar
>
> 1½ to 2 cups (7 ounces) toasted nuts, room temperature (to toast almonds see page 254; for hazelnuts, see page 227; to toast whole walnut or pecan halves, follow the directions for toasting whole almonds)

Place the water in a medium saucepan, add the sugar, and set the pan over medium heat. Stir constantly with a wooden spoon or swirl the pan frequently until the sugar has dissolved and the liquid is clear. Turn the heat to high and boil rapidly, swirling the pan occasionally (do not stir at this point) so that the sugar cooks evenly, until it turns a deep golden brown. Remove the pan from the heat and immediately add the toasted nuts, stirring with the wooden spoon just until they are evenly coated with the caramel. If the caramel solidifies after the nuts are added, set the pan back over medium heat and stir until it becomes liquid again.

Quickly pour the mixture out onto the baking sheet, spreading it with the spoon until the nuts are in a single layer. Let the praline cool completely. Break into pieces and use as desired. To grind finely, place the pieces of praline in a food processor and process to the consistency of fine crumbs, about 40 to 60 seconds.

Store in a dry, airtight jar or storage container at room temperature. The praline will keep for at least 2 to 4 weeks but will eventually soften and form a solid mass.

Double-Lemon
Ice Cream

makes 1 generous quart

The ice cream equivalent of a tall, tingly glass of lemonade on the hottest day of summer, this is the most refreshing dessert I know of. An infusion of flavor from lemon zest plus a generous amount of juice makes this a cold, creamy, bracingly tart finish that is perfect for a sticky summer evening and just as welcome after a hearty meal on a cold winter's eve. The Meyer lemon is a particularly fragrant variety that is grown in home gardens all over California, and it is the lemon I use most in dessert making. If you can't find Meyers, don't worry—supermarket lemons (the Eureka variety) are excellent in this ice cream.

EQUIPMENT AND ADVANCE PREPARATION: An ice cream machine • If you have a frozen canister–style machine, allow 24 hours for the canister to freeze.

> 2 cups (16 ounces) heavy cream
>
> 1 cup (8 ounces) half-and-half
>
> 1 cup plus 2 tablespoons (8 ounces) sugar
>
> Zest of 3 lemons, in strips
>
> 5 large egg yolks
>
> ¾ cup (6 ounces) freshly squeezed and strained lemon juice

To flavor the custard, place the cream, half-and-half, sugar, and lemon zest in a medium saucepan. Warm over medium-low heat to just below the boiling point, stirring several times with a wooden spoon to dissolve the sugar. Turn off the heat, cover the pan with a lid, and allow the mixture to steep for 30 to 40 minutes.

To finish the custard, place the pan back over medium-low heat and reheat the mixture to just below the boiling point. In a small bowl, lightly whisk the egg yolks, just to blend. Whisking constantly, slowly add about 1 cup of the hot cream to the yolks. Pour the yolk mixture back into the saucepan and cook, stirring constantly with the wooden spoon, until the custard thickens and coats the back of the spoon (about 170°F on an instant-read thermometer). Do not let the mixture boil, or the eggs will curdle. Immediately pour the custard through a fine-mesh strainer into a large bowl, pressing firmly against the lemon zest with a rubber spatula to remove as much liquid as possible. Discard the zest. Stir the custard gently for a minute or two, just to cool it slightly. Cover and refrigerate until the custard is very cold, then stir in the lemon juice.

Freeze in your ice cream machine according to the manufacturer's directions. Immediately transfer the ice cream to a storage container, cover, and place in the freezer.

SERVING AND STORAGE NOTES: If possible, let the ice cream "ripen" slightly in the freezer, about 2 to 3 hours. Homemade ice cream may get very hard after 1 to 2 days in the freezer. If this happens, let it soften in the refrigerator for 15 to 30 minutes before serving.

GETTING AHEAD: The custard may be prepared up to 4 days in advance, but do not squeeze or add the lemon juice until the day it is to be frozen. Keep the custard refrigerated in an airtight container.

VARIATION

Double-Lime Ice Cream: Follow the recipe above, substituting lime zest and lime juice for the lemon.

Meyer Lemons

I'm lucky enough to have two large Meyer lemon trees in my yard. In the spring and late fall the air is exquisitely perfumed with their blossoms, and shortly thereafter the tiny green globes swell in size, turn from yellow to an almost egg yolk color, and become heavy with their characteristic sweet-sour-floral juice. My grandmother, a lemon purist, turns up her nose at Meyer lemons and calls them "that orange lemon," but I, like many Californians, have always preferred their unique flavor to that of standard supermarket lemons.

The Meyer lemon was introduced to California in 1908 by Frank Meyer, who found it in Beijing while searching for new agricultural possibilities for the U.S. government. He failed to note the name of the citrus, so it became known as the Meyer lemon. It is not a true lemon (like the Eureka or the Lisbon); at some time in its history it was intimate with either a mandarin or an orange. It was an immediate success in California because of its slightly sweet juice with floral undertones, as well as its beautiful ornamental quality, with dark green leaves, pink-white flowers, and deep yellow-orange fruit. This variety is hardier than true lemons and able to withstand temperatures down to the low 20s, so its popularity spread even into the areas where lemons once dared not tread.

Unfortunately, the original Meyer lemon was vulnerable to the virus tristeza, a threat to the state's commercial citrus groves, which accounts for why such a popular home fruit has never been grown on a large scale. More recently the University of California at Riverside has developed a virus-resistant tree named Improved Meyer, which may encourage larger-scale plantings of this extraordinary fruit. In California the trees are fruitful almost year-round, with the heaviest harvests in the winter and early summer. Watch for them at these times, for the Meyer is gaining in popularity and can occasionally be found in gourmet markets around the country (see Mail-Order Sources, 327).

Lemon and Almond Macaroon Ice Cream Sandwiches

serves 8

Lemons and almonds are a Mediterranean match made in heaven, and here they are paired in a chewy, invigorating variation on an American favorite.

1 recipe Double-Lemon Ice Cream (308)

1 recipe Almond and Hazelnut Chip Macaroons (250)

This dessert is easiest to make when the lemon ice cream is soft and malleable—ideally, right out of the ice cream machine. If the ice cream has hardened in the freezer, either soften it in the refrigerator for 15 to 30 minutes or place it in the bowl of an electric mixer fitted with the paddle attachment and beat it on low speed briefly, just until soft enough to scoop.

To assemble the ice cream sandwiches, turn over half of the macaroons so that their flat side is up. Place a generous scoop (about 2½ ounces) of ice cream in the center of each macaroon. Place the remaining cookies, flat side down, on top of the ice cream, pressing lightly to force the ice cream into an even layer that ends at the cookie edges. Wrap each sandwich tightly in plastic and freeze until serving time, at least 2 hours.

SERVING AND STORAGE NOTES: Serve straight up and unadorned, encouraging guests to pick them up with their hands and lick their fingers when done.

GETTING AHEAD: The ice cream may be made up to 1 week in advance.

The macaroons may be made up to 1 month in advance (see directions, 251).

The ice cream sandwiches may be assembled, individually wrapped tightly in plastic wrap, and frozen for up to 2 weeks. You may need to soften the sandwiches in the refrigerator for 10 to 15 minutes before serving.

Pomegranate Ice Cream

makes about 1 quart

Ice cream is an ideal vehicle for pomegranate molasses, a thick, heady syrup of concentrated pomegranate juice, because its deep, acerbic flavor gives tartness and complexity to the creamy richness of ice cream.

EQUIPMENT AND ADVANCE PREPARATION: An ice cream machine • If you have a frozen canister–style machine, be sure to allow 24 hours for the canister to freeze.

1½ cups (12 ounces) heavy cream

1½ cups (12 ounces) half-and-half

4 large egg yolks

¾ cup (5¼ ounces) sugar

3 to 4 tablespoons pomegranate molasses (71), to taste

FOR SERVING
Lacy Sesame Crisps (267)

To make the custard, place the heavy cream and half-and-half in a medium saucepan. Warm over medium-low heat to just below the boiling point. In a small bowl, whisk together the egg yolks and sugar—the mixture will be stiff at first but will eventually smooth out. Whisking constantly, slowly add about 1 cup of the hot cream to the yolks. Pour the yolk mixture back into the saucepan and cook, stirring constantly with a wooden spoon, until the custard thickens slightly and coats the back of the spoon (about 170°F on an instant-read thermometer). Immediately pour the custard through a fine-mesh strainer into a large bowl. Stir the custard gently for a minute or two, just to cool it slightly. Cover and refrigerate until the custard is very cold. Stir in 3 tablespoons pomegranate molasses. Taste the mixture and add the remaining molasses if needed, teaspoon by teaspoon, until you like the flavor. Keep in mind, though, that the mixture should taste a bit sweeter than you want it to because freezing reduces our perception of sugar.

Freeze in your ice cream machine according to the manufacturer's directions. Immediately transfer the ice cream to a storage container, cover, and place in the freezer.

SERVING AND STORAGE NOTES: If possible, let the ice cream "ripen" slightly in the freezer, about 2 to 3 hours. Homemade ice cream may get very hard after 1 to 2 days in the freezer. If this happens, let it soften in the refrigerator for 15 to 30 minutes before serving.

GETTING AHEAD: The custard may be prepared up to 4 days in advance, but do not add the pomegranate molasses until the day it will be frozen. Keep refrigerated in an airtight container.

Sorbets and Granitas

Sorbets and granitas (*granite* in Italian) showcase the pure, clean flavors of fresh fruit in an exquisitely simple frozen dessert. In fact, the same lightly sweetened fruit juice or fruit puree can be used to make either sorbet or granita—the difference is in how the mixtures are frozen. Sorbets are churned in an ice cream machine, making them smooth and almost creamy in texture, while granitas (from *grana* in Italian, meaning grain or, in this case, grainy) need no special equipment—they are simply placed in a pan in the freezer and stirred occasionally with a fork or whisk until they have frozen to an icy, slush-like texture. When these fruit ices are made at home with ripe, fresh-from-the-market produce, they are infinitely better than the commercial varieties and limited in flavor only by the season and your imagination.

About Sugar Syrup

Used to sweeten sorbets and granitas, sugar syrup (318) is a briefly cooked mixture of sugar and water. It is a snap to make and will keep for at least a month in the refrigerator, so make a batch ahead to have on hand for these easy frozen desserts. If you need to make sugar syrup the same day, be sure to cool it thoroughly before adding it to the fruit mixture, or the heat will slow the freezing process dramatically. To cool the syrup quickly, pour it into a bowl, then set the bowl into a larger bowl filled halfway with a mixture of ice and cold water.

Because sorbets and granitas are made with fresh fruit, you may need more or slightly less sugar syrup than noted in each recipe, depending upon the ripeness and variety of your fruit. Remember, though, that sugar is a key element in creating good texture in sorbets and granitas. Sugar lowers the freezing point of the fruit juice, making it softer and more supple and preventing it from freezing into a solid block, so don't be tempted to leave it out or reduce it drastically. If you feel the mixture is too sweet with the sugar syrup called for, add a bit of freshly squeezed lemon juice or pomegranate molasses (71) both to enhance the fruit flavor and to reduce the sensation of sweetness. Keep in mind that the final fruit mixture should taste a little sweeter than you want it to because freezing reduces our perception of sweetness. Too little sugar can make a sorbet or granita taste flat.

Solutions for Iciness

Homemade sorbets and granitas can become hard and icy within a few days, but this is easy to remedy because they can be thawed and refrozen without damaging the flavor or texture. This is also good to remember if you find, after freezing, that you need to adjust the sweetness or acidity balance of the mixture. If you don't have time to thaw and refreeze a granita that has frozen into an unscoopable block of ice, there are a couple of other solutions: either break it into pieces and puree it in the food processor (do this right before serving) or let it sit at room temperature for 10 to 20 minutes, until it is soft enough to scrape into shavings with the edge of a large spoon, then place the shavings in a container, cover, and freeze until serving time.

Serving Suggestions

I love to combine a sorbet and a granita in a single dessert. In a small bowl or compote dish, place a generous layer of granita, then put a scoop of sorbet or ice cream in a contrasting flavor and color on top. The sorbet looks like a beautiful round egg sitting in a jeweled nest. It's also fun to mix two granitas, for they resemble a blend of giant, glittering colored sugar crystals (stir together quickly and gently, just before serving). Or combine the two serving suggestions and mix two granitas of contrasting colors, then place a scoop of sorbet on top. As you look at the list, remember that a sorbet can become a granita (and vice versa) by exchanging the way the mixture is frozen,

Here are a few ideas for combining the recipes in this book:

- A scoop of pastel orange Tangerine Sorbet (317) in a nest of deep purple Pomegranate Granita with Rose Water (325) or Blackberry Sorbet prepared as a granita (320)

- A scoop of ruby Blood Orange Sorbet (318) in a nest of Tangerine Sorbet prepared as a granita (317) or Raspberry Sorbet prepared as a granita (320)

- A scoop of ice-pink Quince Sorbet with Lemon (323) in a nest of brilliant Pomegranate Granita with Rose Water (325)

- A scoop of palest yellow Lemon Verbena Sorbet (321) in a nest of sanguine Blood Orange Sorbet prepared as a granita (318) or Raspberry Sorbet prepared as a granita (320)

- A scoop of scarlet Raspberry Sorbet (320) on a cloud of Lemon Verbena Sorbet prepared as a granita (321) or a mixture of Tangerine (317) and Blood Orange Sorbets prepared as granitas (318)

- Tangerine (317) and Blood Orange Sorbets prepared as granitas (318), gently stirred together

- Pomegranate Granita with Rose Water (325) and Tangerine Sorbet prepared as a granita (317), gently stirred together

- A scoop of pale Pomegranate Ice Cream (312) in a bright nest of Pomegranate Granita with Rose Water (325)

- A scoop of Crème Fraîche Ice Cream (302) in a ruby nest of Raspberry Sorbet prepared as a granita (310)

- A scoop of Double-Lime Ice Cream (309) in a dramatic purple-black nest of Blackberry Sorbet prepared as a granita (320)

Tangerine Sorbet

makes about 1 pint

Perhaps I'm a jaded Californian, spoiled by the almost year-round availability of oranges from the tree, but I think fresh tangerine juice is infinitely more interesting than orange (the exception is blood orange, see variation below). The extra bit of acidity helps to give tangerines their very special flavor, and it certainly adds to their appeal in a vividly refreshing sorbet. Tangerines are available winter into spring—if possible, ask for a taste before buying, as their quality can vary greatly. Honey tangerines are especially rich and sweet, while satsumas (a seedless loose-skinned variety I love) lean more toward a complex, sweet-sour flavor. This recipe can be doubled. The sorbet mixture can also be made into a granita by following the directions for freezing under Pomegranate Granita with Rose Water (325).

EQUIPMENT AND ADVANCE PREPARATION: 1 recipe sugar syrup (318) • An ice cream machine. • If you have a frozen canister–style machine, be sure to allow 24 hours for the canister to freeze.

> **2 cups (16 ounces) freshly squeezed and strained tangerine juice (see Note)**
>
> **7 to 8 tablespoons sugar syrup (318), to taste**
>
> **1 tablespoon orange liqueur, such as Grand Marnier or Cointreau**
>
> **1 teaspoon freshly squeezed lemon juice**

NOTE: If you buy freshly squeezed juice instead of squeezing the fruit yourself, be sure to buy a little extra to make up for the pulp you will need to strain out and discard.

Place the tangerine juice, 7 tablespoons sugar syrup, orange liqueur, and lemon juice in a medium bowl and whisk gently until well blended. Taste and adjust the flavor by adding a little extra syrup or lemon juice if needed, remembering that the mixture should taste a little sweeter than you want because freezing reduces our perception of sweetness.

Transfer to your ice cream machine and freeze according to the manufacturer's directions. Immediately transfer the sorbet to a storage container, cover, and place in the freezer.

SERVING AND STORAGE NOTES: The sorbet is best served the same day it is made. If it becomes too hard or icy after several days, remember that you can always melt it down and refreeze the mixture.

VARIATION

Blood Orange Sorbet: Blood oranges, with their hint of raspberry and gentle kick of acidity, make an especially good sorbet—even better if you can find oranges that are deeply colored for a dramatic red hue. Follow the recipe above, substituting strained, freshly squeezed blood orange juice for the tangerine juice. For an extra level of flavor, substitute pomegranate molasses (71) for the lemon juice.

Sugar Syrup

makes about 1½ cups

Sugar syrup is used for sweetening sorbets and granitas, as well as for moistening cake layers and sweetening fresh fruit sauces (like raspberry sauce, 149). It holds very well in the refrigerator for at least 1 month.

1 cup (8 ounces) water
1 cup (7 ounces) sugar

Place the water and sugar in a medium saucepan over low heat and warm slowly, stirring several times with a spoon, until the sugar has dissolved and the liquid is clear. Turn the heat to high and bring the mixture to a rolling boil. Cook without stirring for 1 minute. Cool (if you need to cool the syrup quickly, pour it into a bowl, then set the bowl into a larger bowl filled halfway with a mixture of ice and cold water). Transfer to a storage container, cover, and refrigerate until needed.

VARIATIONS

Infused Sugar Syrups: To add another layer of flavor to sorbets and granitas, the sugar syrup can be infused by placing a flavoring from the list below in the pan with the water and sugar, bringing it to a boil as described above, then covering the pan, removing it from the heat, and allowing the mixture to steep for 15 minutes, almost as if you were making a tea or tisane. Taste the syrup to see if you like the flavor—if it needs to be a little stronger, let it steep for another 5 to 10 minutes, but keep in mind that the infused flavors should complement the main fruit flavor, not overwhelm it. Once you like the flavor, pour the syrup through a fine-mesh strainer into a storage container. Let the syrup cool, then cover and refrigerate until needed.

When infusing a sugar syrup, be sure to choose a flavor that will complement the fruit in your frozen dessert. Here are some suggestions, but once you get the idea, feel free to improvise your own combinations with flavorings from the list below. For tangerine, use lime zest and fresh ginger; for blood orange, a mixture of cinnamon, clove, and star anise; for raspberry, a mixture of lemon zest and lemon verbena or a mixture of orange zest and vanilla bean; for blackberry, a mixture of lemon zest and rose geranium or a mixture of black peppercorns and lavender; for pomegranate, a combination of mint and black peppercorns or a mixture of fresh ginger and cloves; for lemon verbena, fresh ginger or a mixture of lemon zest and rose geranium.

- Black pepper—½ teaspoon whole black peppercorns, crushed (I use the edge of a heavy saucepan, pressing down firmly on the peppercorns.)
- Cinnamon—1 cinnamon stick
- Citrus—zest of 1 large orange or 2 medium lemons or 2 medium limes, in strips
- Cloves—¼ teaspoon whole cloves
- Ginger—4 nickel-size slices fresh ginger (about ¼ inch thick), unpeeled
- Lavender—2 fresh lavender sprigs (91) or ¼ teaspoon dried lavender (unsprayed, not for craft purposes)
- Mint—6 medium fresh mint leaves
- Rose geranium—4 medium fresh rose geranium leaves (158)
- Vanilla—½ vanilla bean, split lengthwise and scraped, seeds added to the pan

Raspberry or Blackberry Sorbet

makes about 1 pint

The essence of summer, a berry sorbet has the intensity of fruit picked at its peak of ripeness. This recipe can be doubled. The sorbet mixture can also be made into granita by following the directions for freezing under Pomegranate Granita with Rose Water (325).

EQUIPMENT AND ADVANCE PREPARATION: 1 recipe sugar syrup (318) • An ice cream machine • If you have a frozen canister–style machine, be sure to allow 24 hours for the canister to freeze.

> 2 half-pint baskets (about 12 ounces) raspberries or blackberries
>
> ½ cup (4 ounces) sugar syrup (318)
>
> 2 teaspoons freshly squeezed and strained lemon juice or pomegranate molasses (71)
>
> 1 to 2 teaspoons framboise eau-de-vie (raspberry brandy)

Spread the berries out on a baking sheet, then pick through and discard any debris or moldy fruit. Place the berries in the bowl of a food processor with the sugar syrup, lemon juice, and 1 teaspoon framboise. Process until the mixture is smooth. Pour through a fine-mesh strainer set over a medium bowl, pressing firmly with a rubber spatula to remove as much liquid as possible. Taste and adjust the flavor with additional sugar syrup, lemon juice, or framboise if needed, remembering that the mixture should taste a little sweeter than you want because freezing reduces our perception of sweetness.

Transfer to your ice cream machine and freeze according to the manufacturer's directions. Immediately transfer the sorbet to a storage container, cover, and place in the freezer.

SERVING AND STORAGE NOTES: The sorbet is best served the same day it is made. If it becomes too hard or icy after several days, remember that you can always melt it down and refreeze the mixture.

Lemon Verbena Sorbet

makes about 1½ quarts

Lemon verbena definitely tastes of lemon, but it also has sweet, almost floral overtones and a delicate note of "green." This sorbet captures its elusive flavor beautifully. The sorbet mixture can also be made into granita by following the directions for freezing under Pomegranate Granita with Rose Water (325).

EQUIPMENT AND ADVANCE PREPARATION: An ice cream machine • If you have a frozen canister–style machine, be sure to allow 24 hours for the canister to freeze. • For maximum flavor, start this recipe 24 hours before you want to serve it.

> **2 cups (14 ounces) sugar**
>
> **4 cups (32 ounces) water**
>
> **1 cup (¾ ounce) tightly packed fresh lemon verbena leaves (322)**
>
> **⅔ cup (5¼ ounces) freshly squeezed and strained lemon juice**

Place the sugar and water in a medium saucepan. Cook over medium heat until the mixture comes to a boil, stirring several times to dissolve the sugar. Allow the syrup to boil without stirring for 5 minutes. Then remove the pan from the heat and pour the syrup into a stainless-steel bowl or storage container. Immediately add the lemon verbena leaves, crushing them in your hand before adding them to the hot liquid and stirring them into the liquid with a metal spoon. Cool to room temperature, then cover and refrigerate. Let the leaves steep in the syrup for at least 6 to 8 hours, though 24 hours is best.

Pour the syrup through a medium strainer into a bowl, pressing firmly against the leaves to remove as much liquid as possible. Discard the leaves. Stir the lemon juice into the flavored syrup. Freeze in your ice cream maker according to the manufacturer's directions. Immediately transfer the sorbet to a storage container, cover, and place in the freezer.

SERVING AND STORAGE NOTES: The sorbet is best when served within 2 to 3 days. If it becomes too hard or icy, remember that you can always melt it down and refreeze the mixture. Pair with Pistachio, Sultana, and Anise Biscotti (278).

Lemon Verbena

Lemon verbena, known as *verveine* in France, is one of my favorite herbs. Its sweet, lemony fragrance is soothing and invigorating, and whenever I pass the bush outside my back door, I crush a leaf between my fingers and inhale deeply—talk about aromatherapy!

Native to Central and South America, lemon verbena made its way to this country and to Europe with the help of Spanish explorers. Its long, pointed, light green leaves sprout from woody stems, and when flowering, each curving branch is topped with lacy spikes of white flowers tinged with pale lavender. Though best known for its use in making teas and infusions, lemon verbena can be used in many desserts, as long as there is a step where it can be infused in a hot liquid, for the crinkled leaves, tough and prickly, are unpleasant to eat. Ice creams and sorbets are popular choices, but consider custards, mousses, and poached fruit.

Lemon verbena (*Aloysia triphylla*) is a hardy deciduous plant that is practically impossible to kill if its needs for full sun and well-drained soil are met. In cold climates, plant it in a pot and bring it indoors during the winter, because frost is its nemesis. It takes forever to grow from seed—either buy a small plant from the nursery or take a stem cutting from a friend's plant. The tiny plant I bought three years ago is now seven feet tall! Sometimes during the winter or after a plant has been moved, it will drop its leaves and look dead to all the world, but be patient—after a period of dormancy, it will begin to sprout again. Sources for lemon verbena plants and fresh lemon verbena can be found on page 327.

Quince Sorbet with Lemon

makes about 1½ quarts

The quince is an ancient fruit, related to the apple, that needs long, slow cooking to bring out its special flavor, which is reminiscent of apples blended with pineapple and citrus. Popular for centuries in the Mediterranean and in early America, quinces have declined in popularity here during the last 50 years, but I'm on a campaign to bring them back to our kitchens. Their exquisite flavor and gorgeous rose to burnt red–orange color are a unique and delicious addition to the autumnal table, as can be tasted in this unusual frosty pink sorbet. Quinces can often be found in farmers' markets from late fall into winter (see Mail-Order Sources, 327). The sorbet mixture can also be made into granita by following the directions for freezing under Pomegranate Granita with Rose Water (325).

EQUIPMENT AND ADVANCE PREPARATION: An ice cream machine • If you have a frozen canister–style machine, be sure to allow 24 hours for the canister to freeze.

> 4 medium (about 2¼ pounds) quinces
>
> 8 cups (2 quarts) water
>
> 1½ cups (10½ ounces) sugar
>
> Two 3-inch sticks cinnamon
>
> 2 strips lemon zest, removed with a vegetable peeler
>
> 2 strips orange zest, removed with a vegetable peeler
>
> 6 to 8 tablespoons (3 to 4 ounces) freshly squeezed lemon juice, to taste

To prepare the fruit, peel the quinces with a sharp vegetable peeler or a small, sharp paring knife. Be patient—the skin is tenacious. Use a sharp, heavy knife to cut each fruit in half through the stem. Use a melon baller to scoop out the cores. Save the skins and cores. Chop the quinces into 1-inch pieces, place in a medium bowl, and set aside (the pieces will turn brown but don't worry—this discoloration disappears during the prolonged cooking process).

To cook the quinces, place the 8 cups of water in a large saucepan. Add the quince skins and cores. Place the pan over high heat and bring the mixture to a boil. Turn the heat down to medium and cook at a low boil for 30 minutes (the trimmings are highly flavored and will infuse the liquid with their flavor). Pour the liquid through a medium strainer and discard the quince trimmings. Return the liquid to the pan (you should have about 6 cups) and add the sugar and cinnamon sticks. Scrape off any of the white pith remaining on the back of the lemon and orange zests with the edge of a knife. Add the cleaned zests to the saucepan. Cook over medium heat, stirring frequently with a wooden spoon, until the sugar has dissolved.

Add the chopped quinces to the liquid and return the mixture to a simmer, then cover the top of the liquid with a round of parchment or wax paper to keep the fruit submerged, and continue to cook at a simmer until the fruit is tender and a lovely pink to orange color, about 1½ to 2 hours, depending on the variety and ripeness of the fruit. Do not simply cover the pan with a lid and cook— the parchment paper allows you to monitor the fruit's progress and watch that the liquid does not boil rapidly. Even more important, it also lets moisture evaporate and concentrates the fruit flavor.

Remove the pan from the heat, discard the paper, and let the mixture cool for 30 minutes. Discard the cinnamon sticks and lemon and orange zests. Puree the quince with the poaching syrup in batches in a blender (a food processor may be substituted, but the blender results in a smoother texture). Place the pureed mixture in a container and refrigerate until cold. Stir in the lemon juice to taste. Freeze in your ice cream maker according to the manufacturer's directions. Immediately transfer the sorbet to a storage container, cover, and place in the freezer.

SERVING AND STORAGE NOTES: The sorbet is best when served within 2 to 3 days. If it becomes too hard or icy, remember that you can always melt it down and refreeze the mixture. Serve accompanied by Toasted Almond and Dried Sour Cherry Biscotti (274).

Pomegranate Granita
with Rose Water

makes about 5 cups

Beautiful deep magenta crystals, like tiny shimmering garnets, explode with the bright fla-
vor of fresh pomegranate juice, which tastes like a fusion of blackberries, raspberries, and
deep purple grapes. Make this in the fall when markets are overflowing with the fruit. This
mixture can also be made into a smooth sorbet when frozen in an ice cream machine.

EQUIPMENT AND ADVANCE PREPARATION: 1 recipe sugar syrup (318) • An 8 x 8-inch
nonaluminum pan and a whisk, both placed in the freezer at least 1 hour ahead of time.

> **2 cups (16 ounces) freshly squeezed pomegranate juice or pure bottled**
> **pomegranate juice, no sugar added (available in stores catering to a**
> **Middle Eastern clientele)**
>
> **8 to 10 tablespoons sugar syrup (318), to taste**
>
> **1 teaspoon pomegranate molasses (71) or freshly squeezed lemon juice**
>
> **¼ teaspoon rose water (260)**

Place the pomegranate juice, 8 tablespoons sugar syrup, 1 teaspoon pomegranate
molasses, and the rose water in the cold baking pan and whisk gently until well
blended. Taste and adjust the flavor by adding a little extra syrup or molasses, if
needed, remembering that the mixture should taste a little sweeter than you want
because freezing reduces our perception of sweetness.

Place the pan on a level surface in the freezer and whisk the mixture every
30 minutes, breaking up any ice crystals that form around the edges and stirring
them into the liquid. Leave the whisk in the pan between stirrings. After about 3
hours, you should have a slushy mixture, stiff enough to spoon, with lots of large ice
crystals. Transfer the granita to a storage container, cover, and return to the freezer.

SERVING AND STORAGE NOTES: Serve in small goblets or compote dishes accompanied by Lacy Sesame Crisps (267) or butter cookies. When frozen in an ice
cream machine for sorbet, this recipe makes about 1 pint.

GETTING AHEAD: The granita may be prepared in advance and stored in an airtight container in the freezer for up to 3 weeks. If you find the granita has become
too hard during storage, refer to the notes on page 315 to salvage the mixture.

Mail-Order Sources

General Baking and Pastry Equipment and Supplies

King Arthur Flour Company
The Baker's Catalogue
P.O. Box 876
Norwich, VT 05055
(800) 827-6836 Catalog available
www.kingarthurflour.com
A catalog specifically for bakers, with a wonderful assortment of ingredients and equipment for pastry making and bread baking, including pans, flours, sugars, chocolates, extracts and vanilla beans, dried fruits and flower waters, and much more. Friendly, knowledgeable customer service. Their newsletter is a treasure trove of information and fun.

New York Cake and Baking Distributors
56 West 22nd Street
New York, NY 10010
(800) 942-2539 or (212) 675-CAKE
Catalog available
www.newyorkcakesupplies.com

Oriented toward the professional, this source offers lots the home baker can use, from "how did I ever live without those" cake cardboards to specialty pans and equipment for wedding cakes. Plus chocolates (Callebaut, Valhrona, and Van Leer) and cocoa.

Sur La Table
Catalogue Division
410 Terry Avenue North
Seattle, WA 98109
(800) 243-0852 Catalog available
www.surlatable.com
An incredible soup-to-nuts kitchenware store with a superb selection of baking pans, cutters, rolling pins, ceramic ware, and more—it's enough to make a pastry chef drool. Plus cookware, equipment, beautiful dishes and linens, books, and specialty food items. Lots of great gadgets. Once a year they put out a special catalog especially for bakers—don't miss it.

Williams-Sonoma
Mail-Order Department
P.O. Box 7456
San Francisco, CA 94120
(800) 541-2233 Catalog available
www.williams-sonoma.com
Everything for the kitchen and table, including cookware, bakeware, scales, dishes and tabletop accoutrements, mixers, juicers, toasters, and much more, all of beautiful design and the highest quality. Also some cookbooks and specialty food items. Their Christmas catalog, filled with luscious food offerings in addition to their usual bounty, will make your mouth water.

Antique Apples

Treemendus Fruit Farms
9351 East Eureka Road
Eau Claire, MI 49111
(616) 782-7101
www.tree-mendusfruit.com

Antique Apple Trees

Sonoma Antique Apple Nursery
4395 Westside Road
Healdsburg, CA 95448
(707) 433-6420 Catalog available
www.applenursery.com

Southmeadow Fruit Gardens
P. O. Box 211
Baroda, MI 49101
(616) 422-2411 Catalog available
http://membersataol.com/
Southmeadowfg/South.html

Butane Torch

(see Sur La Table or Williams-Sonoma entry)

Cheeses

The Mozzarella Company
2944 Elm Street
Dallas, TX 75226
(800) 798-2954
www.mozzco.com
A wonderful selection of cheeses, including mascarpone, whole-milk ricotta, cream cheese, crème fraîche, mozzarella, and more. All made without gums or artificial preservatives and delivered in two days.

Chocolate

Scharffen Berger Chocolates
914 Heinz Avenue
Berkeley, CA 94710
(800) 930-4528
www.scharffen-berger.com
An American chocolate company that rivals Europe's best. Excellent bittersweet and unsweetened chocolate, as well as natural cocoa. (For these and other chocolates, see entries under General Baking and Pastry Equipment and Supplies, 327.)

Coconut Milk

Thai Kitchen Pure Coconut Milk
Epicurean International
229 Castro Street
Oakland, CA 94607
(800) 967-THAI Catalog available
info @ thaikitchen.com

Cookbooks

The Cook's Library
8373 West Third Street
Los Angeles, CA 90048
(213) 655-3141
www.cookslibrary.com
A vast selection of cookbooks on all subject matters, with a great selection of Mediterranean, baking, and California cookbooks. Wonderful, knowledgeable staff. Unusual and out-of-print titles, plus interesting books from Europe.

Dried Sour Cherries

American Spoon Foods
P.O. Box 566
(Retail store at 411 East Lake Street)
Petoskey, MI 49770
(800) 222-5886
www.spoon.com

(see also King Arthur Flour Company entry)

Eaux-de-Vie

St. George Spirits
2900 Main Street
Alameda, CA 94501
(510) 769-1601
www.stgeorgespirits.com
California's oldest eaux-de-vie distillery produces spirits of exceptional quality, including framboise, grappa, kirsch, quince, and pear William. The royales (a line of fortified dessert wines) will knock your socks off, especially the framboise or the poire. St. George products are available in many fine liquor shops and may also be ordered directly from the company.

Filo, Fresh Sheets

Fillo Factory
P.O. Box 155
(Retail store at 74 Courtland Avenue)
Dumont, NJ 07628
(800) OKFILLO
www.fillofactory.com

Filo, Shredded (also called *Kunafeh* or *Kataifi*)

Sultan's Delight
P.O. Box 253
Staten Island, NY 10314
(800) 852-5046 Catalog available

Fresh Herbs (Plants)

Nichol's Garden Nursery
1190 North Pacific Highway NE
Albany, OR 97321
(541) 928-9280; fax: (800) 231-5306
Catalog available
www.nicholsgardennursery.com
Organically grown plants, including lavender, lemon verbena, and rose geranium.

Honeys

Oakville Grocery Mail-Order Company
860 Napa Valley Corporate Way
Suite A
Napa, CA 94559

(800) 973-6324 Catalog available
www.oakvillegrocery.com
A good selection of honeys, including chestnut honey, as well as an inspiring array of foodstuffs and wine.

Dean and DeLuca
560 Broadway
New York, NY 10012
(800) 221-7714 Catalog available
www.deananddeluca.com

(see also Kermit Lynch Wine Merchant entry)

Medjool Dates

Melissa's/World Variety Produce Inc.
P.O. Box 21127
Los Angeles, CA 90021
(800) 588-0151 Catalog available
www.melissas.com

Meyer Lemons

Melissa's/World Variety Produce Inc.
P.O. Box 21127
Los Angeles, CA 90021
(800) 588-0151 Catalog available
www.melissas.com

Orange Flower Water and Rose Water

Sultan's Delight
P.O. Box 253
Staten Island, NY 10314
(800) 852-5046 Catalog available

(see also King Arthur Flour Company entry)

Peaches and Nectarines

Frog Hollow Farm
P.O. Box 872
Brentwood, CA 94513
(888) 779-4511
www.froghollow.com

Pear Corer

(see Sur La Table entry)

Pomegranate Molasses

Dean and DeLuca
560 Broadway
New York, NY 10012
(800) 221-7714 Catalog available
www.deananddeluca.com

Sultan's Delight (and pomegranate juice)
P.O. Box 253
Staten Island, NY 10314
(800) 852-5046 Catalog available

Quinces

Melissa's/World Variety Produce Inc.
P.O. Box 21127
Los Angeles, CA 90021
(800) 588-0151 Catalog available
www.melissas.com

Semolina and Tapioca Flour (and Cornmeal, Too)

Bob's Red Mill
5209 Southeast International Way
Milwaukie, OR 97222
(800) 553-2258 Catalog available
www.bobsredmill.com

(see also King Arthur Flour Company entry for semolina)

Spices

Penzeys, Ltd.
P.O. Box 1448
Waukesha, WI 53187
(800) 741-7787 Catalog available
www.penzeys.com
A vast selection of very fresh, high-quality spices and dried herbs and a catalog that is fascinating reading.

Tartaric Acid

Oak Barrel Winecraft, Inc.
1443 San Pablo Avenue
Berkeley, CA 94702
(510) 849-0400
www.oakbarrel.com
Everything you need for wine and beer making, including tartaric acid, which is also used to make mascarpone.

Victorinox Zester

Surfas
8825 National Boulevard
Culver City, CA 90232
(310) 559-4770
email: surfas@pacbell.net
No catalog available
A great open-to-the-public restaurant supply store with everything from stoves to cookware and rows of foodstuffs. If you know exactly what you want, and it carries it, the store will ship it to you. It also carries the Victorinox bread knife (the best) and my favorite cocoa—Cacao Barry Extra Brute (in a 2.2 pound bag).

Wines and More

Kermit Lynch Wine Merchant
1605 San Pablo Avenue
Berkeley, CA 94702
(510) 524-1524 Newsletter available
Wonderful wines hand-picked in the Mediterranean, plus a select offering of groceries, including olive oils and lavender honey. An absorbing newsletter that is one of my favorite pieces of mail to receive.

fig(s), dried (*cont.*)
    snake pastry with
        almond paste, lemon
        and, 233–36
    Tuscan bread pudding,
        188–89
fig(s), fresh, 78
    with espresso-sambuca
        sabayon and shaved
        chocolate, 137–38
    stuffed with goat cheese
        served with raspberry
        and caramel sauces,
        148–50
filberts, 227
Fillo Factory, 329
filo (phyllo), 199
    apricot tart with pista-
        chios and, 97
    frozen, 207
    mail-order source for, 329
    working with, 207–8
    see also baklava and filo
        desserts
filo, shredded (*kunafeh* or
    kataifi), 96, 208
    apricot tart with pista-
        chios and, 95–97
    cinnamon apple and
        sweet cheese in, 243
    fresh cherries and sweet
        cheese in, 241–43
    galataboureko with
        spiced blood orange
        caramel sauce, 229–31
    konafa with tangerine
        lime syrup, 238–40
    mail-order source for,
        329
flaky tart dough, 74, 110–13
flan:
    bonet, 175–77
    chestnut honey, 182–84
    pumpkin, with spiced
        pecans, 178–80

fool, apricot, with almond
    cream, 194–95
Fracchia, Louis and Ellie, 79
framboise, 18
Frangelico, 19
    whipped cream, 54
fregolotta with almonds and
    jam, 45–46
French cuisine, 15
    flavors of, 16–17
Frog Hollow Farm, 161,
    330
fromage blanc, poached
    quinces with, 131–33
frosting, chocolate, 27, 28
frozen desserts, *see* ice
    creams; granitas;
    sorbets
fruit brandies, *see* eaux-de-vie
fruitcake, California, with
    dates, apricots, and
    walnuts, 35–36
fruit desserts, 125–61
    apricots, caramelized,
        with pistachio ice
        cream, 147
    cherries poached in red
        wine with rose gerani-
        um and blackberries,
        157–58
    citrus compote in spiced
        champagne broth,
        140–41
    dates, mascarpone-
        stuffed, with spiced
        blood orange caramel
        sauce and seeded pra-
        line, 134–35
    figs stuffed with goat
        cheese served with
        raspberry and caramel
        sauces, 148–50
    figs with espresso-sambuca
        sabayon and shaved
        chocolate, 137–38

fruit desserts (*cont.*)
    peaches and raspberries,
        summer, with
        Essencia sabayon,
        159–60
    pears, roasted, with
        spiced sabayon,
        128–30
    plums in port with clove
        cream, 152–53
    quinces, poached, with
        fromage blanc, 131–33
    raspberry and cannoli
        cream parfaits, 155–56
fruits:
    buying, 126
    dried, 37
    seasonal guidelines for, 21
    shopping for, 21
    see also specific fruits
Fusco, Joanne, 26

G

galataboureko with spiced
    blood orange caramel
    sauce, 229–31
ganache, chocolate, 86–87,
    170, 171
garnishes:
    candied lemon or orange
        zest, 236–37
    caramel-coated walnut,
        148, 149
    chocolate curls, minia-
        ture, 106
    praline, 306–7
    spiced pecans, 180–81
gelato affogato, 301–3
geraniums, scented, 19
    see also rose geranium
gianduia, 26, 29
ginger:
    sugar syrup, 319
    whipped cream, 54

ingredients, discussions of:
(*cont.*)
brandies, 18
candied lemon or orange
zest, 236–37
cardamom, 278
chocolate chips, minia-
ture, 274–75
citrus, 142–46
cocoa powder, 262–63
coconut, 93
coconut milk, 192–93
cornmeal, 85
crème fraîche, 303–4
crystallized sugar, 244
dates, 136
dried fruit, 37
eaux-de-vie, 18
filo (phyllo), 207–8
goat cheese, 150–51
hazelnuts, 227–28
herbs, 19
for ice cream, 297–98
lavender, 91
lemon verbena, 321
liqueurs, 18–19
macadamia nuts, salted, 93
Meyer lemons, 309–10
mint, 172
olive oil, 281–82
orange flower water, 260
orange oil, 31
pistachios, 212–13
plums, 153–54
pomegranate molasses,
71–72
praline, 306–7
quinces, 217–18
rose geranium, 158
rose water, 260
sesame seeds, 100–101
Insalata's (San Anselmo,
Calif.), 279
Italian cuisine, 15
flavors of, 17

J

jam, fregolotta with
almonds and, 45–46
jasmine, 12
jelly, champagne, with
raspberries, 196–98

K

Kahlua, 19
Kamman, Madeleine, 250
kataifi, see filo, shredded
King Arthur Flour
Company, 327
kirsch, 18
Kleiman, Evan, 35
konafa with tangerine lime
syrup, 238–40
Krahling, Heidi Insalata, 279
kunafeh, see filo, shredded

L

lacy sesame crisps, 267–69
lavender, 19, 91
and almond praline ice
cream, 305–6
cherry, and red wine tart
with crème fraîche,
89–91
sugar syrup, 319
lavender gems, 141, 144
citrus compote in spiced
champagne broth,
140–41
layer cakes:
nectarine mascarpone, 42
pistachio, with nougat
cream, 30–33
strawberry mascarpone,
38–42
lemon(s), 144
and almond macaroon ice
cream sandwiches, 311

double-, ice cream, 308–9
Meyer, 309–10
Meyer, mail-order source
for, 330
quince sorbet with,
323–24
and rose madeleines,
258–59
snake pastry with fig,
almond paste and,
233–36
zest, candied, 236–37
lemon balm, 19
lemon verbena, 19, 322
sorbet, 321
lime(s), 144
brûlée tartlets with
coconut macadamia
crust, 92–94
caramel sauce, coconut
rice pudding brûlée
with mango in, 190–92
curd, 92, 93
double-, ice cream, 309
double-, ice cream,
grilled coconut cake
with, 55–57
tangerine syrup, konafa
with, 238–40
liqueurs, 18–19
Amaretto di Saronno, 177
sambuca con la mosca,
138–39
whipped cream flavored
with, 54
Kermit Lynch Wine
Merchant, 331

M

macadamia (nuts):
coconut crust, lime
brûlée tartlets with,
92–94
salted, rinsing, 93

macaroon(s):

almond, and lemon ice cream sandwiches, 311

almond and hazelnut chip, 250–52

almond and pine nut, 252

double-almond, 252

madeleines:

lemon and rose, 258–59

orange, with orange flower water, 259

Madison, Deborah, 180

mail-order sources, 327–31

mandarins, 143–44

mango, coconut rice pudding brûlée with, in lime caramel sauce, 190–92

marbleized chocolate velvet tart, 104–6

marbleizing ice creams and sorbets, 299–300

mascarpone:

black and white, parfait, 185–87

double-raspberry tart, 88

making, 42–44

nectarine layer cake, 42

raspberry tart with chocolate crust, 86–88

rum, cream, chocolate soufflé roll with, 47–50

strawberry layer cake, 38–42

-stuffed dates with spiced blood orange caramel sauce and seeded praline, 134–35

Medici, Lorenza de, 188

Mediterranean:

creating desserts inspired by, 13–15

Mediterranean (*cont.*)

flavors common to, 15–19

influences of, in California, 12, 13

Medrich, Alice, 263

Melissa's/World Variety Produce Inc., 330

meringue, pistachio, 68, 69–70

Middle Eastern cuisine, 15

flavors of, 17

mint, 19, 172

and chocolate pots de crème, 170–71

liqueur, 19

sugar syrup, 319

mocha chiffon cake with cinnamon and orange, 64–66

Moors, 16

mousse, black and white mascarpone, parfait, 185–87

Mozzarella Company, 328

N

Napa Valley, orchards and vegetable patches in, 78–79

nectarine(s), 83

mail-order source for, 330

mascarpone layer cake, 42

see also peach(es)

New York Cake and Baking Distributors, 327

Nichol's Garden Nursery, 329

noga, *see* nougat

nonna's rugelach, 255–57

North African cuisine, 15

flavors of, 17

nougat (torrone, turron, or noga), 33–34

cream, pistachio layer cake with, 30–33

nuts:

chopping, 200–201

macadamia coconut crust, lime brûlée tartlets with, 92–94

praline, 306–7

see also almond(s); hazelnut(s); pecan(s); pine nut; pistachio(s); walnut(s)

O

Oak Barrel Winecraft, Inc., 331

Oakville Grocery Mail-Order Company, 329–30

olive oil, 281–82

and spice biscotti, Spanish, 279–81

orange(s), 142–43

brown sugar and almond biscotti with cinnamon and, 286–88

caramel, date, and sesame tart with, 99–100

cardamom syrup, pistachio and apricot baklava with, 209–12

chocolate, and almond torte, 29

chocolate, and hazelnut torte, 26–29

chocolate, and walnut torte, 29

cornmeal rosettes with apricot jam, 264–66

cornmeal wafers, 266

orange(s) (*cont.*)

    hazelnut, and chocolate
        chip biscotti, 274

    lacy sesame crisps,
        267–69

    liqueur, 19

    madeleines with orange
        flower water, 259

    mocha chiffon cake
        with cinnamon and,
        64–66

    naval, in citrus compote
        in spiced champagne
        broth, 140–41

    oil, 31

    snake pastry with apri-
        cots, almond paste
        and, 236

    whipped cream, 54

    zest, candied, 236–37

orange(s), blood, 142–43

    caramel sauce, spiced,
        231–32

    caramel sauce, spiced,
        galataboureko with,
        229–31

    caramel sauce, spiced,
        mascarpone-stuffed
        dates with, 13435

    citrus compote in spiced
        champagne broth,
        140–41

    sorbet, 318

orange flower water, 260

    mail-order sources for, 330

    orange madeleines with,
        259

    and pine nut armadillos
        with apricot sauce,
        51–53

    whipped cream flavored
        with, 54

Ottoman empire, 16

oven temperature, 20

oven thermometers, 20

P

panforte, 107

parfaits:

    black and white mascar-
        pone, 185–87

    raspberry and cannoli
        cream, 155–56

pasta frolla (shortcrust
    dough), 74, 114–17

peach(es), 161

    choosing, 83

    and cornmeal tart with
        crème fraîche ice
        cream, 83–85

    mail-order source for,
        330

    summer raspberries and,
        with Essencia sabay-
        on, 159–60

pear(s):

    brandy (poire William),
        18

    brown butter tart with
        vanilla bean, 102–3

    roasted, with spiced
        sabayon, 128–30

    Tuscan bread pudding,
        188–89

    and walnut whole wheat
        biscotti, 289–90

pear corers, 130

    mail-order source for, 330

pecan(s):

    praline, 306–7

    spiced, 180–81

    spiced, pumpkin flan
        with, 178–80

    toasted, caramel sauce, 67

Penzeys, Ltd., 331

peppermint, 172

pepper sugar syrup, 319

phyllo, *see* baklava and filo
    desserts; filo

pie pans, 73

pies, tarts vs., 73

pine nut:

    and almond macaroons,
        252

    and orange flower
        armadillos with apri-
        cot sauce, 51–53

pistachio(s), 212–13

    apricot, and cardamom
        biscotti, 276–78

    and apricot baklava with
        orange cardamom
        syrup, 209–12

    apricot tart with shred-
        ded filo and, 95–97

    buying, 213

    ice cream, 294–95

    ice cream, caramelized
        apricots with, 147

    ice cream, in gelato
        affogato, 301

    layer cake with nougat
        cream, 30–33

    meringue, 68, 69–70

    pomegranate dacquoise,
        68–71

    sultana, and anise biscotti,
        278

    toasting, 213

plum(s), 78, 153–54

    choosing, 154

    and hazelnut tart with
        port wine glaze,
        76–78

    in port with clove cream,
        152–53

poached:

    cherries in red wine with
        rose geranium and
        blackberries, 157–58

    plums in port with clove
        cream, 152–53

    quinces with fromage
        blanc, 131–33

poire William, 18

About the Author

CINDY MUSHET has been a pastry chef for the last fourteen years and has taught numerous classes to both the home baker and the aspiring food professional. She attended Tante Marie's Cooking School in San Francisco, apprenticed at Chez Panisse, and later became the pastry chef of Oliveto Restaurant and Café in Oakland. She moved to Los Angeles and has continued to bake and consult for restaurants in both southern and northern California. For five years Cindy wrote and published the acclaimed quarterly baking journal *Baking with the American Harvest*. She was a contributor to the new *Joy of Cooking,* the *Joy of Cooking Christmas Cookie Book,* and the upcoming *The Collective Wisdom of the Bakers Dozen.* She is a member of the Bakers Dozen, the International Association of Culinary Professionals, and the James Beard Foundation. She holds a degree in anthropology from UCLA and a certificate in sustainable agriculture from UC Davis. She lives in Los Angeles with her husband, Miguel, and daughter, Isabella.